REWATCHING ON THE POINT
OF THE CINEMATIC INDEX

REWATCHING ON THE POINT OF THE CINEMATIC INDEX

Allen H. Redmon

University Press of Mississippi / Jackson

The University Press of Mississippi is the scholarly publishing agency of the Mississippi Institutions of Higher Learning: Alcorn State University, Delta State University, Jackson State University, Mississippi State University, Mississippi University for Women, Mississippi Valley State University, University of Mississippi, and University of Southern Mississippi.

www.upress.state.ms.us

The University Press of Mississippi is a member of the Association of University Presses.

Copyright © 2022 by University Press of Mississippi
All rights reserved

First printing 2022

∞

Library of Congress Cataloging-in-Publication Data

Names: Redmon, Allen H., 1972– author.
Title: Rewatching on the point of the cinematic index / Allen H. Redmon.
Description: Jackson : University Press of Mississippi, 2022. | Includes bibliographical references and index.
Identifiers: LCCN 2022010500 (print) | LCCN 2022010501 (ebook) | ISBN 9781496841810 (hardback) | ISBN 9781496841827 (trade paperback) | ISBN 9781496841834 (epub) | ISBN 9781496841841 (epub) | ISBN 9781496841858 (pdf) | ISBN 9781496841865 (pdf)
Subjects: LCSH: Motion pictures—Aesthetics. | Motion pictures—Philosophy. | Film adaptations—Philosophy. | Digital media—Influence. | Reality in motion pictures. | Reality—Philosophy.
Classification: LCC PN1995 .R3995 2022 (print) | LCC PN1995 (ebook) | DDC 791.4301—dc23/eng/20220607
LC record available at https://lccn.loc.gov/2022010500
LC ebook record available at https://lccn.loc.gov/2022010501

British Library Cataloging-in-Publication Data available

Written with appreciation and gratitude to those who support the mission and operations of the Ronald McDonald House of Dallas.

CONTENTS

Acknowledgments ix
Introduction 3
Chapter 1: The Index 13
Chapter 2: (Cinematic) Reality 57
Chapter 3: Trauma 101
Chapter 4: Adaptation 142
Works Cited 185
Index 197

ACKNOWLEDGMENTS

I am grateful to so many who supported me while I explored the ideas that shape this book. Ryan, Geoff, and Aaron helped me articulate my ideas when they were just an intuition. Amy, Homer, and Walter asked insightful questions or shared what intrigued them most about my project as it was taking shape. Dear colleagues gathering at various conferences, but especially those hosted by the Literature/Film Association and the Southwest Popular/American Culture Association presented papers or offered comments to my work that clarified key concepts. Greg reminded me at the right time to be bold. Marc, Dave, and John provided enthusiastic responses to the project as it was finding its final form. I offer each of you a sincere thank you.

I also want to thank those at my home institution, Texas A&M University Central Texas. I am especially grateful to my students, whose ideas and reactions to the process of ongoing adaptation I ask them to consider always suggest something new to consider. I am grateful to my faculty colleagues whose own scholarly pursuits inspire me. I am grateful to our librarians, who are always so quick to secure the resources I need. I am grateful to my Dean and Provost, who ensure I have the favorable work conditions I do. I am grateful to my President and the A&M University System for, among other things, the faculty development leave they approved and supported that allowed me to complete this project.

I very much appreciate the University Press of Mississippi for their support. This is our second endeavor together, so I already know just how wonderfully they support authors at every stage of a project. I do appreciate all they do. This project is better because of them.

Finally, and most essentially, I want to thank my family. I so very much appreciate the way my wife chases after the fullness of an idea or a concept with me. I value the way my eldest son and daughter discuss or feel a film. I prize the pure enjoyment or comfort my two youngest children feel as they watch and rewatch a movie. Each of these responses provides me my favorite seat in the house.

REWATCHING ON THE POINT
OF THE CINEMATIC INDEX

INTRODUCTION

Movies have always served as instances of rewatching. The earliest films, which came to be known as "actualities," were simply an opportunity to see common activities that had already occurred suddenly set in motion on a screen: "a baby eating, a train arriving at a station, workers leaving a factory, photographers arriving at a conference, a snowball fight, the demolition of a wall" (Doane 2002, 22). Doane explains that the only requirement for something to be put on film was that it was "filmable," which made nearly every detail of life a possibility (22). The early camera very often documented these details from life and brought them to a screen. As the public became more familiar with moving pictures, filmmakers began to repeat the most popular scenes in new scenarios, creating what Amanda Ann Klein (2011) calls the first film cycles. Klein recalls William Heise's (1896) film, *The John C. Rice-May Irwin Kiss*, or, more simply, *The Kiss*, as it is later identified, as the initiator of one such cycle. Heise's film is little more than an actuality that shows two people kissing, but it becomes something else as others begin to bring the intimate moment to the screen in new circumstances. Klein cites Alfred Moul and Robert W. Paul's *The Soldier's Courtship* (1896), British Mutoscope and Biograph Company's *The Amorous Guardsman* (1898), Robert W. Paul's *Tommy Atkins in the Park* (1898), George Albert Smith's *Hanging Out the Clothes* (1897) and *The Kiss in the Tunnel* (1899), James Bamforth's identically titled *The Kiss in the Tunnel* (1899), Siegmund Lubin's *Love in a Railroad Train* (1902), and Edwin S. Porter's *What Happened in the Tunnel* (1903) as some entries in what eventually constitutes the kissing cycle. The films in this cycle not only allowed audiences to see again some everyday scene, but to see that scene anew as well. Film's two most generalizable ways to invite rewatching, seeing that which had already happened in some other place and seeing the same scene again in some new context, were enacted.

As filming and editing techniques became more sophisticated, new opportunities for rewatching emerged. Tom Gunning's (1986/2006) groundbreaking essay argues that early cinema's ability to make "images seen," and by extension to be seen again, served as the primary attraction of early films (381). This ability to show a scene even trumped the cinema's ability to tell a story. For Gunning, early cinema was "less [a] way of telling stories than [it] was a way of presenting a series of views to an audience" (382). The point of the early cinema, especially, Gunning explains, is to "solicit spectator attention, inciting visual curiosity, and supplying pleasure through an exciting spectacle" (384). One can see how the emergence of a film cycle around something as simple as two people kissing would satisfy this three-part expectation. Cinematic techniques like the closeup or other forms of "cinematic manipulation (slow motion, reverse motion, substitution, multiple exposure)" could capture something familiar, but also typically held out of view, only to bring it forward to an audience, and to do so where they could see something new in the moment (384). Spectators could watch an event again and anew.

One of these cinematic manipulations, crosscutting, seems especially noteworthy to those interested in considering how movies always involve some form of rewatching. Crosscutting not only changes what an audience is watching, but how they would understand what they were watching just before the cut carries them to some new context. The happenings in one place would alter the audience's understanding of what is happening in some other part of the diegesis. Edwin S. Porter's *The Great Train Robbery* (1903) realizes this possibility. The film begins with two robbers gagging and binding a telegraph operator. The plot cuts to the men as they board a train and rob the mail car of its safe and the passengers on the other cars of their valuables. The robbers escape the scene, first by boarding the train's locomotive, then by finding the horses they have waiting for them in the woods. The images even suggest the men have successfully executed their heist until the plot executes a crosscut that returns the audience to the opening scene and the telegraph operator. A second scenario begins to unfold that eventually leads to the capture of the presumed escapees. The use of crosscutting allows the audience to experience the robbers' escape and their capture. An instance of watching turns into an act of rewatching, and does so in the way the plot delivers the narrative.

A similar sort of dual experience occurs in what Kristin Thompson (1985) terms "the more conventional 'rescue' pattern of crosscutting, involving two persons or groups who eventually meet" just in time (211). Thompson mentions Vitagraph's *The 100-to-One Shot* (1906) as an example of this scenario. The film tells the story of a man who wins the money his family needs to satisfy a debt to a lender. As the film pushes toward its dramatic ending, the plot crosscuts between the man rushing to deliver the money and the family being evicted by the landlord. The alignment of the two scenarios through crosscutting changes the audiences' experience of the landlord's actions. Every scene gains more than one sensibility. The exact significance any moment realizes is always already a combination of the event that existed before the camera, the editor's manipulation of those events, and, ultimately, the spectator's understanding of them. All three realities exist as well as every reality that extends beyond them. The realities on the screen become their own reality with their own indexical point.

Over time, this new reality, born in the images as they appear on screen and the indexical point created, diminishes the documentary aspects of the cinematic scenario. The elements begin to operate in their own time and space. In keeping with Gunning, the documentary sensibility "goes underground, both into certain avant-garde practices and as a component of narrative films" (382). Gunning specifically mentions genre films as one instance of how some way of seeing emerges alongside the images brought to the screen. A genre film is, in the end, a way of seeing and a way of telling. As Christine Gledhill (1985/2007) remarks, genres, "each with its own recognizable repertoire of conventions running across visual imagery, plot, character, setting, modes of narrative development, music, stars," become one of "the earliest means used by the industry to organize the production and marketing of films, and by reviewers and the popular audience to guide [its] viewing" (252). This generic guidance gives audiences the opportunity to see existing films under new systems of meaning. After all, even a film that comes to be seen as a genre film enjoys some life outside that generic understanding. Audiences only come to associate a particular film with a particular genre as the ideas of that genre become more recognized, at least in the earliest periods of a genre. Rick Altman's (1999) discussion of the musical serves as an example. Many of the films that audiences would eventually deem musicals were released before the term *musical* as a category of film existed. Altman asserts that only after the steady decline of musical films between 1929 and 1932—"55 musical films in 1929 and 77 in 1930 . . . to 11 musical films in 1931 and 10 in 1932 . . . did the term 'musical' regularly" appear in discussions of the format (32). Altman further contends that it was not "until 1933, with the merger of the music-making and romantic comedy, would the term 'musical' definitively . . . appear . . . as a generic noun" (33). Only after 1933, then, would audiences return to films like *Weary River* (1929) or *Hearts in Dixie* (1929) with the understanding that these earlier films were musicals. In this way, these films became reacclimated to new categories as they were also being reexperienced or rewatched.

A similar sort of reassessment happens around the movie star. As the narrative film came into prominence, and some forms of cinema began to set aside its documentary sensibility as the primary sensibility, an appreciation for the performer, the actor, the person bringing life to the character in a narrative, began to take shape. Richard deCordova (1991) attributes the attention given the star as one of the things that leads to "the institutionalization of the cinema" (23). Audiences began to identify and associate movies through the actors who starred in them. Films became more than a technological feat. They served as a site of performance. They offered an actor space to move within a particular story, which, according to de Cordova, also allowed audiences to move beyond the "magic of the machine or the socio-cultural interest of the thing photographed . . . to explore . . . the possibility of discriminating—at the level of performance—between specific films" (23–24). Audiences began to regard films intertextually, linking otherwise unrelated films to one another simply because the same actor appeared across the set of films. The star begins to operate in a manner similar to a genre. Both concepts invite intertextual relationships. Both allow spectators to play not only with what they see on the screen, but with how to relate those things to other things they had seen in other movies. Each new instance of intertextuality offered audiences the opportunity to reconsider, to rewatch films according to some new association. The details on the screen gained points of significance that were only born after their performance, which is to say long after the camera had captured them as they existed in some real world.

Across these early decades of cinema, filmmakers were also permitting still another kind of rewatching as they brought familiar literary sources to the screen. Judith Buchanan (2012) notes that 861 literary authors have had their work "adapted to film in the first twenty years of the industry" (21). These texts were rarely treated with any sense of totality. Buchanan explains that the uses of literary sources in those early years were more like "visual quotations from a [literary] work" (21). Buchanan further argues that "choosing key moments from the inherited story . . . gave the advantage of speedy intelligibility for a picture-going audience," which was expected to be able to set the temporarily isolated moment in some larger context (21). In this way, the literary reference gave way to an imaginative project performed by spectators as they extended scenes either to their sources, if they knew those sources, or in whatever direction their imagination carried them. The act brought a second life to familiar stories, affording audiences the chance to imagine or reimagine the text they had known before their cinematic encounter with it.

This opportunity to imagine and reimagine, to watch and to rewatch, a literary source remains even after the references to literary texts begin to work across traditions of reception rather than with just a single source.

Timothy Corrigan (2007) explains that early cinema turned to the literary texts of Shakespeare, Goethe, Hugo, Dickens, and Wagner, among others, to lift its material "out of the vaudevillian heritage towards the promise of the higher cultural position associated with theater and literature" (34). Corrigan notes the emergence of a cycle of prestige pictures in the 1930s and a cycle of heritage films at the end of the twentieth century that were especially keen at performing this service. Corrigan concludes that both cycles provided audiences "comfortable images of a literary past [that] often represents a therapeutic nostalgia for 'traditional' national values, while at the same time marketing those values to foreign audiences as a self-contained, stable, and unified vision of another culture" (36). Studios might back these sorts of projects purely to produce a profit, but, as Corrigan reminds his readers, filmmakers "author" these films for their own reasons (37). Artists inject earlier texts with their own concerns; and, even if this were not the case, subsequent audiences certainly bring the texts from the past to their present. An adaptation experienced as an adaptation, which is to say with the awareness that this text exists in some other time and place, is an adaptation open to being displaced or of being rewatched in a variety of ways. In this way, a film adaptation is but an instance and exaggeration of that which all film is always already doing, namely, displacing some reality so that it can be rewatched either in relationship to that earlier reality or entirely independent of it. The choice ultimately belongs to the spectator.

Film, then, provides spectators an opportunity for rewatching. While scholars have long recognized that movies involve some form of rewatching, no one has developed an adequate way to discuss this aspect of the cinema. Part of the explanation for this gap is the narrow way in which film theorists have discussed cinema's indexicality. Far too often, scholars imagine the cinematic index to be nothing more than the resulting image of a reality that exists before the lens-based camera. Such a focus leads a media scholar like Lev Manovich (2002) to conclude that cinema is "an indexical art, an attempt to make art out of a footprint" (295). From this perspective, cinema's indexical qualities extend from a mechanical process. These aspects dissipate the moment digital technologies enter the filmmaking process. No longer reliant on an actual world, movies can invent rather than deliver images of the world. Movies begin to arise from the same inventive processes that produce more traditional paintings. The present project works against these ideas by pushing for a broader understanding of the index, one that more properly matches the idea of the index proposed by Charles Sanders Peirce and the uses of this idea in other fields of art. This broader understanding insists that the images in a moving picture maintain their potential to function indexically regardless of whether they are produced analogically or digitally. The chief argument of this book is that cinematic images maintain their indexical qualities anytime the spectator perceives them as indices, and that it is on the point of those indices that the most significant instances of rewatching occur.

Two relatively recent developments justify the timing of this study. The aforementioned advent of digital technologies is one development. Mary Ann Doane (2007) concludes that "confronted with the threat and/or promise of the digital, indexicality as a category has attained a new centrality" within film studies (129). Paul Willemen (2013) intensifies the claim, waging that "*the* most urgent problem on the agenda for film theory today is the need to address seriously C. S. Peirce's triadic classification . . . and, specifically . . . indexicality" (127). The call from both theorists to revisit what it means to call cinema an indexical art echoes Tom Gunning's (2007) suggestion that "it remains unclear . . . how the index functions within a fiction film" (47). This study responds to the above sense of urgency and uncertainty, and it does so by focusing on those contemporary films and filmmakers willing to showcase the indexical qualities of their films. This focus leads to the second recent development, namely, that contemporary films have become particularly interested in visualizing stories that turn on the point of a cinematic index, and especially when that point marks the divide between enduring trauma or ongoing adaptation. One sees this interest across any number of films that spin around some issue of personal or collective trauma. The films of Richard Linklater and Christopher Nolan deserve special attention for the way their narrative elements and plot points can turn on a cinematic index that pivots between trauma and adaptation. Linklater showcases the ways in which the cinematic reality is always set within a push to document and a pull to animate. Nolan exploits the opportunity these tensions create to rewatch and reimagine various types of reality. In the case of these two filmmakers, and most of the films discussed in this book, the cinematic index serves as an opening to a process of ongoing adaptation. The characters will perform the process of ongoing adaptation herein described, as they remake rather than merely receive the reality they once experienced. In so doing, they relocate the cinematic index, bringing it beyond the original moment of registration so that it becomes a prompt for ongoing negotiation and adaptation.

This study argues that the cinematic index always invites an active response, one that dislodges the resulting image from any fixed reality. On the point of what this study deems, in turn, the impoverished, the indefinite, the intertextual, or the imaginative index, spectators can pursue the reality the cinematic index will ever only suggest rather than realize. Such a conclusion addresses some of the concerns film theorists have about the cinematic index in the digital age. It also addresses apprehensions in trauma studies and adaptation studies, especially as they relate to the idea of a founding event or an original. Those conversant with the current discussions of the index in film studies might not be surprised by this connection. The leading discussions of the index, the ones provided by Mary Ann Doane (2002) or Laura Mulvey (2006), ultimately treat the index as a marker of some trauma. The cinematic index either records or preserves a reality that would otherwise be lost. These instances of preservation can unsettle an already unsteady existence. "The event" as it is understood in trauma studies, or "the original" as exists alongside an adapted text in an instance of adaptation, can pose a similar threat. Both realities can emanate an authority that overwhelms the potential for new expressions. The cinematic index being championed in this study refuses to be overwhelmed. It extends from realities that can never be known with certainty, and, just as importantly, that lead to realities that can only ever be suggested. The cinematic index as it is conceived in this study becomes a site of negotiation rather than veridiction.

The project exists four parts. Chapter 1, "The Index," traces the discussion of the index film and media theorists have had before contrasting that view against the ideas of the index first developed by Charles Sanders Peirce. The distinction confirms Tom Gunning's (2007) claim that film theorists have adhered to a "diminished concept of the index" (30). Surprisingly, an adherence to this limited concept of the index causes rather than uncovers the threat digital technologies supposedly bring to cinema. A more comprehensive view of the index, like the one art historian Kris Paulsen (2013) describes, shows that an index can exist regardless of whether the image is digital or analog. In keeping with the suggestions of Paulsen and the intent of Peirce, one can begin to see an indexical potential in onscreen images that arises anytime spectators approach an image as an index. The chapter pays particular attention films that feature characters that come to see their own realities from an indexical rather than actual vantage point. The shift allows the characters to perform the very process of ongoing adaptation on the point of the index spectators can enter when they approach the cinematic image as an index. By way of example, the chapter ends with a discussion of John Lee Hancock's *Saving Mr. Banks* (2013).

Chapter 2, "(Cinematic) Reality," discusses the ways in which a revised notion of the cinematic index can contribute to a more nuanced discussion of cinematic reality. The central idea in chapter 2 is that moving images rarely bring forward a reliable depiction of reality; instead, they exist as a site where reality can be negotiated. This idea is not entirely foreign to film theorists. The chapter considers the ways in which three theorists have articulated aspects of a negotiated cinematic reality, including Christian Metz's (1974) insistence that cinema is only ever providing impressions of reality, Berys Gaut's (2010) nuanced understanding of cinematic realism, and Richard Rushton's extended discussion in *The Reality of Film* (2011). The survey creates space for a less oppressive understanding of cinematic reality, one that sits between a push to document and a pull to animate what it depicts. Central to the discussion is the idea that the cinematic index is most vibrant when it sits between these two impulses. The chapter supports this proposal by looking at the films of Richard Linklater, a director who most explicitly creates films that openly balance a desire to document and to animate the reality set on screen. Linklater's emphasis draws spectators into the very process of meaning-making that has been described by theorists from Hugo Münsterberg (2001) to David Bordwell (1989). The chapter argues that Linklater's films move on the point of an index that performs and permits an ongoing process of adaptation the spectator can enter if they choose to do so.

Chapter 3, "Trauma," explores the ways in which contemporary filmmakers have begun to show characters moving through trauma, and to do so on the point of a cinematic index. As trauma scholars have shown, the current propensity of films featuring trauma is such that one can, as Janet Walker (2005) has, speak of a "trauma cinema." Most of the films that fit within this phase of production allow the narrative and stylistic choices to replicate traumatic symptoms. The films that most interest this study show characters rewatching their trauma to remake it. They feature characters that eventually break from "the event" that had earlier overwhelmed them. The chapter offers Michel Gondry's *Eternal Sunshine of the Spotless Mind* (2004) as one concise example. The main character, Joel (Jim Carrey), enters a process of adaptation that allows him to reimagine rather than reexperience earlier traumas. The chapter ends by drawing a contrast between three 9/11 films: Paul Greengrass's *United 93* (2006), Oliver Stone's *World Trade Center* (2006), and Stephen Daldry's *Extremely Loud and Incredibly Close* (2011). The idea is that the first two films remain in their traumas and that they do so indexically, repeating familiar details to recreate the experience of the initial trauma. Daldry's film, on the other hand, stages a main character, Oskar (Thomas Horn), who learns to renegotiate his earlier experiences, which allows him to break himself from his earlier trauma. In this way, Oskar becomes a further example for the spectatorial response the cinematic index encourages.

Chapter 4, "Adaptation," explores what this process will look like, using insights from adaptation studies that treat adaptation as a process rather than a product. The chapter insists that cinema, as an indexical art, encourages spectators to enter a process of ongoing adaptation rather than mere observation. The key idea of this chapter is that the cinematic index can extend to spectators an opportunity to engage in some new way the reality set on screen. The chapter further argues that one can best realize this possibility when one responds to the indexical, rather than symbolic or iconic, characteristics of cinema. The task of the spectator, to play on the ideas and title of Walter Benjamin's seminal article "The Task of the Translator" (1921), becomes, on the point of the index, an opportunity to redress the images set on screen, to create a reality that has not yet been realized. In this way, the spectator comes to watch and rewatch a film that they might otherwise only witness. The chapter ends with an extended discussion of the ways Christopher Nolan routinely plays on the point of the index. The discussion focuses on three films most especially, *Dunkirk* (2017), *Inception* (2010), and *Memento* (2000), in part, for the ways all three films resist a final form. The images placed on screen serve as an initial rather than final. There is, in fact, no final reality in these films; instead, there is the chance to continue further adaptation of the reality the point of the index suggests without ever fully realizing.

No part of the above discussion means to deny the existence of a diminished index; rather, it is to explore the ways in which other types of indices also exist, indices that might more properly account for the spectatorial response cinematic reality invites. When movies invite rewatching in whatever form—the chance to see a reality that existed before the camera; the enjoyment of seeing something familiar in some new context; the ways in which certain film techniques momentarily manipulate one's sight so that something is seen in a specific way; or the chance to undo more customary ways of seeing by setting a story in a genre, around a star, or in a moment of cinematic adaptation—they set that invitation on the point of the cinematic index. The cinematic index can lead one to a specific place in the world at a particular moment in time, but that record will always be impoverished and incomplete. It will be an approximation that can only gain fuller expression through the imaginative work of the spectator. One might more properly construe even this index as an indefinite sign, something like an indefinite pronoun, which indicates a class of proper nouns rather than any one specific noun. In most cases, the specific reality indicated by an indefinite pronoun is not even as important as the sign itself, the word, which speaks of a somebody or an everybody. The cinematic index can work similarly. It can also work intertextually or imaginatively. It can be the instigator to a process of ongoing adaptation that the spectator can enter each time the index is encountered. The opportunity cinema provides for rewatching occurs most fundamentally, in other words, on the point of an index, which, as this book will show, is something more than a record of some actual reality. It is an opportunity to participate in the ongoing adaptation of whatever reality the index suggests.

Chapter 1

THE INDEX

Alfonso Cuarón creates an irony in *Children of Men* (2006) that his source-text, P. D. James's (1992) novel by the same name, cannot have. Cuarón ends the infertility those in his diegetic world suffer by bringing a digital rather than actual baby into their barren domain. A novel can tell a story that has a digital baby in it, but such a story would not challenge the status of the novel in the way digital images have threatened the status of film. The traditional novel is under no obligation to deliver any actual reality to its reader. The novelist can fashion her reality around whatever bits of fantasy or reality she chooses. The traditional filmmaker has a different responsibility, at least according to those who deem the cinema a certain kind of indexical medium. For these, cinema can only be cinema when it brings some image of some actual reality to the screen. Lev Manovich (2002) most aptly articulates this position, arguing that any movie given to digital tricks is an instance of animation, "a subgenre of painting," rather than cinema (295). His claim assumes that cinema is, after all, as mentioned in the introduction, "the art of the index; an attempt to make art out of a footprint" (295). Such a view matches those who have long celebrated cinema's ability to do what no other art can, namely, to bring to a screen a moving image of the world as it actually existed. Digital practices undo this achievement. The digital filmmaker no longer requires a foot to make a footprint, a reality to show a reality. The diegetic world can be drawn on a computer and presented as a reality. Cuarón's choice to birth a digital baby illustrates as much.

Cuarón does not draw attention to the fact that the baby he sets on the screen has been "painted" into his world with a digital brush. The image of the child is photorealistic, which is to say that it looks like an actual baby. The audience may not even realize the digital trick has occurred as they watch the newborn move and cry. The fact that the trick is not immediately perceptible may actually make it worse to those who want the cinema to deliver actual realities. A false reality seems worse than no reality. For others, the moment might account for part of the appeal of the film. Audiences that learn about the digital child find the film performing a cultural anxiety about technology rather than simply advancing the story. They find themselves, in other words, rewatching their own anxiety on the screen. David Sutton and Peter Wogan (2009) suggest that such an opportunity may very well explain why some movies become blockbusters. The cultural anthropologists' analysis of *Jaws* serves as an example. Their discussion of that film begins with the question, "Obviously the shark in *Jaws* (2005 [1975]) instills fear, but fear of . . . what social anxieties does *Jaws* play on, and what does the shark symbolize?" (117). Sutton and Wogan offer that the film can perform a number of anxieties, most notably, the fear of sneak attacks and a fear of the Other. The representation of these fears propels the film to the success it realizes.

Peter Chumo (1995) explains the popularity of *Forrest Gump* (1994) in a similar way. For Chumo, *Gump* becomes the success it does because it resolves any number of societal divides circulating in society at the time of its release. Forrest's (Tom Hanks) story reconciles racial divides, divides the Vietnam War created, and even class divides. Chumo offers: "for a nation often bitterly divided and fragmented, even unsure of its role in the world, *Forrest Gump* is a reassuring fantasy of a man who, in an almost mythic way, can transcend our divisions and heal the scars of the past" (7). Such a view reaffirms Sutton and Wogan's argument that a blockbuster film often allows audiences to watch and rewatch their anxieties play out on the screen.

Cuarón's *Children of Men* can be shown to do something similar, albeit without the comfort Robert Zemeckis or even Steven Spielberg offers in *Forrest Gump* or *Jaws*, respectively. *Children of Men* quite directly plays into rather than alleviates the anxieties, actions, and acclimations that arise in the West in a post-9/11 world. Cuarón achieves this feat by refusing to distance his diegetic world from the world his viewers occupy. He sets the action in what Samuel Amago (2010) describes as "an utter realism" that is one part present-day London and another part "Bush II-era United States"; the two worlds meld together to form a "dystopian future/present" that is both a specific place and a no-place, a site that is being rewritten even in the moment it is being realized (216). Terryl Bacon and Govinda Dickman (2009) continue this line of thought by describing the world Cuarón places on screen as a sort of "*Here/Now* recycled from atropic, iconographic, and symbolic references . . . that constitute a . . . decrepit London-much-like-London" (147–48). The result is a plot that places viewers before a world that looks and feels much like theirs, not only as it appears, or at least as one could imagine it appearing in the not-to-distant future, but also in terms of the societal ills one might expect to find in such a place. Cuarón's film settles into a place and a non-place, a site that is what it is in the moment it is brought to the screen, but that is also just as much a place that is only being imagined. It is *there* to be recognized and to be reimagined and rewritten. Cuarón's world documents a reality, while, at the same time, animating a world that can only be on his screen.

A similar reading could be offered for Cuarón's digital baby. The appearance of a digital baby can do more than just mark the presence or absence of a cinematic index. It can capture an irony that speaks to the story Cuarón fashions. This irony works on at least two levels. The first level of irony operates on the level of the story. The preference for a digital baby refuses to solve the immediate problem facing Cuarón's diegetic world. The infertility that Cuarón's world suffers remains even after a digital baby appears. A digital baby is, after all, virtually the same as no baby at all. The child cannot save the world from its eventual extinction. Even if those factors frustrating a more proper biological reproduction relent, the world Cuarón brings to the screen is sure to become extinct due to a clear commitment to violence, an idea that is dramatized soon after the appearance of the baby. The characters that occupy the space Cuarón places on screen are spiraling faster and faster toward their own extinction because of their violence. The introduction of a baby to this world, digital or otherwise, can slow that spiral, but it can only slow it. It will not break it. The world set on screen will eventually absorb any child it receives into the violence that governs it.

Cuarón visualizes this aspect of his story by having the news of a pregnancy and the birth of the child temporarily reconcile differences that exist in this world. As it relates to the pregnancy, the news of Kee's (Clare-Hope Ashitey) pregnancy pulls the primary protagonist, Theo (Clive Owen), from his despondency. It infills the Fishes, the primary resistance group in the film, with a new sense of urgency. The most dramatic effect of the baby occurs just after the child is born. Theo and the new mother move from their makeshift delivery room. They pass through a hall occupied by resistance soldiers and, eventually, into the street filled with those they are resisting. The state army freezes. They stand in awe of the child. All fighting stops as Kee and the child move through what would otherwise be an open competition between two ideological spaces. The child's presence causes a literal, albeit temporary, cease-fire.

The fighting resumes in full force the moment Theo, Kee, and child are clear of the immediate consequences of such conflict. What is most interesting about the resumed conflict is how quickly it escalates. One side fires a rifle. The other side fires a missile from a tank. The response is disproportionate. In two or three quick moves, one can imagine the two sides obliterating each other. The fact that a baby occupies this world can hardly save it. The immediacy of the violence shows that there is no real way to stand clear of the overwhelming violence. An apocalyptic-minded commitment to violence will bring the world to an end before infertility has time to realize its most devastating outcome. One could read Cuarón's decision to give such a world a digital baby as a kind of protest to this world's commitment to violence. The staging of the supposed reverence this world gives a newborn baby, as if to honor life—only to return in the next moment to the violence that will almost certainly bring about that child's death—provides the basis for such a protest whether it is intended or not.

The first level of irony leads to a second, or at least to paradox, depending on how one sees it. The audience watching *Children of Men* has the chance to imagine a post-human world, which is to say both a world without humans and, more properly, a world devoid of the human structures that have defined recent human history. Such a world runs counter to the hope that motivates most of the action in the film, and certainly to any hope the final moments of the film suggest. Cuarón most succinctly captures the first frustration when Luke (Chiwetel Ejiofor), the self-promoted leader of the Fishes, murders Jasper (Michael Caine) outside his self-sufficient home in the woods after the recluse refuses to tell the leader where Theo and Kee have gone. As it relates to the present argument, the most important aspect of this scene is what the spectator watching it imagines as the event unfolds. Jasper's world, the safe haven he has created for himself and others, will be lost to the woods in short order after his death. Cuarón's choice of framing as the event unfolds begs audiences to imagine this loss. Theo watches atop a hill, moving to find a clear view through the trees. From a distance, he, and the audience with him, struggles to distinguish the house from the vegetation that surrounds it and even stretches across its roof. The image encourages spectators to imagine the house completely beneath the vegetation that is already engulfing it, which is to say a time when any trace of humanity will be lost.

The image as it emerges through the trees and vegetation in this scene is especially interesting. It might be one of the few scenes without much digital brushwork. The scene accepts a higher measure of indexical accuracy as it is most normally considered. Still, the image as it exists before the spectator champions a cinematic reality over any actual reality. The scene is a mix of what is there in front of the camera and what the spectator imagines will exist as that world moves forward. The final scene of the film works in a similar way, with the sea replacing the vegetation. Theo has brought Kee and her baby, Dylan, to the place where they are to meet the ship, *Tomorrow*, that promises them safety. The dinghy the three characters occupy floats in the vast ocean. The water creates a dense mist that is literally rising and blocking one's ability to see the characters. The humans begin to disappear from the screen and do disappear just before the screen goes black. The sounds of children laughing and playing on the soundtrack can be heard, but this sound refuses to promise any certain future. The source of the laughter is entirely undetermined. It could be almost anything, and, perhaps, most disturbingly, it could exist at any time. It could, in other words, be a memory as much as a sign of some salvation. It could index a desired hope as much as a distant past. The index, in this moment, can extend from some imagination or revert to some reality. The index points in at least two directions if not more.

The digital phantom that is the baby Dylan can work similarly. It can project to some unrealized reality or mark some existing one. It can simultaneously point toward both realities. As it relates to the irony or paradox the digital birth brings to the story, any sense of spectatorial hope will be qualified the moment they learn Dylan is a digital phantom. His numerical status undermines any optimism. As Nicole LaRose (2010) notes, "a digital subject . . . conceives of reproduction outside of biology" (9). Set within a story where the most natural forms of biological reproduction no longer work, either due to infertility as the film would have it, or sterility as the novel has it, technology provides the only path to survival. That solution does not, as LaRose explains, "solve the biological infertility of the dystopian world [, . . . rather it] introduces a new form of kinship that makes . . . biology relational to technology" (17). Humans can only survive to the extent that technology enables their survival, which is, at least on an individual level, only temporarily. Every individual, if not the whole of the civilization that supports them, will pass. Such awareness, LaRose argues, creates a digital angst that arises as much from an absence as from an ongoing presence. The digital image is *there* even when no one is *here* to see it.

Julian Murphet (2008) picks up on this suggestion by describing what makes Cuarón's preference for a digital baby so haunting: "Cuarón has opted, correctly, to put in the place of the transfigurative infant not a 'real' screaming baby, but the film's most subtle and perfect digital effect" (114–15). For Murphet, the choice performs "the traumatic effect of the digital-Real, a curvature of indexical space, right at the empty centre of the film's articulation . . . who is . . . suddenly more animate than any of the actors" (115). The appearance of the digital baby reperforms the anxieties audiences see on display for those who live in the worlds imagined in Ridley Scott's *Blade Runner* (1982) or, more recently, Alex Garland's *Ex Machina* (2015). Both of those worlds have lost their ability to distinguish the difference between human and nonhuman life. Murphet suggests this loss very nearly guarantees that machines will win. Nonhuman life has all the advantages. It is the "fittest" of the two forces, or so the worry would go. Cuarón plays into this worry, albeit in a more subtle way than does Scott or Garland, and does so through the introduction of the digital baby. Most the film's central characters die over the course of the film. As already mentioned, Theo dies in the closing moments. The digital baby, of course, lives. The digital child will not be able to reproduce, so it cannot correct the issue confronting Theo's world, but it can outlive everyone in that world, just as it very nearly has done even before the film stops.

The finale is an interesting reversal of the scenario that is played out a couple of years later in the early parts of Pixar's *WALL-E* (2008). The Earth in *WALL-E* has become as inhabitable as *Children of Men* imagines it to be. The "wake-up call" E. Ann Kaplan (2016) sees Cuarón's film making, for "audiences to attend to what their actions are doing to the species and the Earth—to the real dangers of climate change and other global economic and social conditions," has gone unanswered (78). Human beings have jettisoned the planet on corporate spaceships meant to provide humans a home while a corporation restores the planet. In their absence, a host of Waste Allocation Load-Lifter: Earth Class (WALL-E) trash compactors cull the debris. What is most interesting about this movie as it relates to the present discussion is the way movies appear in *WALL-E*, and especially Gene Kelly's *Hello Dolly!* (1969). The lone operational WALL-E begins to take on human characteristics as he completes his years of work. One marker of that humanity involves him playing a VCR of *Hello Dolly!* in his makeshift abode. The technology brings a live-action clip into an otherwise fully animated world. The moment reverses the more usual shift from human to nonhuman played out in *Children of Men*. In *WALL-E*, the live action sequence finds a way through the animation. Something human transforms the machine. And all of this happens through a movie, which would seem to reverse the tide that Manovich imagines washing over cinema, which the theorist claims will bring film to its end. In *WALL-E*, the animated, the painted, gives way to the analog.

The two moments—the one from *WALL-E* that has a machine in an animated film watching a live-action analog film, and the other from *Children of Men* that brings a digital baby into what otherwise appears to be an actual world—enter the same indexical fight. There are those like Manovich who claim that the emergence of the digital photograph annihilates the cinema, returns it to its pre-nineteenth-century conditions. As it relates to *Children of Men*, the digital baby, and every digital detail that forms the diegetic world that surrounds it (as the baby is just one of many digital tricks in the film), mark the end of cinema. For Manovich, the digital child occupies a space on the screen with the same mix of presence and absence that every digital image manages. The image is *there* on the screen, but it has never been *there* in a world in front of a camera, which means to Manovich and those of the same mind that the detail is uncinematic. One finds a concise example of this thought from Bruce Kawin (2011). Kawin compares the ending of two movies, Abel Gance's *La Roue* (1922) and James Cameron's *Avatar* (2009). Gance's film ends with "a real-world image" of clouds moving around a mountain (196). Kawin considers the moment a stroke of luck. The movement of the clouds and mountains showcase the symbolic core of Gance's film. Kawin deems Gance's image "a complete cinematic sign, with iconic, indexical, and symbolic elements that are clearly expressed and plainly interdependent" (196). Kawin finds Cameron's ending to be lacking, at least indexically speaking. Cameron concludes his film with an image that also captures the symbolic core of his film. The director presents the image of a computer-generated dragon flying through an equally computer-generated cloud-filled sky. Like Gance's image of clouds and mountains, Cameron's image brings the film to a fitting ending, but it does so through digital tricks performed on a computer. Kawin judges Cameron's image to be "a representative digital composite. . . . iconically, it resembles the event it portrays; symbolically, it evokes Earthly images . . .; indexically, it is nowhere" (197). Cameron's images may be photorealistic, but they are not realistic, and that denies them their indexicality, or so argues Kawin.

Some film theorists have resisted the idea that the digital image threatens the very existence of cinema. Tom Gunning (2008), for instance, wonders to what extent the means of production impacts how one interprets an image. Gunning submits, "I am not sure we ordinarily approach photographs semiotically . . . as signs"; rather, most photographs simply function as "an image of the world" (46). Gunning argues that digital photographs can provide such an image; they do it all the time. They provide viewers an image of the world, in part, because the image, itself, is never held entirely in the frame. Every image, Gunning argues, makes us imagine "something else, something behind it, before it, somewhere in relation to it" (46). Gunning insists that digital images, especially when grouped as Manovich would have it with animated images, can spark this same sense of imagination. They have been doing so throughout the history of cinema. And, in keeping with the spirit of Gunning's argument, so too have animated films. As such, even if a digital film were deemed an animation, it would, as every animated film before it, spark the imagination of the viewer that watches it, at least as long as the film plays in front of a human imagination.

By also emphasizing the relationship images forge with a viewer, Niels Niessen (2012) indirectly extends the argument Gunning begins. Indexical arguments tend to emphasize the relationship the image on screen had with the reality that existed before the camera. While not denying that relationship, Niessen claims it is not the only one, and not the most important relationship, not even when addressing the indexical qualities of an image: "at least as important is the relation between viewer and image" (161). Niessen reminds readers that "for Peirce, the index par excellence is the pointing finger.... it takes hold of our eyes ... and forcibly directs them to a particular object and there it stops" (165). That may be where the index stops, but it is not where the viewer's imagination stops, especially not in the cinema. The cinematic index is simply where the spectator's imagination begins. The interpolation that symbols and icons perform, dependent as they are on social convention and the need to resemble that which they denote, does not exist with the index. The index is always yet-to-be-determined, not-yet-interpreted, not-yet-known. It directs one's attention to a specific object, but it does not establish "the nature of its object" or even itself (165). Niessen insists that this sort of cinematic index can exist in both the digital and the analog frame. For Niessen, both modes of registration index something, and they do so deictically and in relationship with a viewer. After all, the significance of index at any moment can only ever be explored by a viewer. The index only admits the existence of something beyond itself.

The question becomes, what sort of index do spectators watch when they watch movies, digital or otherwise? According to the long discussion film theorists have had of the index, one might most properly conclude that audiences watch a diminished index. This is the view Gunning (2007) takes toward the discussions of the cinematic index he reads. Gunning claims that the discussion of the index he reads limits the camera to only ever bringing forward a trace or an impression of reality. Both possibilities reduce film to little more than a substitute for something that once was the real, but not as something that can realize its own reality or even the reality the image means to depict. The camera can, after all, never capture the whole of a reality. The filmmaker can only bring to the screen a slice of the reality that stood in front of the camera, if for no other reason than because some decontextualization will always occur. Some distance from an actual time will always be traveled, which means that the reality on the screen will never be the reality in the world, and neither does it mean to be, Gunning argues. The cinema is always already dealing with impressions of realities rather than reality itself.

Gunning's summary is not a reason to abandon the idea of the index, even if Gunning himself seems inclined to do just that. It is, however, a reason to reconsider the cinematic index. That is the aim of this chapter and this book. As this project will show, contemporary cinema often plays on the point of complex index. The image on the screen is a mix of real and imagined realities. Both types of realities can function as indices. To help identify the different ways the cinematic index can function, this project explores four types of indices beyond Gunning's diminished index. Contemporary filmmakers play on the point of the impoverished index, which is most like the diminished index. The difference between the impoverished and diminished index is that the impoverished index knows that it is only an approximation of a reality, and one that can never lead one back to any actual reality, even if it does lead to some reality in some past. The second index, the indefinite index, works similarly. The indefinite index is situated in some past, but it points to a class of realities rather than an individual one. It is an "everyone" rather than a specific "one." The last two indices work even more generally. The intertextual index suggests a relationship between two or more otherwise independent or loosely associated realities. The intertextual index serves as a bind between these realities, rather than a sign of some specific reality. The last type of index, the imaginative index, points to a reality, but it is a reality that the spectator must construct. In this way, the imaginative index remakes whatever aspect of reality is brought to the screen, and it does so through the imaginative work of the spectator. The imaginative index becomes the most interesting index of the mix, at least as it relates to this study, because it most explicitly enters the process of ongoing adaptation this book insists an indexical cinema can perform and permit. An example of this process can be traced through any number of contemporary films. One specific example will appear at the end of the chapter. Before turning to that example and discussing the ways in which all four indices emerge in it, some additional justification for moving beyond the diminished index is in order.

Regardless of where one lands on the debate on whether digital technologies erase or recast the cinema, one does well to admit that the advent of digital technologies gives theorists a reason to reconsider the cinematic index. Mary Ann Doane (2007) proposes that scholars must either look to recover the index that has been lost to them or altogether abandon the concept. Doane looks to recover some sense of indexicality by emphasizing, as Niessen will after her, "the deictic index," the "this" that at once "points to and verifies an existence" (146). For Doane, the cinematic index works the way a relic works: it reminds those who see it that something *was*. However, unlike those who claim the cinematic index verifies itself through an actual relationship with the world, Doane determines that the cinematic index verifies cinema itself. Every image, even the digital image, Doane reasons, participates in "representation and reviv[es] the idea of a medium" (148). This, for Doane, means that the advent of digital technologies changes rather than threatens the medium. This is the point Niessen ultimately makes as well: "cinema as a medium ... is inherently transforming[,] ... giving expression to people's changing relationships with the world" (174–75). Niessen and Doane, then, both see cinema surviving, and doing so with its indexical qualities intact. The index that matters most to Doane (and to a lesser extent Niessen, if only because of his primary interest in the relationship between the image and the viewer), however, is the one that points to a medium that lives regardless of mode of registration.

Paul Willemen (2013) reaches a similar conclusion even as he looks to redirect the concept as it typically arises in film studies. Willemen welcomes the idea of an index that operates as a pointed trace; he just encourages scholars to let that trace mark different periods of the movie-making industry rather than anything in the real world. The index that matters most to Willemen is the one that demonstrates "the industry's power and competitive aspirations ... connected as they are to particular pieces of equipment and particular phases ... all of them indexing a moment or phase in the organization and development of an industrial sector" (128). From this view, digital tricks do not fail to reference reality. They do, however, most essentially reference a reality not on the screen. Cinematic tricks of all kinds mark the industrial, technological, and economic attributes of the epoch that enables them. As a matter of explanation, Willemen offers, "what De Mille, and, before him, Griffith, and before that, Pastrone, put on display in their historical epics [are] the means of production at the disposal of the industry"; these filmmakers create images that are "indexing or anchoring the text's relation to an actual moment in the 'history' of a social formation" (119–20). The index remains. So, too, does the cinema.

Gunning (2007), as already admitted, seems readier to abandon the idea of the index from film theory, unsure what the concept offers those who want to appreciate more fully the experience of watching a movie. Gunning argues that film scholars have long assumed cinema to be an indexical art, even if they have failed to articulate what that means. Gunning suggests that film theorists have generally been content to support arguments for the reality of the cinema through an "abstracted" rather actual understanding of the index as it emerges across the writing of Charles Sanders Peirce (30). For many film theorists the index has become little more than a declaration that the image brought to the screen from a lens-based camera had some direct connection to the reality that existed before that camera. Both senses of *before* matter here. The discussions describing a diminished index stress the fact that the images on the screen occurred in front of a camera. They also emphasize the way in which the realities captured in an image existed earlier than the image itself. The two conditions presumably twice-load the image with an authority it would not otherwise possess. Gunning estimates that an overemphasis on these two aspects of authority reduces the index to little more than "the existential trace or impression left by an object" (30). The image on the screen becomes fixed in the past that supposedly produced it. Gunning cautions that this static description of the cinematic image misses the significance of motion in a moving picture. Gunning bargains that movies engage spectators the way they do because they move rather than that some part of what is on the screen ever existed in the world before they subsisted on the screen. Gunning explains that motion invites "the empathic participation, both imaginative and physiological, of viewers"; it permits the spectator to be "absorbed not by a 'has been there' but by a sense of 'There it is!'" (46–47). Any assessment of the way cinema engages spectators would need to account for the difference between these two utterances.

Gunning openly wonders whether an appeal to the index can capture much about the experience one has watching a movie. He suggests that the index may have "been entrusted with tasks it cannot fulfill and that reading it back into classical realist theories of the cinema probably obscures as much as it explains" (47). Gunning is probably right, at least as long as the diminished version of the index he bemoans is the only version of the index informing considerations of the movie-watching experience. Interestingly, film scholars struggle to discuss any other index even when they mean to do so. Manovich and Kawin imagine the digital index being a trace to nowhere, which is still a trace. Doane and Willemen cast an index that marks a medium or an industry. What is most helpful about these proposals is the way they reconceptualize the index. The index becomes something more than just an assurance of some lived reality lifted from some past, which is what has so often been the case, if only because this is the aspect of the index Peter Wollen (1969) most emphasizes when he introduces Peirce's index to film theorists through André Bazin.

Wollen is the first theorist to directly discuss Peirce's index, icon, and symbol as they relate to the cinema. Admittedly, his reasons for doing so have less to do with establishing the cinema as a realistic medium than with determining whether or not the cinematic image is a complete sign in a Peircean sense. Most of what Wollen writes works to distinguish an incomplete cinematic sign from a complete one. Wollen provides examples only of indexical, symbolic, or iconic thinking about film. Wollen deems Bazin indexical, Christian Metz symbolic, and Josef von Sternberg iconic. Each of these instances of cinema is incomplete. Wollen insists that an image on the screen must realize each side of Peirce's trichotomy for there to be a complete cinematic sign:

> The aesthetic richness of the cinema springs from the fact that it compromises all three dimensions of sign: the indexical, the iconic and the symbolic. The greatest weakness of almost all of those who have written about the cinema is that they have taken one of these dimensions, made it the ground of their aesthetic, the "essential" dimension of the cinematic sign, and discarded the rest. This is to impoverish the cinema. Moreover, none of these dimensions can be discounted: they are co-present. . . . it is only by considering the interaction of the three different dimensions of the cinema that we can understand its aesthetic effect. (141)

Wollen ends his discussion of Peirce's trichotomy by praising the films of Jean-Luc Godard, who Wollen believes develops a complete cinematic sign. Wollen suggests that Godard creates "Peirce's perfect sign . . . an almost equal amalgam of the symbolic, the iconic and the indexical[,] . . . conceptual meaning, pictorial beauty and documentary truth" (154). This final point is rarely introduced in a discussion of Wollen's index, which is unfortunate. Wollen writes about the index, the icon, and the symbol to show that the cinema possesses all three forms, and that all three forms can cooperate within a single frame. Wollen wants to guard against the deprivation of cinema. Unfortunately, theorists have tended to focus on comments on each aspect of the sign, which are overly reductive at times, rather than his fuller idea, namely, that all three sides of the sign must exist to have a complete cinematic sign. As it relates to the index, scholars see a trace or an impression to some fixed reality rather than something more complex. In so doing, they ignore the broader aspects of the index Peirce proposes. Such a valuation turns the screen into an archive and the image into a record. This rendering of the index does not capture the way in which the cinema can engage the spectator on the point of the index.

To see how this diminished index emerges, one does well to follow Wollen's remarks about the index a bit further. Wollen prefaces his remarks about Godard's films as a complete cinematic sign with a discussion of the symbol, the icon, and the index that (overly) emphasizes the unique qualities of each form. The discussion exaggerates the qualities of each form to the detriment of the shared qualities between the three expressions of signs. As signs, all three forms express "something that stands to somebody for something in some respect or capacity" (Peirce 99). Wollen sets aside the general idea of the sign, and with it the need to consider each form as one instance of the sign, to consider the unique qualities of each. As it relates to the index, this means setting aside the more nuanced aspects of the index.

The only aspect that matters to Wollen by the end of his discussion is the relationship the index has to something in the real world. Wollen means to show how the index arises "by virtue of an existential bond between itself and its object" (122). Peirce's index has other functions and even more significant qualities. Chief among them is the way the index exists independent of the kinds of social negotiation and recognition that govern icons and symbols. For its part, the index does not negotiate its subject; it simply indicates its existence. The meaning of that object is *yet-to-be-determined*. As a sign within a series of signs, one could say the same thing for the subject, the indexical sign itself. It also carries a meaning that has yet-to-be-determined. It simply exists, and, in so doing, bears witness to the existence of some other reality, which the index can only ever suggest. In this way, the index is always explicit rather than symptomatic. Its reality is never in dispute even if its significance is never irrevocably established. The index remains open to be explored, and to be explored in a variety of ways. Or, more properly, this is what the cinematic index could be. One must recover this sense of the cinematic index, however, for it to exist.

Wollen, perhaps inadvertently, shifts Peirce's discussion of the index to a diminished index when he relates Peirce's concept to an overzealous reading of Bazin's (1960) "Ontology of the Photographic Image." Wollen links passages from that piece to parts of Peirce's discussion. For instance, Wollen understands Bazin's comparison of the photographic image to a variety of objects that touched their subject, "a mould, a death mask, a Veronica, the Holy Shroud of Turin, a relic, an imprint," to align with Peirce's idea that indices will bear some literal relationship with their object (125). To be fair, Wollen's point is not to establish a proper way to discuss the index. Wollen wants to distinguish the index from the icon and the symbol, even to show the consequences of championing one aspect of Peirce's trichotomy over another. In other words, as already admitted, Wollen wishes to expose the limits of an incomplete sign. To bolster that argument, Wollen tilts Bazin's argument in ways that emphasize the world over an image, reality over the cinema. Wollen justifies this approach by reminding readers that Bazin wanted to create "an aesthetic . . . that . . . asserted the primacy of the object over the image, the primacy of the natural world over the world of signs" (126). Such an emphasis explicitly values the object in the world over the image on the screen. The best images, Wollen finds Bazin to say, are the most natural. Wollen offers Bazin's evaluation of Vittorio de Sica's *Bicycle Thieves* (1948) as the exemplar of Bazin's aesthetic: de Sica's film serves as the "first example of pure cinema . . . as Bazin would have it. . . . No more actors, no more plot, no more *mise en scene* . . . no more cinema" (131). With de Sica,

Bazin sees reality brought to the screen. The viewer does not need to work to see this reality. It exists to be recognized.

Unfortunately, this view of the index mischaracterizes Peirce's index if not Bazin's aesthetic. Peirce's philosophy is a philosophy of signification, not revelation. Wollen's discussion of Peirce, especially as it emerges through his connections to Bazin, misses the more general function of the index, if for no other reason than because it sets aside the active spectator. Wollen assigns Bazin's aesthetic an unmistakable, and regrettable, passivity. Wollen warrants this reading of Bazin by holding that the theorist meant to highlight "the passivity of the natural world rather than the agency of the human mind" (131). Wollen does admit that Bazin eventually moves beyond the position he assigns him. Wollen writes that Bazin's emphasis on the interrelationship of "the interior and the exterior, the spiritual and the physical, the ideal and the material" leads Bazin to conclude "that films should be made, not according to some *a priori* method or plan, but like those of Rossellini, from 'fragments of raw reality, multiple and equivocal in themselves, whose meaning can only emerge *a posteriori* thanks to other facts, between which the mind is able to see relations'" (132). In this way Bazin does imagine an active spectator; but this spectator does not serve Wollen's argument the way the passive one does, so it is not the subject of his discussion. Wollen focuses on those passages from Bazin that consider a more passive spectator. Wollen prefers a blunt index to a robust one. He emphasizes one sense of being-there that the index isolates while ignoring others. The index does, of course, carry a sense of being-there with the object that gives it shape. It also maintains from the moment it is placed on screen a sense of being-there in the plot. This sense of being-there in the plot is critically important; this sense exists the longest, and ultimately matters most. It is also the sense of being-there that removes the index from some originary moment and does so as soon as the image is brought into existence. In this way, the image carries with it a distance from the original reality that gave it shape. It is this sense of distance that allows the cinematic index to exist as an index that leads to another index rather than a fixed reality. Unfortunately, it is this sense of distance that has most often been glossed by theorists. Most theorists consider the sense of being-there with some reality that existed before the camera rather than a sense of being-there in the plot. The four types of cinematic index being proposed in this study depend on some recognition of the reality the image itself acquires. Such indices only ever exist in a now, which is to say in the moment the image is encountered.

A sense of now returns the discussion to Gunning's interest in film spectatorship, and it does so indexically. Somewhat surprisingly, Gunning (2007) provides the first step toward such an index when he notes the extent to which Christian Metz's "cinematic impression of reality depends on 'forgetting'" (47). Some sense of "forgetting," Gunning argues, is what enables the "there it is" to be expressed. Chang-dong Lee's *Burning* (2018) has a wonderful moment early in the film that can directly speak to this sort of forgetting as it relates to the indexical qualities of moving images and the opportunity spectators have to respond to those qualities. Hae-mi (Jeon Jong-seo) sits center screen at a table in a bar with her hometown mate, Jung-su (Yoo Ah-in). As the two characters talk about Hae-mi's upcoming trip to Africa, Hae-mi sets her glass of beer on the table to her left. She turns to her right to grab an object that does not visibly exist. Hae-mi pulls in front of her what she imagines to be a bowl. She reaches into its center and retrieves an object. She turns the palm of her hand upward, as if to leave the item sitting in her hand for a few seconds. She, then, begins tossing the object into the air. With each pitch, Hae-mi follows with her whole face what would be the rise and fall of the item. The camera cuts to Jung-su, whose eyes, at first, stay with Hae-mi's face, before eventually simulating Hae-mi's motions as if he sees what she sees. Only after she has Jung-su's attention does Hae-mi explain her eccentric behavior: "This is pantomime," she says as she peels the skin of a tangerine. Jung-su wonders if she is taking classes to become an actress. Hae-mi scuffs at that idea. She says she is learning the skill just for fun, and justifies her decision by declaring, "Look! I can eat tangerines whenever I want." Jung-su is impressed. He tells Hae-mi that she has talent. Hae-mi protests: "This has nothing to do with talent." The trick, she insists, is simply to forget that the tangerine is not really there. "The important thing," she further clarifies, "is to think you really want one. Then your mouth will water, and it'll really taste good." Hae-mi proves her point by pantomiming one more especially delicious bite and enjoying the sensations her performance produces until the two characters burst into laughter.

The scene imagines a central object, the tangerine, which becomes an index where those emphasizing the diminished index would say no index exists. The standard discussion would insist that there can be no index where there was not first some reality. If one cannot speak of the index for a digital baby or a computer-generated dragon, then one certainly cannot speak of the index for a purely imagined tangerine. Remarkably, the short story on which the film is based, Haruki Murakami's (1983/1991) "Barn Burning," and the script Jung-mi Oh and Chang-dong Lee adapt from that story suggest you can speak of such things. As it relates to Murakami's story, the performance in the author's short story creates space for the narrator to comment on how different writing about something differs from seeing it. The narrator describes the young woman's performance peeling, eating, and discarding the seeds in each bite of tangerine. The narrator ultimately admits to being dissatisfied with his own description: "when you try to put it in words, it doesn't sound like anything special. But if you see it with your own eyes for ten or twenty minutes (almost without thinking, she kept on performing it) gradually the sense of reality is sucked right out of everything around you" (52). For Murakami's narrator, the absence of reality the performance creates frustrates his ability to present the event with accuracy. Hae-mi's performance becomes more significant than any description of it can be.

Lee's cinematographer, Kyung-pyo Hong, reasserts this same idea on the screen. The performance invites one to see a prop regardless of whether that prop is actually placed on the screen or not. Hae-mi's performance leads the audience to imagine the tangerine just as Jung-su eventually imagines it. The prop materializes on the screen. The piece of fruit is *there* if only by impression in the broadest sense of the word, to return to Gunning. As Gunning explains, "cinema works with images that possess an impression of reality, not its materiality" (44). Moreover, the cinematic impression always exists in the present rather than in some past. It demands a spectator who is also present, just as Jung-su eventually becomes present before Hae-mi's tangerine. Once present, the character, as the spectator with him, is ready to help determine rather than merely receive the significance of the image observed on the screen. In this way, the performance manufactures what is real. This feature of the performance is visualized the moment Jung-su averts his eyes to see the object Hae-mi pretends to hold in her hands. In keeping with Hae-mi's earlier claim, the image is real if the performers, or the filmmakers behind them, or the audience in front of them, want it enough. As it relates to the spectator, one could argue that the image becomes real the moment spectators participate in its existence through their experience of it. This idea brings one back to Gunning's desire to understand more fully the "extreme spectator involvement that movement can generate," and it does so on the point of the index (47–48).

Gunning's desire is not entirely unrelated to the broader opinion Manovich wants to develop. One can reduce the essential idea in the above arguments from Manovich, Willemen, and Doane to one statement: the appearance of the digital requires a reassessment of the cinema. For Manovich, this reassessment demands a return to earlier ideas associated with movies. One must again emphasize motion in the moving picture, an emphasis that Manovich claims cinema loses in the early days of its development as it disassociates itself from animation and artifice. Manovich reminds readers that what cinema did better than "numerous other nineteenth-century pro-cinematic devices . . . [like] magic-lantern slides[,] . . . the Phenakisticope, the Thaumatrope, the Zootrope, the Praxinoscope, the Choreutoscope . . . [is that it] cut all reference to its origins in artifice" (296, 298). The cinema began to "pretend to be a simple recording of an already existing reality" (299). Every other pro-cinematic device had to leave visible the means by which it represents reality. Manovich argues that this pretense paradoxically robs cinema of its early vitality. It fixes reality in a frame that meant to free it. Digital painting, the term Manovich chooses to describe digital cinema, corrects this misstep by allowing reality to function "as raw material for further compositing, animating, and morphing" (301). Reality becomes the starting point of a movie in digital cinema rather than the essential point.

Such images, Manovich maintains, comprise a double code. One part of the code, the real, references some reality. The other, the digital, reminds, or at least has the potential to remind, viewers how to negotiate that reality because, in some ways, it is no reality at all. Cuarón's digital baby actually serves as one example for how this can work, and especially for those who know the baby is alphanumeric. The artificial baby confronts the reality placed on screen in such a way that audiences can begin to scrutinize the reality Cuarón constructs or, more properly, reconstructs it from James's novel. Cuarón's (re)construction can only ever really be the first in a series of reconstructions. Spectators will perceptually reconstruct the image and place it in the plot each time they see it, either affirming prior constructions or building new ones. A series of resulting constructs emerges either way. The actual image on the screen becomes one entry in a series of entries between some alpha and omega. The image on the screen returns the spectator to a middle, to a site of negotiation, to a reality that disrupts the reality that came before the image (the real) or the reality that came after it (the imagined). A bidirectional index sits at the center of the two, pointing the spectator in one direction or the other. The image becomes an instance of Manovich's double-code, which is equal parts reality and code, which means it is also an open sign rather than a closed certainty. In some cases, like that of George Lucas's *The Phantom Menace* (1999), this mix is concealed, hidden from the audience. In other cases, like Vuk Ćosić's *ASCII History of the Moving Image* (1998), the mix is brought to the foreground. In both cases, the mix of reality and code is present, which allows the image on screen to function as something other than a simple record of reality.

Manovich argues that the particular pairing of reality and code that Ćosić devises "evokes not only a peculiar episode in the history of computer culture but a number of earlier forms of media and communication technologies as well" (332). As Manovich explains, ASCII code extends from earlier technologies like Baudot code and Morse code. The two earlier codes convert symbols into sounds of regular durations, which is just what ASCII accomplishes. The more comprehensive code embodies for Manovich each of the earlier technologies, so that ASCII serves as a compression of a series of technologies rather than simply a technology unto itself. Manovich maintains that Ćosić's *ASCII* compresses a series of technologies in just the way a digital image compresses a series of realities. The double acts of compression result in what Manovich deems "an 'artistic compression'; that is, along with staging the new status of moving images as a computer code, [Ćosić] also 'encodes' many key issues of computer culture and new media art in these images" (333). Here, one finds oneself alongside Willemen's reconstituted index. Ćosić's compression locates his moving image in a particular era of cinema in the same way De Mille, Griffith, and Pastrone locate their moving images in their epochs, even if that compression simultaneously acknowledges other realities as well. There is room, then, for more than one index.

One should be noted that the industrial index Willemen most especially favors does champion one reality over another. The reality of an industry displaces the significance of every other reality, indexically speaking. The reality or impression of reality in the image on the screen hardly matters. The image is little more than a period, which is to declare it both an epoch and a full stop. The sense of contiguity the index should favor is displaced by a moment of completion. To return to Cuarón's digital baby, when left under the most extreme versions of an industrial index, the entry of a baby formed in a computer becomes mostly, if not only, a piece of evidence for the circumstances occurring at or around the release of *Children of Men*. In the case of the former, the birth of the digital child reminds audiences of the presumed death of cinema; in the case of the latter, it signals the dawn of a new period of filmmaking, which, one could understand as another kind of death. One epoch ends as another begins. The old is gone. The new is here. In these instances, the industrial index marks a moment that passes in some period around the release of a film rather than as an opportunity to participate in the ongoing construction of a reality that exists on the screen or just beyond it, to remain with Gunning's idea of the importance of offscreen space. This more limited view tranquilizes rather than motivates active forms of spectatorship. The index of a different sort can do better, and it can do better by functioning as an index each time it is perceived.

To recover this broader index, one does well to return to Peirce's proposal of the index. Albert Atkin (2005) stipulates that any discussion of a Peircean index must be grounded in Peirce's more general idea about signs. For Peirce the sign exists as "something which stands to somebody for something in some respect or capacity"; the point of the sign "addresses somebody, that is, creates in the mind of that person an equivalent sign, or perhaps a more developed sign," which serves as the "interpretant of the first sign" (163). Atkin finds three critical ideas about the sign in this definition. The first idea is that every sign stands for something else, which is to say, among other things, that the sign is not the object it means to stand for. The sign is always an indication of the object. Just as importantly, the sign is also always invocative, which is to say that it brings about a subsequent sign in the mind of the person who perceives it. In this way, the sign is never an endpoint; rather, it is the start of a process. In keeping with Paul de Man's (1982) assessment, "the interpretation of a sign is not, for Peirce, a meaning but another sign; it is a reading, not a decodage, and this reading has, in its turn, to be interpreted into another sign, and so on *ad infinitum*" (9). This process is always relational, an instance of contiguity, which accounts for the third critical idea Atkin finds in Peirce's definition. At minimum, the more developed sign in the mind of the observer relates to the first sign, which itself stands in relationship to rather than realizes what it signifies, and it does so either as a symbol, an icon, or an index.

Daniel Chandler (2016) provides a useful overview of each of these three potential signs, as well as the manner in which the symbol, the icon, and the index relate to its object. The symbol relates to its object through convention, which is to say through social agreement. Chandler lists the following examples of symbols: "language in general (plus specific languages, alphabetical letters, punctuation marks, words, phrases, and sentences), numbers, Morse code, traffic lights, [and] national flags" (40). Each sign that falls in these categories indicates what it does because some societal rule has determined it should. It only continues to relate to that specific entity for as long as that societal determination holds. In this way, symbols are always arbitrary. They symbolize what they do to whom they do only for as long as they do. A sign that symbolizes economic power to one group, for instance, can symbolize economic diminution to another; and it can indicate something else entirely to still a third group. The World Trade Center in New York is a clear example of this polysemy. As Robert Patrick and Amy MacDonald (2012) describe, the Twin Towers suggested one thing to Western audiences before the tragic events of 9/11, and something else entirely to some non-Western audiences. They came to signify something else still to audiences after 9/11. As a symbol, the significance of an image of the Towers evolves with the attitudes and perceptions that evolve around it.

Chandler discusses icons in a similar way. Icons relate to their object through some "perceived *resemblance* or imitation" (Chandler 40, emphasis in original). Chandler offers "a portrait, a cartoon, a scale-model, onomatopoeia, metaphors, realistic sounds in 'programme music,' sounds effects in radio drama, a dubbed film soundtrack, [and] imitative gestures" as some common examples of icons (40). Each sign indicates what it does as an icon because, and only to the extent, that it looks or sounds like the object. An image that functions as an icon today may not some time later. Bazin's discussion of the family album in the "Ontology" essay discloses this possibility: "those grey or sepia shadows, phantomlike and almost undecipherable, are no longer traditional family portraits but rather the disturbing presence of lives halted at a set moment in their duration" (Bazin 8). Such shadows lose their iconic value over time. The opposite occurrence can also transpire. An image can come to resemble a person if some audience comes to accept that image as a likeness of that person. This possibility is partly what motivates Picasso to respond to Gertrude Stein the way he does when viewers claim she does not look like herself in his painting. Picasso simply responds, "she will" (Stein 12). Picasso's comment indicates an awareness that likeness is based on perception, and that perception changes. A sign's ability to function as an icon changes as perceptions change.

Indices, as Chandler describes them, would seem to be less temporal and less temperamental since they exist independent of interpretation. They are what they are regardless of whether they are perceived as such or not. Icons and symbols, conversely, must be perceived as icons or symbols. They exist as a matter of opinion. Indices exist "a matter of fact . . . because . . . there is a real connection" between the sign and the object it indicates (Chandler 51). Chandler illustrates this aspect by creating several categories of indices:

> "natural signs" (smoke, thunder, footprints, echoes, non-synthetic odours and flavours), medical symptoms (pain, a rash, pulse rate), measuring instruments (weathercock, thermometer, clock, spirit-level), "signals" (a knock on a door, a telephone ringing), pointers (a pointing "index" finger, a directional signpost), recordings (a photograph, a film, video or television shot, an audio-recorded voice), personal "trademarks" (handwriting, catchphrases). (40)

Such categorization is interesting if only because it shows that there is more to an index than film theorists typically admit. The index can be more than a trace or an impression. Indexical traces and impressions are, at best, a subset of indices. A footprint is a trace, as is a recording, but one would rarely speak of smoke or thunder or an odor or a knock as a trace. The impressions of each of these signs disappear almost as quickly as the object they indicate.

The one quality each of the indices in the above list share is that each sign captures the attention of the person who perceives it. Chandler explains this sense of the index when he writes, "unlike symbolic and iconic sign relations, indexical relations do not represent or symbolize things but act as a stimulus directing our attention toward them ... 'anything which focuses the attention ... which startles us is an index'" (50). The image on the screen, then, can be an index, not because it has some basis in reality but because it directs one's attention to some reality and does so in some specific way. The index Chandler describes oscillates between a reality that exists in the sign and one that points to a yet-to-be-determined reality. Both realities matter, but the yet-to-be-determined reality might be the most significant, as it is the reality that triggers the pursuit of a reality only the index can trigger. This reality is only ever constructed. It is never recovered. Any sense of recovery can only corrupt the process of ongoing construction the index means to trigger, and to trigger each time it is encountered.

The whole of this project explores the above sentence. Several other qualifications still need to be registered, however, before that exploration begins most properly. One such qualification occurs when Chandler cautions scholars against treating the index, icon, or symbol as types rather than forms. A sign is never inherently a symbol, an icon, or an index; instead, a sign comes to function as one of these three forms. The sign an object tolerates can be designated a symbol to the extent that the sign functions as a symbol, which is to say as a sign that relates to its object through some convention. That same object could also tolerate an iconic or indexical relationship. Chandler offers a map as an example: "a map is indexical in pointing to the location of things, iconic in representing the directional relations and distances between landmarks, and symbolic in using conventional symbols" (54). One can scrutinize a map as an instance of all three forms. A coin can also function in any of the three forms. As an index, the coin signifies a specific minting process. As an icon, it assumes the likeness of a face or a building. As a symbol, the object denotes some specific increment of currency. Chandler contends that Peirce intends for his system to remain flexible enough that the function of a sign is never fixed. It is to be negotiated each time it is encountered, and renegotiated through a process of signification where signs can be interrogated anew each time they are encountered as symbols, icons, or indices.

One can rightly attribute some eagerness to treat cinematic signs as *either* symbols, icons, or indices as one of the primary explanations for how film scholars come to favor a blunt rather than urbane notion of the index. The more one emphasizes the uniqueness of each mode, the more limited each mode necessarily becomes. This unnatural narrowing is especially unsettling for the index, which is more nuanced than the symbol or icon. To return to Atkin (2005), one can attribute five features to the index: "1) indices use some physical contiguity with their object to direct interpretation to that object; 2) indices have their characteristics independently of interpretation; 3) indices refer to individuals; 4) indices assert nothing; [and] 5) indices do not resemble, nor do they share any law-like relation with their objects" (163–64). The first feature accounts for the two attributes of indexicality most often discussed in film theory. Following Atkin's use of smoke as an example of an index, one can speak of the physical connection smoke has to fire, which is to say its existence can lead one to a fire, but this is not the primary function of the smoke. As already above discussed, the primary function of the smoke as it exists indexically is to direct one's attention toward a fire. In this way, the smoke becomes an instance of deixis. Atkin argues that the smoke "merely *suggests* the presence or existence of its object"; it does not, as the icon or symbol might do, "generate or characterize the object for our understanding" (164). This suggestion realizes the first feature of the index.

In addition to suggesting a reality, the index also remains independent of any interpretation, which brings Atkin to the second feature of indices. Atkin avers that the index bears its "characteristics independently of any interpretation" (165). This is another way in which the index differs from the icon and the symbol. Icons and symbols only are what they are when they are interpreted as such. A peace sign, by way of example, is not a sign for peace unless it is recognized as such. Smoke, on the other hand, is always smoke. It is the physical element it is, and it extends from the physical element it does, regardless of whether or not it is recognized as such. The same is true of any index. It is what it is, independent of interpretation, even if what it points to is less certain.

Just as importantly, every index maintains its indexical qualities even if it also accepts iconic or symbolic qualities. These other qualities do not negate the indexical qualities of the index. To return to the examples of the coin and the map, a coin and a map can maintain some standing as an index even if it can also be an icon and a symbol. Atkin turns to a quote from Peirce to emphasize this aspect of the index: "an index . . . is a real thing or fact which is a sign of its object . . . quite regardless of its being interpreted as a sign" (165). This statement at once suggests two things. On the one hand, an index is an index even if it is not recognized as such. And, on the other hand, it remains an index even if it is circulated as another type of sign. In keeping with the second condition of the index, the index exists independent of any interpretation.

Atkin further explains three other features of the index. The third feature, which Atkin designates the "singularity feature," acknowledges that indices will refer to one thing, which is to say that the index deals in particulars rather than generalities (165). Atkin explains, "the sky-track left by a jet plane is an index of that *particular* jet plane. So too with smoke and fire; a *particular* plume of smoke is an index of a *particular* fire" (165). This third feature leads to a fourth, what Atkin designates the "indicatory feature," which accounts for the way the index will "show or indicate their objects rather than describe them"; in this way, an index is "purely denotative; it refers to its object without describing that object" (165). As such, the index enjoys what Atkin terms a "phenomenological feature," the fifth feature of the index, which is another way to emphasize the index's "brute existence" (165). As a brute reality, the index does not have to be like the object it depicts to function, nor does its ongoing existence depend on some convention. The index simply is and its being indicates something specific, even if that something specific is yet-to-be-determined. In fact, by virtue of being an index, it can never be fully determined. It can only be indicative.

Atkin admits that not every index will have all five features. Atkin contends that Peirce creates space for partial indices when he devises three categories of the indexical form, which are the index, the sub-index, and the precept. Those forms that fit the first category will have all five features. The weathercock exists as an example of what Peirce would deem an index:

> The weathercock exemplifies the significatory feature because a physical contiguity [exists] between it and its object[,] . . . the independence feature[,] . . . because it . . . would still point westward whether I interpret that as a sign[:] . . . the singularity feature by being an index of an individual object, or at least, an object treated as an individual[;] . . . the indicatory feature . . . by indicating nothing more than . . . the direction or presence of the wind[; . . . and] the phenomenological feature since the essential connection between the direction of the weathercock and its object is down to the brute existential connection between it and the wind. (170–71)

Sub-indices and precepts will only bear some of these features. Atkin distinguishes sub-indices like "I," "he," "she," "this," and "that" from ideal indices by noting the "strong symbolic content" in the pronouns and demonstratives (171). These signs only make sense by virtue of "habit and convention . . . by . . . our agreement about how to interpret them" (171). As such, these signs are not truly independent, nor are they phenomenological like ideal indices. They are, however, in line with the other three features. They do bear some physical contiguity with their object; they do also refer to a single object; and, finally, they do "assert nothing," which fits the indicatory feature (172). Atkin concludes, then, that sub-indices "have the generality of symbols, but they are able to circumvent that generality and *show* their object on a particular occasion of use" (172). Hence, one can discuss their indexical qualities.

Atkin finds the same tolerance toward precepts, which, by virtue of giving direction or offering to make a selection, create "indexical actions or experiences" (174). Atkin states: "the precept is meant to result in an indexical experience, and ... it is from this intended result that its denotative power is supposed to come" (175). These experiences may occur through some shared quality, which occurs with the sub-indices "I," "here," and "now." All three signs mean what they mean by virtue of their sharing some similarity with a speaker, a place, or a time, respectively, which limits their impact as ideal indices; but these virtues do not empty these forms of their indexical qualities. These forms still exhibit features one, three, and four of indices (physical contiguity, singularity, and indicatory features). As such, these less-than-ideal indices can be treated as indices, and they should be. One would miss some part of what the sign can do if one ignores the indexical qualities of a less-than-ideal index.

Atkin's allowance for a less-than-ideal index, which he attributes to Peirce at every turn, challenges the legacy of the index as it arises within film studies. Film theorists tend to refer to an index only to account for the lens-based camera's ability to bring some reality before the camera to the screen. Kris Paulsen (2013) develops a different sort of indexical image, and she does so with rather than against the digital image. Paulsen admits that the digital image lacks the certainty, the authority of a lens-based recording. The art historian suggests that this doubt is partly what makes digital images so meaningful. Paulsen proposes that as digital images "extend sight and hearing, and reach into far-off places, we are given reason, or at least permission, to doubt what we see" (83). This "digital doubt" gives viewers space to explore contingencies more authoritative depictions mean to settle, and it does so indexically (85). For Paulsen, this means locating the image in the present. The index does, after all, "always establish a forceful present-tense connection with its receiver," in part because, unlike the symbol or the icon, the index exists as a sign that is yet to be interpreted (85). This lack of an interpretation leaves the sign open for interpretation(s). Any significance it realizes will only be temporary, as the next encounter can give rise to some other significance.

Paulsen reminds readers that the digital image is not so different from analog images. Both types of images can remain open for interpretation. Paulsen explains, "while a photograph usually represents something very specific—it provides a clear image of a certain moment in space and time—any photograph can be used in a variety of ways and testify to multiple, and [even] contradictory things" (89). From this view, the same opportunity exists for spectators when they are confronted with the mountain either Gance or Cameron supplies. Both structures represent something specific. Each specificity belongs to a particular time and place. Just as importantly, each specificity also remains open to alternative possibilities, possibilities that neither filmmaker could have meant in the original moment of registration. As such, both images tolerate the indexical exploration the point of every index invites, an exploration that exceeds every intended meaning.

Paulsen adds a second point to this initial one: the digital and the analog image alike remain open to a variety of uses and meanings. Their placement in a narrative may limit those possibilities in just the way Kawin (2011) shows they can be limited. The fact that they are understood to represent the symbolic core of the film is one kind of limit. An examination of these same images as indices will exceed these limits by reopening other points of significance. To this last possibility, Paulsen (2013) contends, "the index, like its subspecies, the photograph, has always been an indeterminate sign that relies on context and narration for its ability to serve as evidence or to testify to a particular event or action. Indices are, by nature, always open to interpretation and doubt" (89). One allows this process of interpretation to linger a little while longer to the extent that some doubt remains in the image. The moment the image securely signifies what it signifies is the moment the sign forfeits its indexical status.

Paulsen champions the digital image's ability to reintroduce doubt into the frame, which preserves rather than threatens its indexical status. The image, digital or otherwise, accomplishes the work of the index as Paulsen understands Peirce to describe it whenever that doubt is present. Quoting Peirce, Paulsen writes, "Indices . . . are in the imperative, or exclamatory [mood], as 'See there!' or 'Look out!' They focus the receiver on the present situation. . . . 'they call upon the hearer to use his powers of observation, and to establish a real connection between his mind and the object'" (94). Paulsen further explains that this connection takes place in some context, in a present tense: "the index is a sign that calls all three terms—the sign, referent, and receiver—into a contextual, present-tense situation. . . . the index must, then, be understood not as a mark of resemblance, proof, or truth, but rather as an instance of rationality, interpretation, and decision" (95). A moment of doubt about what one sees will only ensure these three aspects remain. Doubt leads spectators to discover the cause of the symptom conveyed in the index, a point Peirce himself emphasizes when he describes indices as "indexes of something" (95). The task of the spectator is to pursue this something. Paulsen contends that "the digital revolution has not destroyed or undermined the index; instead, it has called attention to the index's true identity as a sign from which one is separated, with a meaning one must guess" (99). It has reestablished a sense of doubt, which leaves space for the emergence of any number of alternative possibilities and meanings.

The typical assessment of cinema's indexicality differs from Paulsen's in both its focus and its final claim. One sees both differences in Laura Mulvey (2006), who describes the index as "an incontrovertible fact, a material trace that can be left without human intervention" (10). Mulvey maintains that the cinematic index has always delivered a fact, only audiences could not see those facts due to the incessant motion of the action and the (over)contextualization of the narrative. The introduction of new ways to watch films, which bring with them the ability to delay or even stop the flow of the film, restores the viewer's ability to see the facts that otherwise would have been lost. Once stilled, spectators see past the image the narrative requires them to see and they see into the moment of time at which the image was taken. Audiences can return to "privileged moments [that can be] paused and repeated, the cinema itself finds a new visibility that renders [these moments] special, meaningful, pleasurable" (165–66). Mulvey relates this return to the pleasure Freud finds children experiencing when repeating a favorite song, story, or game. Mulvey's viewers return to specific films or individual moments in those films to take possession of something that could only have been grasped at earlier. These returns initiate a "process of discovery . . . that . . . work[s] perversely against the grain of the film" (166). This process of discovery is always an instance of recovery rather than creation. The importance of this difference will be made plain shortly.

Mulvey's insight might begin to align with the points Paulsen will make after her, but Mulvey ultimately moves in a different direction. Mulvey aims to uncover the ways in which digital technology permit spectators to gain some primacy over an image that would otherwise overwhelm them. As Mulvey explains it, in the unnaturally stilled frame, "the male figure is extracted from dominating the action and merges into the image. In so doing, he, too, stops rather than drives the narrative[,] . . . stripped of the power to organize relations between movement, action, and the drive of the plot . . ." (166). The power to pause a film, then, allows the audience to see the index for the first time, but it is a specific rather than more general kind of index. It is an index set in a particular past. Mulvey offers a moment at the beginning of *Imitation of Life* (1959) as an example: "halting the duration of the extended take, breaking up its elegant continuity, reveals further details that could not be registered within the shot's movement[,] ... which allows ... the time of registration to come to the fore" (184). The still frame awakens what Mulvey terms an "aesthetic of delay," which promotes "the thoughtful reflection of the film image ... [as] a way of seeing into the screen's images, shifting them and stretching them into new dimensions of time and space" (192, 195). This reflection is relatively passive, however, depending as it does on recognition rather than revising. The moment requires one to connect what one sees to the time it represents. The spectator is ultimately left under an image, which is, itself, left under time.

Interestingly, Mulvey finds in Bazin's "Ontology" essay, and specifically his discussion of the family album, the basis for the reflective posture she advocates. Mulvey pays particular attention to Bazin's claim that the photograph "embalms time" (56). Mulvey sees in this description Bazin privileging the moment of time arrested in a photograph the moment the photograph is taken: "Once time is 'embalmed' in the photograph, it persists, carrying the past across to innumerable futures as they become the present" (56). The still image, Mulvey argues, actually stills life, which creates a "strange sense of displacement" (57). The observer of a photograph is visually caught in the space between Roland Barthes's (1979/2010) "here" and "there," "this" and "that," "now" and "then" (57). This displacement produces an uncanny effect for Mulvey as the image animates to some degree an object or subject that time has made inanimate. The lens-based photograph becomes a "conflation of life and death, the animate and the inanimate" (60–61). Mulvey maintains that Bazin understood this material quality of the photograph, and that it is this understanding that prompts Bazin to talk about a "photograph as index [that] almost literally 'haunts' the blurred boundary between life and death" (64). This haunting occurs because the index in the photograph (as Mulvey understands Bazin to see it) relates the viewer to the object otherwise lost in time.

Paulsen responds to Mulvey's position with the contention that Mulvey misrepresents Peirce's claim that a photograph bears some link to the time in which it was taken. Paulsen admits that while "Peirce does suggest that the photographic index is a physical trace that results in resemblance, it is, [Paulsen] argue[s], a leap to think Peirce is here defining the index in general" (90). Paulsen charges Mulvey with conflating a discussion of the index with a discussion of the photograph. The two do not invite the same discussion. Paulsen finds Mulvey to be writing about the index when she really means to describe the photograph. The photograph might be "an incontrovertible fact"; it might generate a trace to some past. But these traits belong to the photograph, Paulsen posits, and not to the index proper: "the index possesses no such security. . . . the index is the root of the photograph's openness to interpretation and doubt, not its guarantor of truth" (90). This seems, in fact, to be the point that Bazin wants to make, too, although the theoretical tradition of Bazin's words casts his intent in another role.

A more unconventional reading of Bazin suggests that the theorist is less interested in the past a family photo captures than he is in the extent to which such an image recovers some sense of contingency. For the family member who returns to it, that contingency is buried beneath the reality the person in the image eventually realizes. But the family member can recover that lost contingency should they choose to do so. This return allows the viewer to entertain any number of alternative futures for the person in the photo, each springing from the moment captured in the image. The past in the photograph reintroduces a sense of doubt where certainty would otherwise exist. It permits the viewer to reimagine rather than recover reality.

Mulvey champions a different relationship with the stilled image. Her index serves as a fossil. Mulvey admits as much when she describes the stilled image as "time fossilized" (31). Mulvey's remark is made with Manovich's remark about lens-based cinema being "the art of the index[,] . . . an attempt to make art out of a footprint," in mind (295). Mulvey responds to the implication of Manovich's claim by asserting that even if cinema is a footprint, a copy of some reality, it still deserves examination: "However lacking in artistic aspiration the footprint may be, as an indexical sign it marks an actual moment in time as well as the shadowy presence of an event as potentially significant, for instance as Friday's arrival on Crusoe's Island" (20). From this perspective, one cannot determine the significance of an image without stilling the image to create space to see all that the image captured on film has to show. The intent of such images, Mulvey would argue, is to recognize what the image brings forward rather than to engage it. Paulsen prefers a more inventive response.

Mulvey's view of the index fits the accepted view of the index as passed down from Wollen. One finds the same sort of understanding in Doane (2007), albeit with a different focus. Doane admits that the digitally produced image can no longer serve as a trace, but she insists that it can still perform the deictic operations granted indices. As an instance of deixis, the image "implies an emptiness, a hollowness that can only be filled in specific, contingent, always mutating situations" (2). Doane turns to art critic Rosalind Krauss (1977/1985) to show the benefit of seeing these deictic qualities of the index. Krauss championed 1970s art for its ability to empty art of any sense of "trace or mold"; by circulating and emulating ready-mades, like Marcel Duchamp's *Fountain* (1917), artists "affiliated [their art] with the performative dimension of signification, the pointing finger of the index, and of the shifter in language. . . . they brought onto the scene . . . the sheer affirmation of an existence, the emptiness of 'meaningless meaning'" (3). Contrary to those like Manovich who claim that the advent of the digital undoes cinema's indexicality, Doane suggests that the digital image maintains an indexical quality, but it is now a deictic index, an index waiting to be filled.

Doane (2007) offers that the shift from the index as trace to an instance of deixis asks viewers to adjust how they think about realism: "while realism claims to build a mimetic copy, an illusion of an inhabitable world, the index only purports to point, to connect, to touch, to make language and representation adhere to the world as tangent—to reference a real without realism" (4). Doane (2002) returns to her own idea that every image is at once a "record and performance" (24). From this view, the earliest film actualities, by way of example, both record a time that would be lost were they not captured on celluloid and perform a particular history, namely, the birth of cinema. Doane suggests that these early images establish a record that deals in "shock and surprise," and that ultimately raises questions about representability (24). When acting out its deictic function, Doane contends the index favors one representation over another, which is to say that it favors one way of seeing over another.

Doane admits that this same favor inhabits digital images just as much as lens-based photographs. The instantaneous photograph, in particular, exists as a point to some "exact moment[, . . . to] a halting of time . . . [that] is perpetually 'on the verge of' completion" (217). Doane draws a distinction between the instantaneous photograph and the cinema. The cinema projects an illusion of continuity that hides its exact moment and would appear to complete itself. In the end, however, cinema recovers its ability to halt time with every cut, every break of action. Doane reasons that the cut is the "exemplary cinematic operation," asserting as it does "the instantaneity of the individual photogram," converting time as it does to "something that can be held or possessed in a metaphorical sense" (217–18). In this moment, the indexical dimension of cinema as Doane sees it appears most clearly. The moving image suddenly realizes its status "as the empty deictic signifier, the 'this' or 'that' which can theoretically be filled with any content whatever," although these moments of pure possibility tend to be circumvented by the specificity of their image (223). Doane's idea is that the index satisfies an archival impulse that creates space for the removal of whatever limits one might place on the indexical quality of cinema. One can, after all, always see the artifact in the archive in a new way. This is the hope that returns one to the archive in the first place. It can, from Doane's view, be the hope that returns one to film, too.

For this hope to be realized in film, film theory needs a more sophisticated account of cinema's indexicality. Doane shows why. Doane regards the index as "the imprint of a once-present and unique moment, the signature of temporality" (16). She insists that this signature ultimately remains out of time, which is to say neither in the past nor in the present. The cinematic index Doane describes can seize some details from the moment of its registration, but it cannot hold them entirely. Neither can the image born in the past ever truly enter the present. Doane contends the cinematic image "becomes strangely immaterial; existing nowhere but in the screening for a spectator in the present, [the cinematic index] becomes the experience of presence" (23). Spectators become aware of the passing of time and the contingencies embedded in every moment, but they experience this perception in a space without any truly linear sense of time. They experience these images in a space between time, which produces "the pathos of archival desire" (25). The sense of time Doane's cinematic index delivers exists as a "record and performance" (24). It moves as "an homage to contingency," which, among other things, leaves the record and performance as a "site of newness and difference" (32). Such a site would seem ready to entertain multiple encounters, but Doane denies the cinematic index this possibility. She bases this denial on the juxtaposition of two independent ideas, the idea of the afterimage and the index, as they emerge in the late nineteenth century.

Doane claims that the idea of afterimage and the index, independent though they are, both "circulate around the question of accessibility of the present in representation" (70). Both treat its object, the retina, in the one case, and, the image, in the other, as an archive. Following the ideas that support the concept of an afterimage, the retina records images perceived with "a strong enough force," and retains an impression of those images on the eye even after they are no longer visible (75). In this way, the retina becomes an archive of impressions, although each impression only exists for a moment. The next moment of observation "annihilates the [earlier] retinal imprint in order to make room for its own impression" (76). In this way, the idea of the afterimage leaves the present just out of sight. It also insists that every subsequent act of perception displaces the earlier reality. As such, sight is continually regenerating its vision, and is doing so one impression or series of impressions behind the present moment. This view of perception fits Doane's most specific interests, which can be described as an attempt to understand an array of archives of "impression, imprint, and trace" (88). The cinematic image becomes another example of such archives as they emerge in the late nineteenth and early twentieth centuries.

Doane further justifies her perception of the cinematic image by drawing a comparison between the afterimage and Peirce's index. In truth, one could treat all three sign-types in Peirce's triad of sign as an impression, imprint, or trace. The symbol is impressed by some social convention. The icon is imprinted with some likeness. These signs represent some reality even if they only do so in a general sense. They also remain one step removed from that reality. Where the index distinguishes itself is in its relation to a time for some particular reality. As Doane notes, the index forces "attention to a particular object, *here and now*" (91, italics mine). The index arises from some direct connection with some reality from the past, but its presence on the screen suggests that it brings that past to the present. This suggestion seems reasonable, in part, because the index operates with "singularity and uniqueness[:] . . . the wind blowing at the moment in a certain direction, a foot having landed in the mud at precisely this place, the camera's shutter opening at a given time" (92). In this way, the index would seem to bring those who perceive it at least as close to some reality as the afterimage. Still, the cinematic index, like the afterimage, is always one step behind that reality, at least as it is experienced. It can bring spectators to the edge of some reality, to some present moment, even if the image and the spectator never find each other in the same moment of time.

The trouble with the above assessment, at least as it relates to the cinematic index, is that it treats the cinematic index as little more than a trace. Such a perspective ignores the possibilities for the index to be a trace to some reality, an admission of its own reality, and, most importantly, an indicator of still some other reality entirely. The cinematic index realizes this possibility to the extent that it functions indexically, which is to say to the extent that it directs the spectators' attention toward something other than itself. This something else does not erase what was in front of the camera or what is on the screen. In keeping with Peirce's more general view of the sign, where one sign leads to another sign, one index can and even should lead to another index. This seems especially true of the cinematic index. Remarkably, Doane leaves room for this perspective when she combines her analysis of the afterimage and the index. Doane suggests that by combining these two concepts one finds a way to treat the eye as "a kind of photographic plate . . . [that] momentarily" records the image in the retina the way a filmstrip registers the subject or object of the camera on the filmstrip (69). The analogy is interesting because it reverses the direction the cinematic index normally points; rather than pointing to the past and the reality that existed before the camera, the index points to the spectator, who forms a new image, a new sign in the mind's eye. This reversal returns the discussion of the index to

Peirce's more general conception of the sign, which always produces another sign in the mind that perceives it. From the clearing Doane provides, one can see the cinematic index leading not to the foot that leaves a footprint, but to an index-with-the-spectator an observation of the footprint generates. A sense of *here-with-the-spectator* begins to overwhelm a sense of *there-with-some-reality-beyond-the-frame*. Such a view can move spectators from Doane's "pathos of archival desire" to what this project calls the *Kairos* of ongoing adaptation.

Doane does not make this shift herself. She ultimately leaves the index in a "haunted" space between a sense of "here" and "there" (94). This placement serves Doane's interest in the archive. It also matches Peirce's own doubt about whether or not the present can ever actually be accessed. Doane reminds readers that Peirce supposes "time is a true continuum except at the moment of the actual present" (99). In the actual present, Peirce insists that time is split "between past and future" (99). This split creates space for chance, which disrupts convention. The index, then, exists as chance. Thusly conceived, the index is a sign that is "evacuated of content . . . a hollowed-out sign . . . [that] designates something without describing it ('The index asserts nothing; it only says "There!"')" (92). These comments start to carry Doane to a discussion of the index that film scholars rarely have. Unfortunately, Doane turns from the opening her insights deliver in order to see the index as little more an archive, in part because she insists this sense of chance is disrupted "as soon as one is aware that a film can be viewed again—that this experience of presence can be repeated" (104). In the moment one realizes a film can be rewatched, the image on screen becomes, for Doane, "a record . . . of its own performance . . . a historic present" (104–5). As such, the cinematic index is neither "here" nor "there"; rather, it is left in a contingent space that stands outside of time, in a space that the index can acknowledge but can never truly settle.

Doane's account is endlessly engaging, and it offers a compelling description for the way cinema participates in a societal need to seize time. Given its focus on time and the inaccessibility of the present, it does, however, also fall into the trap that is set for anyone who considers the index as a trace. Such a view leaves the index at one remove from reality. It offers that the index can mark the presence of some reality, but it cannot exist in a reality, at least not with the sense of contingency any reality born in time should enjoy. There is only the index as trace, which becomes a closed sign, fit to shape particular perceptions. This is the idea Mulvey most fully considers. Mulvey claims that the cinematic sign, like the photographic sign, enjoys "a privileged relation to time, to the moment and duration of its inscription[, . . . because there is] a physical relation to the original of which it is the sign" (9). Mulvey compares the image captured on the photo-strip to "the memory left in the unconscious by an incident lost to the consciousness. Both have the attributes of the indexical sign, the mark of trauma or the mark of light, and both need to be deciphered retrospectively across delayed time" (9). As it relates to cinema, the index Mulvey describes exists as "an incontrovertible fact, a material trace that can be left without human invention" (55). Such a description leaves the index as trace, an indicator of a reality that is not onscreen, which is one part of Peirce's index, but only one part.

In all fairness, Mulvey does not necessarily work to use the indexical qualities of the photograph to create some guarantor of truth. The spectator's newfound ability in the digital age to freeze the frame, to halt a film's foreword movement, opens a space to construct a new reality from an old one. Mulvey maintains that the whole of a film changes for the spectator when confronted with "stillness and repetition" (170). The spectator becomes empowered to commit "an act of violence against the cohesion of the story, the aesthetic integrity that holds it together, and the vision of its creator" (171). The tricks of the cinema get revealed and the magic of the movies must be reconsidered. Drawing on the insights of Raymond Bellour, Mulvey writes: "film subjected to repetition and return, when viewed on new technologies, suffers from the violence caused by extracting a fragment from the whole that, as in a body, 'wounds' its integrity. But in another metaphor, this process 'unlocks' the film fragment and opens it up to new kinds of relations and revelations. . . . as it penetrates the film, this new way of looking emasculates the coherent whole of narrative structure, 'wounding' the surface" (179–80). Every return threatens the authority of the author or the image.

Mulvey argues that spectatorial involvement eventually brings the indexical qualities of the cinema back into focus. Each spectatorial disruption stops "the forward movement of the story" (165). The details that were once buried beneath the narrative begin to develop a life of their own, although it is an automated rather than organic life that emerges. Repetition produces familiarity, which makes even natural performances look "mechanical" (171). Mulvey argues that this shift returns the spectator to "the time of the camera," to a "then" that would otherwise be lost beneath a "narrative 'now'" (173). Mulvey maintains that this return reminds the spectator that the world of fiction depends on the existence of a world now lost to time or death. This reminder creates a transfer between then and now that would otherwise be blocked. The spectator can shift between at least two times and two places (if not also in the times and places between those two realities). Mulvey surmises that this alteration occurs because the index exists as a trace. The filmic image suddenly relates to a real world and a real body that would otherwise no longer survive. The image becomes a "ghostly trace of reality," the distance between life and death seemingly evaporating as "the cinematic illusion fuses two incompatible states of being into one" (175). The emergence of the index reminds spectators that what appears on screen is more than a fictional world. It is also a trace to/of an unknown world.

Mulvey claims that these traces will most often move in one of two directions. The trace either "'wounds' ... [or] 'unlocks' ... new kinds of relations and revelations" (179). The trace can wound the narrative, disabling it so that it can never again operate as it did before it was stopped. It can also unlock what Mulvey terms "interactive [or later, pensive] spectatorship" (179). The pensive spectator can use the insights and observations that occur when the film is stopped as opportunities to "reflect 'on the cinema,'" especially those parts of the cinema that are covered by movement (186). This opportunity exists even once the film begins to move again. "The fictional present" can, in the words of Mulvey, "reassert itself" (187). Mulvey asserts that the now moving image can create "continuous transformations of 'nows' and 'thens' as the screen images move forward" again: "the protean nature of the cinema, its affinity with metamorphosis, its transformations from frame to frame, is conjured up" (189). The pensive spectator, given as she is to repeated viewings, "finds consciousness in the present," a way to be in a world that is at once passing and present (191). This idea fits Gunning's suggestion about impressions of reality rather than some literal connection to reality. Reality is always at one remove from the spectator. The cinematic index is always with the spectator. It has yet to be fully realized, in part, because it always remains in motion. This motion creates a sense of presence that calls for a response rather than mere recognition. It demands the spectator negotiate its significance, and it does so, indexically speaking, "here" rather than "there," which is to say at the moment it is perceived instead of the moment it was registered on film.

This last idea begins to approach the idea of rewatching on the point of the index this book encourages. The index can signify more than one object. The index is what it is the moment it is registered but is also whatever it will be as it is brought into other relationships. The cinematic index can, after all, at once index some point in the world, some point in the narrative, some aspect of the filmmaker, an actor, a genre, a film cycle, or a franchise, and even some point in the life of the spectator. The index never points in one direction absolutely. Some new force can always appear that changes how one negotiates the indexical sign. Take the weathercock, Atkin's ideal index, as an example. Left alone, the weathercock will testify to the presence and passage of the wind. A weathercock can be moved "unnaturally," though. It can become the plaything of a child and moved at their whim. Their play does not deny the weathercock its standing as an indexical sign; it does not morph into an icon or a symbol after being exposed to it. It does, however, come to index something other than what it was intended to index. The instrument meant to index the wind suddenly registers children playing, at least to those who know to look for their play.

The same sort of shifts occurs beneath or behind the sub-indices "I," "here," "now," "this," or "that" Atkin mentions. The index remains the same even though the object touching that index changes. The same shifts take place behind the directional and selectional precepts. Both lead subjects to an object, and, as Atkin quotes Peirce as saying, "*that* object is X" (175). The fact that an "X" is provided rather than the specific object indicates that the goal of an indexical object can be a host of things, all of which will be found through the same indexical experience even if what is found differs. What matters as far as determining if one can talk about a sign as indexical or not is how that sign relates to the object to which it relates, not if the relationship being indicated excludes every other relationship. As the above examples demonstrate, the index names provisional rather than permanent relationships.

Contemporary cinema has become especially keen to exploit the provisional nature of its index, and to do so in a variety of ways. The index is treated as an impoverished sign, an indefinite sign, an intertextual sign, and an imaginative sign. One sees all four of these treatments in John Lee Hancock's *Saving Mr. Banks* (2013), and especially in the development of the film's main character, Pamela (Emma Thompson). The Pamela at the opening of the film insists on an impoverished if not diminished index. The character favors an index that remains true to some source. As the film progresses, Hancock begins to place Pamela in a space where key indices begin to index more than one thing. The impoverished index becomes indefinite. The indefinite gives way to the intertextual. By the film's finale, Pamela, and the audience with her, come to see an imaginative index, one that allows the character to adapt her experience rather than to repeat the same experience time and again in the way one suffers trauma. In this way, Hancock's *Saving Mr. Banks* becomes a tidy way to introduce the sorts of indexical play this book proposes contemporary filmmakers enter, and some of the benefits for doing so.

One of the things that makes *Saving Mr. Banks* a great place to begin the present study is the way the film openly tolerates so many superficial indices. Even before the film begins, audiences know the film postures itself as a prequel to Disney's *Mary Poppins* (1964), which marks it as one kind of index. Everything it displays becomes the reality behind the film that most spectators will already know. One might even consider Disney's *Mary Poppins* as a trace to the reality Hancock's film details. Hancock's film rewards those who want to see the film as an accurate history of sorts in a couple of ways. To begin with, as Kevin Stern (2013) details, several scenes occur "where the actual events took place—namely The Walt Disney Studios in Burbank, California in addition to several other locations throughout Southern California." The filmmakers were even granted access to Disney's Photo Library collection, which allows the set design team to revert the already actual site into an even more accurate representation of itself circa 1961. This push for iconicity begins to diminish the indexical aspects of the film. An index does not need to look like its object. In fact, it often will not look like its object. The push to look like the object being represented does bring one closer to the concept of the diminished index, however, which makes every turn Hancock makes from this index that much more interesting.

Hancock creates some distance from the diminished index at the end of his film when he chooses to place some of the aforementioned photographs alongside or within the credits. The first such image appears immediately after John Lee Hancock is identified as the director. A black-and-white photograph of the actual Walt Disney and Pamela Travers appears opposite the credit to the film's screenwriters, Kelly Marcel and Sue Smith. The next credit brings with it an image of Julie Andrews, Walt Disney, and Pamela Travers. Images of photographs and actual sketches of scenes for Disney's film continue to appear throughout the credits. What is most interesting about these images is the extent to which they establish that the images that just appeared in Hancock's film are not iconic. None of the characters are so close a match to the people in the photographs that anyone would confuse one for the other. Neither are the sketches that appear even a near match to something someone would recognize. In this way, Hancock's credit sequence deemphasizes the iconic value of his film, which can reinvigorate an indexical quality to what has just transpired. The resulting images in Hancock's film begin to emerge as an impoverished rather than diminished index, which allows them to operate with a sense contingency that would otherwise be denied.

More interesting than the ways in which *Saving Mr. Banks* champions the indexical qualities over the iconic is the way the film itself plays with its indexical qualities. The plot moves from the impoverished and indefinite index, to the intertextual and imaginative index, all the time moving Pamela through the anxiety she feels about for her father's death, or at least her inability to save him. One sees this invitation to play on the point of the index throughout the film, but perhaps nowhere more plainly than at the pivotal moment of *Saving Mr. Banks*, at least as it relates to the goal-oriented plot of the film.

Walt Disney (Tom Hanks) travels to London in a last attempt to have Pamela give him the rights to her Mary Poppins stories. Walt's visit begins with the moviemaker expressing that he has come to see just how much life has disappointed Pamela. He now understands that Mary Poppins may be "the only person in [Pamela's] life who hasn't [disappointed her]." Pamela responds with the most logical thing anyone would say in such a moment: "Mary Poppins isn't real." Walt disagrees. He insists that Pamela's fictional character is "as real as can be." She is certainly real to all of those who find "comfort" in her existence and in the stories she fills. Walt's words implicitly return the discussion to the debate he and Pamela have already had about animated penguins. Pamela does not want the film Disney makes with her Mary Poppins to be an animated film. Walt accepts that condition, only to propose an animated sequence complete with dancing penguins. For Walt, one can mix live-action and animation and not have an animated film, just as one can accept the reality of a cinematic character. The divide between lived-reality and movie-reality is not as pronounced as Pamela pretends them to be. Both realities, Walt will argue, can be shaped by the imagination in important ways.

Walt illustrates what he means a few sentences later when he admits to Pamela to having his "own Mr. Banks." Walt tells Pamela a story of the winter when he was eight years old. His father, a newspaper circulation owner, would force Walt and his older brother into the harsh Missouri winter twice a day every day to deliver the papers. Walt admits to being motivated by the buckle end of his father's belt, and of finding himself "sunk down in the snow, waking up, 'cause [he] must've passed out for a moment." The details obviously shake Pamela. Walt tries to soften things by saying, "I don't tell you this to make you sad. . . . I love my life . . . and I love my dad . . . but rare is the day wherein I don't think about that eight-year-old boy delivering newspapers in the snow and old Elias Disney with that strap in his fist. . . . and I'm just so tired . . . I'm tired of remembering it that way." Walt proposes that he can remember his dad differently if he can make his *Mary Poppins*. He can save "George Banks," the character in the film, his dad, Pamela's dad, and, in fact, any dad that spectators associate with that character.

Walt ends his pitch to Pamela with a description of storytellers, a description that requires a certain kind of spectator if it is to be accurate. He tells the author, "George Banks will be honored. George Banks will be redeemed. George Banks and all he stands for will be saved, maybe not in life, but in imagination, because that is what we storytellers do: we restore hope with imagination; we instill hope again and again and again." Walt provides storytellers with a good deal of power. The truth is that storytellers can only do the work Walt proposes they can do if spectators participate in stories they tell. Spectators must see, for example, their father in George Banks. They must emotionally participate in the story they might otherwise only witness. In keeping with the proposed language of this chapter, they must play on the point of the intertextual and imaginative indices. Hancock's film builds to this proposal. This invitation to an imaginative index only appears after other forms of the cinematic indices have also been presented. The very contest between these indices is the surest way to the intertextual and imaginative indices, if only because the presence of the contest ensures that one is never only dealing with the diminished index.

Hancock's film is particularly good at visualizing this contest, too. In addition to the disagreements the script stages between Pamela and those at Disney trying to reimagine her story, the cuts in time between Pamela's present and her past, which she experiences as Ginty (Annie Rose Buckley), Pamela's childhood name, also ensure that the index on the screen is always caught between two points in time, space, and perception. These cuts are especially good to show Pamela performing the active forms of spectatorship *Saving Mr. Banks* and most of the films considered in this book perform and openly invite spectators to perform. The flashbacks themselves offer a second type of narrative structure in the film, marking the moves Pamela makes through the various types of indices as she plays the part of character and spectator in and to her own story.

Hancock's film actually opens with two scenes that can, upon reflection or return to the film, signal the careful attention the plot gives to the contest within Pamela. In the first scene, a child, Ginty, sits in the grass with her eyes closed and her face turned skyward. Her knees are pressed into her chest. Her arms are strapped across her legs. The shot holds as the music and opening words from Disney's *Mary Poppins* fill the soundtrack: "winds in the East / Mist coming in / like something is brewing / about to begin / can't put my finger on what lies in store / but I feel what's to happen / all happened before." On the final phrase, a fade carries the audience to London, more than fifty years later. The now adult Pamela, Mrs. Travers, sits at her desk in a close visual match of Ginty in the first scene: her face points skyward, her eyes are closed, her arms are stretched across her chest. A series of quick cuts identify the kinds of items surrounding Mrs. Travers: a book, a statue, and, finally, a photograph of Ginty with her family. The last image connects the child in the first scene with the woman in the second. The strategy to mark this connection through a photograph suggests a significant distance between the two people. The two periods remain very much separated in time. In this early moment of the film, there is Ginty and there is Mrs. Travers. Neither character is *here* per se. Neither are they *there*. They are, at the opening, in that space between time Doane and Mulvey describe. It takes the whole of the film to reconcile this divide, and, in so doing, to display the way storytellers can invite spectators to restore hope through imagination by playing on the various points of the cinematic index.

What is most interesting about the way *Saving Mr. Banks* restores hope is the way the film allows the plot to display the work spectators must perform to realize the benefits Walt suggests storytellers might be able to deliver. In short, the plot explicitly presents the extent to which such restoration will occur as an act of rewatching that will transpire on an index that one learns to adapt. This is precisely what Pamela experiences over the course of the film. In the early parts of the plot, Pamela resists the proposed adjustments to her story. This point is most clearly on display during the screenwriters' presentation of the visuals they want Pamela to consider. The character is given to an impoverished or, perhaps, an indefinite index. The details in her story are fixed to a reality she is not ready to revise, not too much. The renderings on offer by the creative team are clearly not faithful to her story, which turns out to be as much about her actual life as they are elements in her stories. This fact becomes most apparent during the creative team's presentation of the Banks' house. Pamela protests, "oh no, no, goodness me, no . . . the Banks' house doesn't look like that. . . . *My* house is a terraced-house with a pink door, white bricks, and a crack in the gate. . . ." Pamela continues her defense of her vision, saying that the house the creative team proposes is "too grand." Pamela meant the family to be "everyday normal sorts of people." The most important part of the above protest is the possessive pronoun "my," which could work in one of two directions. Pamela could be saying that her vision of the house is simpler, or she could be referring to the family on which the Banks are based. It becomes clear upon reflection or upon literal return to this scene, with the whole of the film in mind, that Pamela's protest is based on just how personal her "fictional" story is. Pamela has yet to become the storyteller Walt describes at the end of the film. She is more of a confessional author, unaware of her own confessions.

This unawareness leads Pamela to other protests. She resists the ideas that Mrs. Banks is "a silly suffragette" and that her first name would be Cynthia. She more strongly rejects the idea that Mr. Banks has moustaches. Upon seeing the first drawing of the character, Pamela pronounces, "This isn't Mr. Banks, this, this isn't him." The lead writer, Don DaGradi (Bradley

Whitford) responds, "uh, yes, that's Mr. Banks." Pamela explains that it cannot be him. Don clarifies that it must be. Don even reminds Pamela that the illustrator of her books gave Mr. Banks moustaches. It only follows that he would keep them, especially because Walt Disney, himself, has asked that he have them. Pamela remains unfazed by this justification. After some more debate, one of the writers, Bob Sherman (B. J. Novak), interrupts what looks to be a never-ending contest to ask, quite pointedly, "Does it matter? Does . . . it . . . matter?" Pamela refuses to answer the question; instead, she insists he leave the room, which he does. Pamela does, too, shortly thereafter, as the plot leaves the rehearsal room to follow Pamela as she returns to her hotel. The story, however, remains in the above moment. The script again cuts to Ginty's childhood. This cut is different, however, in part because it provides the answer to Bob's question.

Ginty's dad, Travers Goff (Colin Farrell), stands in front of a basin and mirror shaving. The character's face appears twice on the screen, once as it exists in the room, and a second time in the mirror. As the father steps back to wash his blade, Ginty's face appears in the bottom corner of the mirror. The image on the screen quite literally serves as a mirror for this memory. The admiring daughter asks her dad, "Why do you do that?" He tells her it is for her: "Which kinds of kisses do you prefer, scratchy ones, or silky ones?" The camera pulls back to place Ginty in two places on the screen, once still in the mirror, and now also with her face at the top of a windowsill outside the washroom. The child answers, "silky ones." The father takes that as his answer: "Well, then, swish, swoosh; a man must shave for as to spare his daughter's cheeks." The plot returns to the film's present and to Pamela in her bathroom in Los Angeles. The now older daughter swipes her hand across a steam-filled mirror as she says, "swoosh," and looks at herself with a sad expression. The sequence provides the answer to Bob's question, but it also begins to bring together Ginty and Pamela in way the earlier memories keep them apart. Pamela finds herself not only remembering a scene from her childhood but also bringing that memory to the present, where it can be reanimated and reperformed.

Each of the crosscuts Kelly Marcel and Sue Smith set in the script for *Saving Mr. Banks* can be shown to be interested in this sort of melding of time. By the time the plot reaches the above moment, the film has performed nine jumps in time, including the two already described. Each jump proposes some sort of parallelism to explain it, but the motive for these shifts in time change as they go. For example, at first, each cut would seem to reveal some comparable moment in Ginty's life to the experiences she is having in her adult life. There is the near visual match between the two time periods already above described in the first jump. The second jump operates more thematically. Pamela admits to wanting to keep her house, and the plot cuts to Ginty playing with some grass and flowers to create a makeshift house in her childhood yard. A later cut occurs as Pamela is on the plane from London to Los Angeles. The plot shifts to the Goff family's move from their house and position in Maryborough, Australia, to start a new life in Allora, which is quite literally at the end of the railway line. Each of these early cuts accepts the logic of an indefinite index. They preserve some reality. When set against the shaving scenes, these jumps begin to appear less like two sets of time, and more like one moment of time from which Pamela cannot escape. Pamela suddenly seems stuck in her past. The audience begins to understand that her preferences for the adaptation of *Mary Poppins* have as much to do with her desire to redeem some past as they do with her preferences for how her story will be adapted. Pamela seems especially caught between a then-and-now, a here-and-there, which leaves her committed to an impoverished or indefinite index. She cannot be moved from her preferences in the present because she herself is still so firmly grounded in a past.

Quite importantly, this revelation does not do anything to settle the torment Pamela feels. It simply marks her location in time, which is always, at this moment in the film, both here-and-there, then-and-now. This idea is especially on display during the rehearsal for the "Fidelity Fiduciary Bank" song the Sherman brothers propose. The scene begins in the rehearsal room, but, as the singing on the soundtrack fades and Pamela turns to look out a window, the plot cuts to the day of a fair during her childhood where her father gave a speech. Unlike other crosscuts in the film, the plot does not remain in one place throughout the duration of the flashback; instead, it alternates between the rehearsal room and the past event. The change in pattern would seem to affirm what the shaving scene at least suggested, namely, that Pamela is neither in one place nor the other. She is most accurately in a haunted place between a clear sense of here and there. A terrific image in the rehearsal room at the middle of the sequence captures Pamela's displaced reality. She stares out the window, but her face also forms on the glass as a reflection that stares back at her. In this moment, Pamela is looking out and from the same window. The two faces quite literally look at one another.

Eventually, Pamela leaves the window to go to the bulletin board where the sketches of Mr. Banks appear. The plot moves from the drawn images of Mr. Banks to Pamela's memory of her father's drunken speech, which quite clearly breaks her mother. As the song finishes, Pamela turns to express her disapproval of the whole vision for Mr. Banks: "Why did you have to make him so cruel? He was not a monster!" Don wonders to whom she is referring, which is a fair question. He asks, "Who are we talking about, I'm confused?" The comment is the most accurate thing anyone could have said in this moment. Pamela is almost certainly not talking about the Shermans' Mr. Banks, no matter how much she insists she is. She is more likely confronting the cruelty of her father's alcoholism, something only the audience could know. The audience is, after all, the only ones seeing the time that pains Pamela. Pamela pleads with the writers to let Mr. Banks be less cruel. She admits to being unable to bear what they are doing to him.

The most interesting aspect of this scene is the way it can mark a shift between the indefinite and the intertextual index. Each of the indices in this scene—the memories, the song, the images on the bulletin board—can index more than one thing. As it relates to the memories, Pamela is quite clearly not remembering the events to understand herself; she is trying to understand something about her father, or at least their relationship. This idea is suggested in her eventual defense of her father. The memory, then, is at least two things, hers and not hers. The song also accepts more than one index. It indexes the characters who are singing the song that will appear in Disney's film, and the words the father says during his speech in Pamela's memory. The sketch of Mr. Banks is just as polysemous. It indexes the character that will be in the film, but it suddenly begins to mark Pamela's father, too. Each of these indices accept the qualities of an intertextual index. The rest of the film turns toward the last of the three indices being proposed, which finally emerges most fully for Pamela, and the audience with her, during the screening of Disney's *Mary Poppins*.

Through a series of six more intercuts interspersed between various ups and downs of the creative process the film retraces as Pamela's Mary becomes Disney's Mary, the script makes clear that Pamela is unable to save her father's life. In the final cut in this particular sequence, Ginty stands beside her father's deathbed. He has died. His death marks the end of the narrative arc the crosscuts themselves constitute until Pamela becomes a spectator in the movie house at the premiere of Disney's *Mary Poppins*. The premiere disrupts any finality, though, in just the ways Walt tells Pamela it will. Hancock allows his audience to see the hope Walt's film gives Pamela by keeping the camera on her throughout much of the premiere. Initially, Pamela repeats the groans and frustration she expressed throughout the creative process. She grimaces when Mary Poppins (Julie Andrews) suggests a spoonful of sugar can make everything better. She refuses to look at the animated sequences. Her responses begin to change as the film begins to engage her emotionally. Pamela smiles as the chimney sweeps perform "Step in Time." She begins to cry as Mary Poppins talks about the limitations of those we love, those things that, "through no fault of their own, [keep them from seeing] past the end of their nose." Full tears fall from her eyes as Burt (Dick Van Dyke) counters Jane (Karen Dotrice) and Michael's (Matthew Garber) argument that their father does not love them.

The genuine emotion has a cathartic effect on Pamela that redirects the cinematic indices on display. The events on the screen assume an intertextual and imaginative point. As Pamela watches Mr. Banks (David Tomlinson) leave his house to keep his appointment with his employers that will almost certainly end his tenure at the bank, Pamela's mind cuts to four memories with her father. The first sees the child slip her father a bottle of liquor. If shown earlier in the film, the playing of this memory might indicate some supposed culpability in her father's death. By occurring in the moment of the plot it does, the detail seems more like an acknowledgment of her father's limitations than a kind of confession. The second memory shows her giving her father a hug at his bank. The third shows Ginty at the window asking her father never to leave her. Her father promises never to leave her, a promise he would seem to be unable to keep—only Hancock's plot cuts to Pamela in the theater. The character-turned-spectator is smiling, which suggests her father has kept his promise to her in some manner. The last cut shows how he might have kept that promise: Pamela first sees her father through the window she was at in the third cut, and then that image fades to a scene of the father and daughter in their yard in Maryborough. The daughter leans into the father, who wraps his arms around her. The camera pans upward before eventually settling on the image of a cloud-speckled blue sky. Walt's film seems to deliver on the promise he made to Pamela in London, which, in turn, allows Ginty's father to keep his promise. As a spectator, Pamela has done what Walt said storytellers can do: restore hope with imagination, and she has done so at the point of the intertextual and imaginative index.

The proposed progression from the impoverished, to the indefinite, to the intertextual, to the imaginative index in *Saving Mr. Banks*, and especially its willingness to let the imaginative index resolve some anxiety or trauma, is indicative of the display contemporary filmmakers have been prone to perform. John Lee Hancock is not alone in his explicit display of this shift and its ability to restore hope with imagination. Each of these shifts sets aside the obligations that extend from an impoverished index, the idea that the image bears some responsibility to a determined reality, in preference of the imaginative index. The impoverished index serves Doane's "pathos of archival desire." The imaginative index arises with the *Kairos* of ongoing adaptation. Spectators perform this act in the now every interpretive moment provides. They realize the point of this moment as they realize alternative objects behind the index set in the plot and look to build their own understanding or interpretation from those objects. During their interpretive work, the minutes or hours, the months and the years registered in the film get displaced by other times. The interpretive moment of the now overwhelms all other senses of time. A relationship forms between the spectator and the object on screen: an index that sparks the imagination, which challenges the original memory, the moment of registration, and the significance of the elements on screen in new directions each time they are encountered. Such is the work of ongoing adaptation the imaginative index occasions.

Chapter 2

(CINEMATIC) REALITY

For rewatching to occur on the point of the index the way the first part of this project suggests it does, one needs to set aside the idea that movies mean to capture or deliver some real-world reality. A reality certainly exists with and on the screen, and it is this reality that this project most wants to consider. This is the reality that proves most gripping in the films discussed in the last chapter, and most especially John Lee Hancock's *Saving Mr. Banks* (2013). The central character of that film, Pamela (Emma Thompson), initially struggles to see the reality the screen can deliver. She is trapped in her own reality. Pamela only comes to appreciate the more participatory nature of the cinematic image as she gains some distance from the idea of an actual and authoritative reality that must be revered. As this happens, the onscreen images begin to command their own reality with their own indexical point. These points lead Pamela to rewatch her past, to adapt it, and to move through the trauma she had experienced.

What makes Hancock's film so noteworthy for this study is the way the film cycles through each of the four cinematic indices being described. The film cycles through the impoverished, the indefinite, the intertextual, and the imaginative indices, and it does so in a way that tempts one to reconsider cinema's relationship to reality. The film begins with a strong commitment to the impoverished index. The impoverished index points to a specific time and place in the real world. It serves as a fact, a brute reality that often means to be accepted rather than negotiated. Hancock provides an example of the impoverished index during the early scenes that show the Goff family's travel to their home in Western Australia. These details are presented as actual moments in the Goff family's reality. The reality of these details is strong enough to overwhelm the deictic quality of the index, at least as it might exist as something other than a pointer to that reality. As Hancock's film progresses, this reality begins to loosen enough that the indefinite index can emerge alongside the impoverished index. The indefinite index also points to a brute reality, but it does so with attention to its own existence.

This is the index Pamela misses when she questions the house the Sherman brothers propose as the Banks' house. Pamela insists that their version is not *their* house. The proposed image may fit the category of English houses, but it is not the Banks' house. It is worth noting that both the impoverished and the indefinite index serve representational ways of thinking. They tend to be emptied of any significance beyond what they explicitly show, which weakens their indexical function, at least when representational ways of thinking are pushed too far. Simple likeness is, after all, a matter of iconicity, not indexicality.

The intertextual and imaginative indices move beyond representational signification. They point to realities that initially rather than irreversibly produce it. Hancock offers a succinct picture of an intertextual index during the "Fidelity Fiduciary Bank" rehearsal. The song being constructed and performed points to at least two realities at once. There is the reality that will be realized in Disney's *Mary Poppins* (1964). There is also the reality Pamela remembers. The index in this moment becomes like a two-lane highway. The direction one travels depends more on the traveler than "the road." The image itself travels in more than one direction, just as Hancock's editing of the scene indicates. One can be in the room where the rehearsals take place, in the past with Pamela, or in the 1964 film that will present the eventual version of the song. The location depends on the spectator. A similar thing occurs with the imaginative index except that it indicates a significance that is always in the making. Its reality is never fixed. In keeping with the traditional language of the index, it proposes a new foot in an old footprint, producing a new reality. This is the index that emerges when one juxtaposes the first and last scenes of Hancock's film. In the first scene, Pamela sits alone as a child. In the last, her father joins her. Pamela has reimagined her reality, or, more properly, her memory of some reality, and she has done so on the point of the index Disney's Mr. Banks (David Tomlinson) provides. Pamela comes to reimagine her past in the presence of the cinematic index. Such is the work of the intertextual and imaginative indices, which set spectators in motion so that they can, in the language of Hancock's film, restore order with imagination, see some part of their past more clearly, more fully, and, above all, more inventively.

Pamela begins to reimagine her past as she distances her memories from a fixed reality. One could claim that Pamela is not remaking her reality as much as misremembering it. If one accepts that either the opening or closing scene in *Saving Mr. Banks* is true, then Pamela has certainly misremembered one or the other. Either her father is, as he is in the first scene, absent, or he is present, as he is in the last scene. He cannot be both present and absent, at least not according to the traditional accounts of reality. Interestingly, recent research on memory would suggest he could be both present and absent in one's memory. As Richard F. Thompson and Stephen A. Madigan (2007) state, "our interactions with the physical world—our sensory experiences, our perceptions, our actions—change us continuously and determine what we are later able to perceive, remember, understand, and become" (1). Memories, in other words, are neither fixed nor are they entirely accurate. As Thompson and Madigan say, they are not "a tape recorder or video recorder, holding a perfectly accurate record of what has been experienced" (6). They change each time they are accessed. Details shift to accommodate new ideas. From this view, it is entirely possible for an adult to remember a day from her childhood where she was with her father in one memory and without him in the other. There is, in fact, no way to say which memory is true and which is false, a point Thompson and Madigan admit: "at present, there is no generally reliable way of distinguishing between true and false memories" (159). Only the one who holds the memory can ever really say, and almost never with absolute certainty. The ultimate significance of a film element, or even the whole of a film, can be just as uncertain. The significance of both can change when spectators reencounter and rewatch them, and especially when they do so on an indexical point.

Any reality or notion of reality set on the screen offers itself as a site of negotiation rather than an act of preservation. Any type of sign can spur this negotiation. Symbols and icons can be reinterpreted and reconsidered. The index invites this (re)negotiation, and this is especially true of the cinematic index. The cinematic index exists as an empty sign within the plot that points to any number of realities. In this way, the cinematic index is always open, which is to say that it is always ready to operate in some new context. This is even true of the indices fixed to some brute reality. The impoverished or indefinite index can give way to the intertextual and imaginative index. They will do so when they stop merely representing reality and start pointing to other realities. Tom Gunning's (2007) insistence that movies offer an "impression of reality" rather than a literal depiction of reality offers one way to move from the former to the latter (29). Drawing on Christian Metz's early essay "On the Impression of Reality in Cinema," Gunning marks the difference between an impression of reality and the delivery of reality. Gunning recommends that cinema leads spectators to exclaim "there it is," rather than "this has been there" (Gunning 41). The motion in a movie implicates the spectator in the present action, which is always distanced from the past. This distance allows spectators to set aside any material significance to the past. The ultimate significance or substance of the cinematic sign, ultimately, depends more on the viewer who participates in its making than on the supposed reality before the camera. A reality in front of the camera can, of course, shape the elements on the screen, but it can only do so provisionally. Spectators will make a more decisive impression on each element, and they will do so each time they see them.

The control the spectator has over the images injects a certain amount of indeterminacy and uncertainty into every frame. The discussion in chapter 1 of what Kris Paulsen (2013) refers to as digital doubt provides the requisite indeterminacy. Paulsen's digital doubt celebrates contingencies rather than resolves them. It refuses to settle on any one particular significance. This unsettling accommodates a certain amount of uncertainty, something film scholars describe in at least two different ways. With his six types of realism in the cinema, Berys Gaut (2010) provides one way to discuss this uncertainty. The first type of realism is what Gaut calls "content realism," which arises anytime one considers in an image "*what* is represented, not *how* it is represented" (61, emphasis in original). Gaut explains that a story has content realism when "the *kinds* of people or objects, and the *kinds* of events represented are those that tend to occur in the real world" (61, emphasis in original). The second type of reality is illusionism. Gaut contends that cinematic stories entertain two types of illusionism: cognitive and perceptional illusions. Cognitive illusions arise anytime the image involves a "false belief" (62). Gaut offers as one example of a cognitive illusion the idea that one is in the presence of the fictive world being depicted on the screen. Perceptual illusions are similar. They arise when spectators take what they see to be literal. Gaut suggests the perception of motion counts as an instance of perceptual illusion. Even when the motion appears real, cinematic motion does not follow the rules of actual motion. Characters can move from one space to another without "occupying all of the intervening points between the start and end points," which makes motion an instance of perceptional illusionism (62). When combined with the first category of cinematic realism, Gaut's first two types of cinematic reality show the ways in which cinema involves representation and misrepresentation.

Gaut mentions photorealism as a third instance of reality in cinema. An image is photorealistic anytime "the animation image of something is visually indiscriminable from how a photograph of that thing *would* look" (66, emphasis mine). Gaut offers an image of King Kong as one example of a photorealistic reality. Such an image can be deemed photorealistic so long as the animal looks on the screen the way he might in a photograph if a photograph were to be taken. It does not matter if a photograph has been taken, only that it theoretically could be. From this view, onscreen images can be photorealistic without being real. This allowance leads into the fourth type of realism Gaut discusses, ontological realism. Gaut counts any image that has a "causal relation to [its] subject" as an image with ontological realism (67). By this logic, a digital image would not have the same sense of ontological realism that an analog photograph would. This idea is worth debating, and that debate will follow. For now, it is enough to say that an idea of photorealism and ontological realism could be combined together to advance the idea that any image that is photorealistic could be taken as an image with ontological reality. The image does, after all, exist, and it does so with a specific kind of being. It should hardly matter if that being is born in reality.

Gaut adds two more concepts of reality to his types of cinematic reality. The fifth notion of realism is epistemic realism. An image is epistemically real any time it "provides strong (though defeasible) evidence that the object or event that it apparently depicts really was like that or really happened" (68). The above debate about Pamela's two memories in *Saving Mr. Banks* illustrates the two parts of this argument. Both memories provide strong enough evidence to suggest they could have happened just as they are depicted. They both did happen on the screen, which can be enough to grant to each some level of epistemic reality. The copresence of two possible realities hardly puts either at risk; instead, they exist as extensions of some accepted core reality. The last type of reality Gaut discusses, perceptual realism, arises under the same conditions. An image enjoys perceptual realism when it is taken to be realistic. In this way, a factually inaccurate image can be perceptually realistic if it is taken to be realistic. From this view, a digital image of a baby, to return to Cuarón's *Children of Men*, will be perceptually real so long as it is taken to be a realistic image. In this way, reality becomes a matter of perception.

What is most interesting about Gaut's types of reality as they relate to rewatching on the point of the cinematic index is the way in which the types of reality correspond to the four cinematic indices. Content realism and illusionism both relate to the ideas that govern the impoverished index. Photorealistic realism recounts to the indefinite index, especially if the image exists as more than a testament to the reality in the image. Epistemic and perceptual reality fit the imaginative index. The only type of reality that begs some additional discussion is Gaut's ontological realism. As Gaut presents it, ontological realism most properly belongs to the impoverished index. If one extends the allowances Gaut provides photorealistic realism to ontological realism, one could relate this type of realism to the intertextual index. Richard Rushton (2013) provides an argument that would allow this extension to occur.

Rushton begins his monograph, *The Reality of Film*, with a query from philosopher Cornelius Castoriadis: "why would we not start [investigations of reality] by positing a dream, a poem, a symphony as paradigmatic of the fullness of being and by seeing in the physical world a *deficient* mode of being" (Castoriadis 1997, 5, as quoted in Rushton, 2, emphasis in Rushton). Rushton introduces Castoriadis's question to challenge the presumption by film theorists that one encounters reality in the world and unreality on the screen. Rushton counters this belief with the bold suggestion that "films are part of reality . . . they are not . . . abstracted from [it]" (2). Films exist as indubitably as any other hard fact in the world: a table, a tree, or a dog. They become part of the world humans occupy. They help humans make sense of that world. They give shape to a shape-shifting world. Films constitute what Rushton terms a "filmic reality," which itself "create[s] things[,] . . . realities[,] . . . possibilities, situations and events that have not had a previous existence" (2, 4). For Rushton, the world on the screen is as realistic as any other reality and should be treated as such.

Within Rushton's compound, filmic reality, exists both a declaration and a concession. In terms of the declaration, the concept of a filmic reality advances the idea that opens this chapter—that film is part of reality. Rushton clarifies that his idea intends to undercut the assumption that film is primarily a representational art. Such a view relegates film to "at best a secondary mode of being" (2–3). It also requires audiences to base their judgment of a film against "how 'true to reality'" that film is, which Rushton offers rarely happens (3). Plenty of films grounded in some "unreality" have captured the attention of audiences. Box office receipts support this claim. The list of the all-time top-ten highest grossing movies worldwide illustrates as much: *Stars Wars Episode VII—The Force Awakens* (2015); *Avengers: Endgame* (2019); *Avatar* (2009); *Black Panther* (2018); *Avengers: Infinity War* (2018); *Titanic* (1997); *Jurassic World* (2015); *The Avengers* (2012); *Star Wars: Episode VIII—The Last Jedi* (2017); and *Incredibles 2* (2018) (boxofficemojo.com). Only one of those films, *Titanic*, grounds its action in anything close to the customary notion of reality.

One could note the date of the top-ten films and conclude that the appeal of some unreality is a new thing. A look at the top-grossing films in the United States for each decade in the sound era tells a different story. As the following lists shows, films avoiding direct representations of reality have appealed to audiences throughout the history of film: *Gone With the Wind* (1939), *Snow White and the Seven Dwarfs* (1937), and *The Wizard of Oz* (1939) in the thirties; *Bambi* (1942), *Pinocchio* (1940), and *Fantasia* (1940) in the forties; *The Ten Commandments* (1956), *Lady and the Tramp* (1955), and *Peter Pan* (1953) in the fifties; *The Sound of Music* (1965), *The Graduate* (1967), and *Butch Cassidy and the Sundance Kid* (1969) in the sixties; *Star

Wars: Episode IV—A New Hope (1977), Jaws (1975), and Grease (1978) in the seventies; E.T.: The Extra-Terrestrial (1982), Star Wars: Episode VI—Return of the Jedi (1983), and Star Wars: Episode V—The Empire Strikes Back (1980) in the eighties; Titanic, Star Wars: Episode I—The Phantom Menace (1999), and Jurassic Park (1993) in the nineties; Avatar, The Dark Knight (2008), and Shrek 2 (2004) in the 2000s; and, Star Wars: Episode VII—The Force Awakens, Avengers: Endgame, and Black Panther in the 2010s (filmsite.org). Only The Graduate and Jaws creates a diegetic world that might be mistaken as a realistic representation of the period in which it was released. Only Gone With the Wind, Butch Cassidy and the Sundance Kid, and Titanic follow the rules of any traditional reality. The rest are either animations, musicals, or fantasies, which is to say that they are films given to some unreality, at least as reality relates to the world beyond the frame.

One finds in the above list another reason to consider Rushton's argument. A review of the most popular movies in any decade suggests that audiences of every generation turn to films for something other than literal representations of reality. This idea returns to the declaration within the compound "filmic reality." Rushton argues that films tend to flourish to the extent that people can "do . . . something . . . with their filmic experiences" (3). The most rewarding films, Rushton continues, "allow [spectators] to make sense of experiences, thoughts and feelings" (5). In other words, movies do something more than grant spectators an alternative reality, an escape from reality. Following Rushton, they bring spectators into contact with their own lived reality, which one might also call their provisional reality. The argument at the end of the previous chapter supports this idea. *Saving Mr. Banks* shows the performative power of film as an instance of reality rather than a representation of it. The one difference between what Rushton suggests and what this project proposes is that it is not enough to lift film from its presumed understanding as a representation of reality. One needs to tether this lift to a revised notion of the index, one that emphasizes the deictic and speculative qualities inherent to the index, and to do so over any perceived physical contact with some actual reality that occurred before the camera. In other words, one needs to develop an indexical account of filmic reality that not only assigns a film some relationship to some reality but that also uncovers how that reality points to speculative realities only the spectator can ever bring into being.

To relate this proposal to the more accepted discussion of the cinematic index, it is worth restating that the two realities before the camera, the one in front of the camera and the one that exists earlier than the one on the screen, are never the only realities the index on the screen indexes, and even more rarely are they the most interesting one. As it relates to Pamela's perceptual and philosophical shift across Hancock's film, it is interesting that her stories have some basis in the author's past, which is to say in some instance of a reality. The status of her fictional character, Mary Poppins, changes a bit when one learns that she emerges from Pamela's real encounters with a real person in her life, her Aunt Ellie (Rachel Griffiths). The same thing happens to how one regards Mr. Banks's profession after one learns that Pamela's father worked as a bank manager. Still, these details create interesting correspondences that try to give the characters some specific meaning. Once they are set in motion, however, these correspondences begin to lose a grip on the character on screen, or even Pamela's memory of them. Some new significance begins to emerge. Following the argument Hancock has Disney (Tom Hanks) make, such things are brought to the screen to be remade, and to be remade each time they are encountered. They are, in other words, always already indices ready to index something more than the first reality that produced them.

In the language of this project, the first reality lingers beneath at least two versions of the index set on the screen. The impoverished and indefinite index can lead one back to those realities, even though both indices distance themselves from the reality, at least as it has existed in some real world. As it relates to the impoverished index, the return to an earlier reality reminds one that what has been in an actual reality could have been something else. It is something else the moment it is represented on screen. The reality before the camera suddenly sits in a new context that can be pursued in new ways, even if those new paths must, for some reason, still return one to the reality before the camera. The appearance of the indefinite index will work similarly, relating to the fixed reality before the camera but encouraging new ways to work from that reality. The person or place in the image is just a "somebody" rather than a specific body. They are like phantoms akin to those set in Bazin's family album. The uncertainty these phantoms permit allow the impoverished and indefinite index to give way to the intertextual or imaginative index. The intertextual index will allow the image to accept new relationships. The imaginative index will realize new realities. Collectively, the four cinematic indices will encourage audiences to reimagine the reality set in the plot. They will (re)direct spectatorial attention to *a* reality rather than *the* reality.

Non-cinematic indices of all sorts can do the same thing, but they rarely realize different realities the way cinematic indices do. A real-world index is too much with the world to tolerate as many possibilities as cinematic indices. A specific foot makes a certain footprint. A particular pain indicates an actual condition. A gust of wind moves the weathercock in one direction. A unique hand forms a characteristic knocking. A recording captures a scrupulous message. Each of these indices in the real world have a specific cause and they respond to that cause. The cinematic index works less specifically. Never the product of one reality, the reel-world index points to a host of realities. There is the reality before the camera, the narrative aim, the impression of a director, a studio, a director, the actor, the genre, the period, and a host of other influences, including, of course, the spectator, who can redirect the cinematic index in whatever ways she is prepared to redirect it. This is the sort of play Pamela comes to stage across Hancock's film. It is the act of rewatching she performs during the screening that follows her collaboration with Disney. As a spectator, Pamela lets the index on the screen point her to new possibilities in her past, and, eventually, she reimagines a memory of her father and her childhood. Hancock bookends his film with these two memories, which most especially marks the work the character-become-spectator begins to accomplish in the movie house as she watches Disney's film and rewatches her own memory. Her effort demonstrates the ways cinematic indices can invite audiences into a process of ongoing adaptation that means to undo the most literal ideas of filmic reality.

Rushton's notion of a filmic reality brings one closer to the performative and invocative ideas of the index this project champions. The declaration in his phrase, that film enters reality as a reality-unto-itself, only pushes for one aspect of what a more comprehensive concept of the index can provide. The confession in the phrase—namely, that film constitutes a *cinematic* reality rather than an objective reality (if such a thing ever truly exists, or, more accurately, is ever really experienced)—gets to other important aspects of the cinematic index. No matter how convincing Rushton's argument is that film is a reality, one has to admit that spectators do different things with the reality on the screen than they do with the reality in the world. If nothing else, there are realities one experiences directly and realities one experiences by proxy. Both of these realities can be real, even as they are also different. To observe the birth of a child is not the same as to hear a story about that birth, even if both the experience and the story are real. In the same way, the experience one has as a child is not the same as the memory of that experience decades later, even though both the experience and the memory are real in an important sense. To Rushton's point, one can treat the real world and a reel world in a similar manner. Both are real, and, just as importantly, neither is subservient to the other. The task of the reel world is never to accurately or truly capture the real world. The reel world moves according to its own rules and priorities, just as the real world moves without any concern for its own representation.

The reel world does move with an important difference from the real world. The world on the screen moves within the tension to document and to animate the story it tells. Such a claim deserves fuller explanation, but even a succinct distinction between the two modes can clarify the critical stakes of this chapter. Documentaries scheme to say something, to show something, or to respond to something. In a word, they want to admit something. Animations, on the other hand, stir this something with imagination; they animate. Amy Herzog (2000) provides a succinct way to see the two sensibilities being herein described and to isolate the two together on the point of the index. Herzog finds within Bergson and Deleuze a "fundamental destabilization of the very idea of a representation, displacing notions of signification and association in favor of acts of creation and images of thought." Herzog further explains that these acts of creation and images of thought extend from images that create their "own fluid movements and temporalities." In other words, rather than representing reality, these moments of creation constitute their own reality. This reality contains its "own unique duration," which is to say its own capacity for change. For Herzog, this reality exists to the extent that spectators explore and expand it, which is to say to the extent that this reality is admitted and imagined, documented and animated.

From this view, one could claim that the reality of cinema emerges on the point of an index that pushes for exploration and expansion, admission and imagination, documentation and animation. This index is not only, or even most interestingly, marking some reality that existed earlier or in front of the camera; rather, it is arranging through memory and return what Dorothea Olkowski (1999) deems "a qualitative multiplicity," the result of an attentive perception that "opens as many circuits as there are memory images attracted by this new perception" (114). The cinematic index becomes a site of negotiation that begins with some admission and that continues to develop through the imagination. *Saving Mr. Banks* provides one example of this type of negotiation. The way in which Richard Linklater so often leaves his spectator between a documented admission and an animated imagination provides another. This chapter ultimately offers an extended discussion of Linklater's films, to discuss the ways in which they consistently move within a desire to document and to animate some reality. Linklater's films also balance themselves on some notion of memory and return, which is to already offer an example of some play on the idea of a real past. Linklater's characters are often coming to terms with a past rather than just accepting that past. Their work matches several ideas throughout film history for how spectators engage the cinema. One of those is Hugo Münsterberg's early suggestions for where movies operate. Another is Rushton's reassessment of André Bazin and Christian Metz. The chapter recounts and relates two discussions before turning to the aforementioned consideration of Linklater's cinematic index and the imaginative response it encourages from his spectators.

Hugo Münsterberg, one of the earliest theorists of the cinema and a prominent Harvard psychologist, insisted very early in the history of cinema that movies deserve scholarly attention because of the role they assign the spectator. Münsterberg argues that even the most simplistic and realistic projections depend on audience participation. So much of the moving image, Münsterberg reasons (1916/2001), occurs in the mind, beginning, of course, with apparent motion, which is "produced by the spectator's mind and not excited from without it" (74). Münsterberg recommends that the essential condition of the cinema is "the mental activity" of the spectator rather than the images themselves: "depth and movement alike come to [the spectator] in the moving picture world, not as hard facts but as a mixture of fact and symbol. . . . spectators . . . see things distant and moving, but [they] furnish to them more than [they] receive" (78). The images are, in other words, as much impressed by the mind that perceives them as is the reality they capture in front of the camera. As such, the meaning of any cinematic image, and especially its significance, depends on an act of perception; it depends on the mind of the spectator. Münsterberg explains:

> The mere perception of the men and women and of the background, with all their depth and motion, furnishes only the material. . . . We must accompany those sights with a wealth of ideas. They must have a meaning for us, they must be enriched by our own imagination, they must awaken the remnants of earlier experiences, they must stir up our feelings and emotions, they must play on our suggestibility, they must start ideas and thoughts, they must be linked in our mind with the continuous chain of the play, and they must draw our attention constantly to the important and essential element of action. . . . our attention must be drawn now here, now there, if we want to bind together that which is scattered in the space before us. (79–80)

From this view, even the most realistic stories accept some element of fantasy. The image itself is incomplete and unrealistic until it is processed by the spectator. The cinema delivers an image, but it is an image that is empty of meaning. The spectator must fill an image with meaning if it is to have any momentous meaning. While not an idea Münsterberg mentions, this is what allows the cinematic image to always maintain an indexical quality.

The symbolic and iconic aspects of every image can always be drained on the point of the index.

Münsterberg's estimation anticipates more contemporary discussions of meaning making in the movies, the sort David Bordwell offers in *Making Meaning* (1989), and Bordwell's framework does inform some of the later moves in the present study. Those steps become more interesting, however, after a fuller discussion of Münsterberg, and especially his belief that movies move as the mind moves. Münsterberg remained especially interested in cinematic framing and editing as models of the interworking of the mind. Münsterberg gives particular attention to the closeup and the flashback or flashforward, and how these two techniques follow the manner of attention and memory, respectively. Münsterberg insists that the closeup models the coordinated operations in the mind that moves one's attention to "the center of [one's] consciousness" (85). For Münsterberg, human attention is more accurately the coordination of attention and inattention. That which has one's attention—a smell, a sight, a sound—is in focus, while everything else temporarily vanishes. The smell and sight disappear for a moment while the sound is held in the ear. The closeup works the same way. All but the hand reaching for the revolver disappears for a moment as a killer moves for a weapon: "the detail that is being watched has suddenly become the whole content of the performance, and everything that our mind wants to disregard has been suddenly banished from our sight" (87). For Münsterberg, the image on the screen has modeled the way attention works in the mind.

In the same way, the flashback (or cutback, as Münsterberg calls it) and the flashforward model, respectively, memory and imagination. The flashback breaks from the present to show some earlier detail in the same way a memory breaks from the present. Münsterberg suggests that even when a memory relates to the present, one must still deem the turn to the memory a break from the current moment. The flashback serves as an example of this operation. Münsterberg provides a scenario to illustrate his point. A husband finds himself in a perilous position. The screen cuts to the moment where he kisses his wife goodbye just before he meets some perilous end. The flashback carries the spectator where memory might. Past and present are brought together. The flashforward does the same thing for the present and the future. The folly of some fool's actions can be stretched across decades so that the outcome of that foolishness can be seen in one leap. In both cases, "the photoplay obeys the laws of the mind," moving across time as attention, memory and imagination operate in the mind (91). The photoplay displays these operations on the screen, performing the way in which they naturally disrupt linear time.

These disruptions in linear time unsettle the laws of physical space as well. Earlier in his argument, Münsterberg considers the ease with which movies can shift between scenes. Backgrounds can be altered in a moment. Locales realistically separated by miles can be artfully set beside one another. Spectators can watch in the most realistic drama a man move from one place to another in one seamless progression. It hardly matters if the man is crossing the street, a continent, or the world. To turn to a phrase from Münsterberg's (1915/2010) "Why We Go to the Movies," it is as if "the limitations of space are overcome" (10). Returning to Münsterberg's argument in *The Photoplay* (1916/2001), the truth is that the movies disrupt space and time equally, and do so in just the way the mind disorders space and time. The mind is not bound to its locale. Neither is it bound to the present. Its memory or imagination can carry it to new places and other times. Münsterberg insists movies can satisfy this human capacity by working in a like manner. They can display the omnipresence the human mind could entertain if it could see beyond itself. After all, Münsterberg reasons, "life does not move forward on one single pathway. . . . parallel currents [of space and time] with their endless interconnections is the true substance of [human] understanding. . . . the richer it is in contrasts, the more satisfaction may be drawn from our simultaneous presence in many quarters" (95). The underlying assumption supporting this possibility for Münsterberg is the certainty that even lens-based movies intend to break from reality rather than to preserve it. These images invite the audience to interact with them rather than receive them. This interaction leads from sign to sign, indexically speaking, which is another way of saying that every reality leads to another reality. The lens-based film has always shown this tendency. The reality before the camera leads to a reality on the screen. The reality on the screen realizes a sense of here that can carry forward to another reality, one the reality on the screen can only point toward without ever naming. In this way, the reality on the screen lingers in a way the reality before the camera cannot.

Münsterberg's discussion of emotions provides one of the ways the sign on the screen lingers on the screen. Münsterberg opens his chapter on emotions with the following claim: "to picture emotions must be the central aim of the photoplay. . . . the persons in the photoplay are to us, first of all, subjects of emotional experience" (99). Münsterberg intends to say more than that the characters in a movie display emotion or that audiences have emotional responses to those displays. The emotions the screen displays exist beyond the human players. The clothes they wear, the setting in which they sit or stand, cry or laugh, and every other aspect of whatever is represented as the frame widens or the soundtrack plays conveys emotion. There are times when spectators feel the emotions the scene portrays. A character is heartbroken or overjoyed or nervous or exhausted, and the spectators' emotions match her feeling. Münsterberg explains spectators "feel as if [they] were directly seeing and observing the emotion itself" (105). The opposite also occurs. A character on screen takes delight in the suffering of a rival, the very same person with whom spectators have attached themselves throughout the drama, and the audience feels contempt or outrage at the character's actions. Münsterberg insists that in either case, when spectators are emotionally aligned or misaligned with the characters and actions on screen, the emotions that the spectators feel emerge from the spectators rather than the moving images. Emotions are "aroused in the mind of the spectator through the subtle art of the camera" (108). The emotions are not on the screen any more than meaning or reality is in the screen. For Münsterberg, emotions, meaning, and reality each occur in the mind of the spectator, and they occur to be experienced and reexperienced rather than merely recognized.

Münsterberg's position blurs the normal lines between reality and the movies in just the way Rushton wants to blur them. If movies operate as the mind operates, then it follows that they also bear some reality of their own, or at least that they are perceived to do so, which following the ideas of perceptual realism is enough to warrant calling something real. Rushton's reassessment of André Bazin and Christian Metz further develops this idea. More importantly, Rushton's reappraisal of Bazin and Metz clarifies how the whole of this discussion can relate to the idea of the cinematic index as it is being developed in this project. As it relates to Bazin, Rushton urges scholars to look to Bazin for something more than a defense of a realist cinema. As a point of contrast, Rushton summarizes the general attitude toward Bazin within film studies to be a reduction of the theorist's ideas. Scholars often suggest that Bazin believes "all a filmmaker need do is point a camera at the world, keep the camera rolling, and the result will be undeniably real" (43). Rushton rightly faults this view as overly reductive. If nothing else, Bazin's belief that "realism in art can only be achieved in one way—through artifice" suggests to Rushton that Bazin understood that "realism can only ever be a construction and never a straight replication, duplication or representation of reality" (44). Rushton offers that Bazin means to create a different sort of divide from what those wanting to use the theorist as a way to cut between realistic and illusionistic films might allow.

Rushton goes one step further to argue that Bazin champions the idea of a filmic reality more than generally gets recognized. Rushton mentions two notable exceptions, Philip Rosen (2001) and Daniel Chandler (2006), as a way to establish a different divide between types of cinema, or, more properly, cinematic engagement. Rushton credits Rosen for rejecting the idea that Bazin believes in "an objective, pure and unmediated reality that is out there" (60). Instead, Rushton finds Rosen appreciating in Bazin a belief in a reality that can only ever be perceived by a subject. Contrary to the received understanding of Bazin, which treats Bazin as the champion for cinema's ability to re-present reality, Rushton finds in Chandler's reading of Bazin a theorist interested in "how the reality of things might be *acknowledged* by human subjects as real" (63, emphasis in original). The discussion between Rosen and Chandler posits a view of reality that depends on social agreement rather than recognition of some objective reality that exists in front of a camera. This turn breaks away from what Rushton deems a false divide between reality and illusion so often attributed to Bazin.

Rushton uses Bazin's discussion of two films, *Germany Year Zero* (1948) and *Voyage to Italy* (1953) (alternately translated as *Journey to Italy*), both by Roberto Rossellini, to illustrate the difference between an interest in reality and illusion and a socially accepted notion of reality. Rushton understands Bazin to view *Germany Year Zero* as an attempt "to start again, to define reality again from scratch, to rebuild senses of a reality worth sharing" (48). Rossellini accomplishes this appeal to a restart by dramatizing the angst that arises when one's actions call into question the ethos that motivated those actions. In the case of *Germany Year Zero*, Edmund's (Edmund Moeschke) despondency after poisoning his father to act out the ideals of his teacher's "survival of the fittest" philosophy dramatizes the end result awaiting those who live in a world that refuses any "notion of reality that can be socially shared... other than... 'every man for himself'" (49). *Germany Year Zero* ultimately stages for Bazin a world unable to agree on a socially accepted notion of reality, which is to say any notion of reality. The film is, in an important way, without reality, a point Rushton observes through a quote from Bazin: "Driven into the street, the kid walks and walks, searching here and there among the ruins; but, one after the other, people and things abandon him" (48). Edmund, and the audience with him, is left without a reality, which serves as something of a call for the audience to create a reality, new possibilities, situations, and events, which is to say, some filmic reality.

Rushton turns to Bazin's praise of *Voyage to Italy* as an example of what this more idealized version of filmic reality would look like. As Rushton recounts, Rossellini's film places a married couple in a foreign culture, which necessarily "unhinge[s] [them] from reality" (49). The couple is left to renegotiate their reality. In the early and middle parts of the film, the couple's need to renegotiate a reality divides them. Before the film ends, however, "a miracle occurs—at least, Bazin refers to it as a miracle... [when] a certain reality comes into being" (49–50). The couple realize a reality "they can inhabit . . . they can share," which, according to Rushton, "is what Bazin's realism amounts to" (50). Bazin's reality is not a reality that exists before the camera or ultimately even on the screen. It is a performance, which, following Münsterberg, is to be realized in the mind of the spectator. The entire process involves more than representation or recognition. In Rushton's words, "far from being a realism of representation or of looking like reality, the reality to which Bazin subscribes is one of placing worth in human actions, of trying to forge agreements about what reality is or should be" (57). The dramas staged in *Germany Year Zero* and for most of *Voyage to Italy* illustrate what it is to exist without an agreed-upon notion of reality. The last part of *Voyage to Italy* illuminates the opposite, and under that light, reasons Rushton, emerges the concept of realism that most interests Bazin.

Rushton's reassessment of Bazin lends some credibility to his notion of filmic reality, and it does so by showing how a plot can perform the reality-making process a movie can initiate. This is what Bazin finds the couple in *Voyage to Italy* doing. It is what this project finds Pamela doing in *Saving Mr. Banks* or, as will be discussed momentarily, Linklater allowing his characters to do. The common denominator across these examples is that movies permit spectators to do something to the reality they watch, and to do so on the point of an index that never tires of moving from sign to sign, index to index. To be fair, one has to move beyond Rushton's ideas of the index to arrive at a clear picture of this process. Rushton twice addresses a less productive idea of the index than the one herein proposed. The first arises during Rushton's discussion of Stephen Prince (2004). Rushton comments on the way Prince makes Bazin "the fall-guy" for an overly simplified concept of "photographic realism" (53). Rushton finds Prince parading an idea of the index that exists "back in the old Bazinian days of photo-mechanical filmmaking" that has since become irrelevant (53). Rushton rejects this antiquated idea, offering that the traditional idea of the index believes too much in the reality in front of a camera. Rushton admits that a proper idea of filmic reality needs "to affirm that [the realities inscribed by the camera] can only ever be generically or socially shared realities" (54). What matters for Rushton, as it is what he sees mattering to Bazin, is that the reality movies create "can be *imbued* with reality" (57, emphasis mine). Rushton freely admits his belief that digital and analog images can be imbued with reality equally well. The literal reality or non-reality of the image on the screen matters much less to Rushton than the fact that the image is on the screen, and, once on the screen, the images can register themselves as a reality.

Rushton raises the matter of indexicality a second time when discussing Rosen. Rushton sees Rosen offering "that there is no intrinsic, objective connection between an indexical sign and its referent" (62). This idea actually fits the arguments Bazin makes in his "Ontology" essay more than either Rushton or Rosen declares. As already described in the first chapter, the received account of Bazin in film studies, especially as it relates to the concept of the index, tends to be mediated by Peter Wollen's presentation of Bazin. Wollen wrestles from Bazin's writing a passive index. The sign can serve as a trace, but it serves the "passivity of the natural world rather than the agency of the human mind" (131). A careful reading of Bazin's words can show that Bazin works toward a different understanding. Bazin's thoughts on the family album provide one example. The image in the family album does not extend to the person whose earlier life can be found in it; instead, it marks a new opening in the past, a moment when the person in the image can begin again and anew. The guarantee of who the person is in the present is set aside in favor of the earlier moment when she could have been any number of other things. From this view, the photograph exists as anything but a connection to a reality that will be. It is a reminder that any eventual reality can always be undone by the image. One is free in the face of the photograph, moving or not, to search out other realities.

A careful review of Bazin suggests that he was also aware that one reality might lead to another. Bazin does emphasize the literal imprint of reality a lens-based camera captures; but he uses this detail in a surprising way, one that challenges the oversimplified reduction of the ideas Rushton protests, even if Rushton stops short of appreciating the insight. Bazin begins his essay with an admission that photography and cinema differ from the ancient plastic arts. The earlier arts were "aimed against death," against "the victory of time," which stole the body and claimed the living for the dead (9). The ancient practice of making mummies or death masks illustrates the intent of these artifacts, which reverse the process of time and return to the living a body lost to death. Bazin admits that it might look like photographs are doing something similar, but he ultimately contends that photographs serve a different purpose. A lens-based photograph records reality in a literal way. The image returned in photograph is the body as it appeared in one particular moment of time. In this way, Bazin claims, the photographer creates what earlier artists could not, "an ideal world in the likeness of the real, *with its own temporal destiny*" (10, emphasis mine). One could, as many have done, focus on the first half of this statement at the expense of the second. Bazin does acknowledge the literal likeness of some reality a photograph delivers. This would be the iconic aspects of the image. Bazin also creates space for the deictic index that can exist as the indefinite, intertextual, or imaginative index. This space emerges in the second part of Bazin's sentence, which argues that the photograph follows its own temporal destiny. It is not, in other words, only a copy of reality. It is a moment of reality captured to be set free from itself.

Bazin's subsequent admission that the photograph and the moving image generate an alternative realism that means to do more than fool "the eye (or for that matter the mind)" would reinforce his desire to describe the new temporal destiny each image generates (12). Cinema's trick is less about creating an alternative reality than it is about exploring the yet-to-be-determined quality of the object found in the frame. Bazin insists the lens-based image stops time not simply to represent that moment, but to initiate a process that tracks a range of possibilities left unexplored by the actual, lived subject. The resulting lens-based image follows a different path than the lived subject follows, which permits the spectator to imagine through such an image something other than some lived reality. In short, the lens-based photograph creates space for exploration rather than preservation. This view can only operate on the point of the index. The iconic values of the sign are set by the reality the image captures. The symbolic elements are also set, born out of social convention and agreement. While Rushton is right to find in Rosen an argument that the index can also "only ever be the result of a learned relation," one must conclude that this assessment runs counter to the idea Bazin (and, for the record, Peirce) promotes (62). The index is the index, in part, because it stands apart from such wrangling. The index is never "mummified," to play on Rosen's idea of the "mummy complex." It is an empty sign, a pointing finger that can be shown to point to different realities.

This idea is more in line with Bazin's ideas than even Rushton explicitly recognizes. To return to the idea of the family album, Bazin is sure that the lens-based photo album delivers a different sort of portrait than the plastic arts could distribute even if the two mediums appear to adhere to the same impulse. The portrait depicted by a painter on a canvas can achieve a kind of likeness that approximates the image of a subject, but Bazin argues that the resulting image leaves the subject in the past. It also returns the observer who sees it to that past. It does so because a painting is, for Bazin, "an illusion," the attempt to reverse time and carry an image from the past into the present to be remembered (12). The photograph works differently because a photograph breaks time by delivering to the present the image of a subject as it has *not-yet-been-known*. It brings the subject of some past, whose person has been disrupted by his/her existence, into the interpretive moment of the present. In this present, the subject entertains a host of contingencies the literal subject in the past had to forsake. This series of new possibilities occurs, according to Bazin, because the photograph delivers a suitable "substitute" for the actual subject: "the photographic image is the object itself, the object freed from the conditions of time and space that govern it. . . . it *is* the model" (14, emphasis in the original). While a painting literally suffers at the hand of the artist, the photograph appears without any such interference. It is *yet-to-be-interpreted* in the same way a landscape has yet-to-be-interpreted either by an audience or by consequence of its own action.

Bazin reemphasizes the yet-to-be-interpreted/realized aspect of a photograph by talking a second time about the sense of presence the image as an object realizes. Bazin contends that lens-based images become "the disturbing presence of lives halted at a set moment in their duration, *freed from their destiny* . . . [the images] embalm time, *rescuing [the subject] from its own proper corruption*" (14, emphasis mine). Having been halted in some specific moment, the subject reacquires an otherwise unacknowledged temporal and narrative freedom. No longer understood along the path the subject's life literally traveled, the photograph breathes new possibilities into the subject. These possibilities are there for the audience to see. The subject awaits a new journey. Those who see the photograph are also freed: the lens-based image strips the subject from the frame of "all those ways of seeing it, those piled-up preconceptions, that spiritual dust and grime with which my eyes have covered it" (15). The image "imitates the artist" and the audience, both of whom can suddenly choose a way to see a subject that has been captured but not fully seen, a subject that is still in the process of being seen for the first time, and that is open to be seen again (15). The image on the screen is always ready to be reseen, to be rewatched.

Rushton arrives at a similar idea, albeit through a discussion of Christian Metz rather than Bazin. Rushton regards Metz's notion of the imaginary as, most accurately, a testament to cinema's reality rather than its status as some sort of illusion. Rushton grounds this opinion in a specific understanding of the imaginary, which Rushton believes to capture what Metz mentions as cinema's greatest achievement, namely, its ability to "provide [spectators] ways of conceiving new and different worlds" (Rushton, 94). The cinema accomplishes this feat through "its curious and distinctive blending of fantasy and reality, somewhere on the border between the two, not purely and simply an illusion which we know to be an illusion, but also not simply a replica of the real which we take as a copy or replica of that real" (95). In other words, the images on the screen are never either real or illusion. They are perpetually somewhere and something in between. They are in their own accepted reality. Of course, the images on the screen are not accepting themselves; instead, they are accepted by spectators. In this way, the spectator is always part of the filmic reality. To this end, Rushton reminds readers that Metz maintained that spectators must "accede to the imaginary 'contract' any film proposes . . . [through] wakefulness, alertness" (100). The spectator must participate in the meaning of the image, but such participation will depend on the image—for there is no other way to honor the contract the film proposes, rather than simply the imagination of the spectator.

The imaginary signifier Rushton wants to recover in Metz, then, sits between two contested spaces. The first contest is between reality and illusion. Rushton maintains that Metz's imaginary signifier is never purely real or illusionary. The image is a reality we accept or reject, but not a reality that bears any singular truth. Neither is the image a strict illusion in a ghostly sense. It exists, and, in so doing, it has something to contribute to the play on the screen. This first contest leads to a second one between the image's space on the screen and in the mind of the spectator. This second contest will have greater significance in the second half of this book. For now, it is enough to admit it exists. The first contest deserves more discussion, however, before the way in which this second contest can mark the difference between trauma and adaptation will matter in the right way. The significance of the real and imaginary must be sorted first. As they relate to cinema, these ideas cooperate with rather than exclude one another. They mark two extremes of what spectators can do with cinema. On the one hand, they admit some reality. On the other, they (re)imagine it. These two possibilities coexist on the screen to produce a field of reception wherein one is free to play on the point of the index, looking for the various realities the cinematic index can reference, while still accepting the presence of this sign in the plot. Herein lies the pushing and pulling of the cinematic index that seems to most interest Linklater.

Before exploring this pushing and pulling as it arises in Linklater's films, one needs to say more about Rushton's reluctance to consider cinema a representational art. Movies very clearly represent something. They represent many things, in fact, and, in keeping with the specific argument of this book, they do so indexically. One must move through and beyond discussions of reality and illusion to see this index properly. The index set within a binary of reality and illusion will almost always result in either the impoverished or the indefinite index. This is certainly what happens when one emphasizes some notion of reality. The image's connection to some literal and quite often fixed reality will be too certain to welcome the intertextual or the imaginative index. A similar thing happens when one emphasizes illusion. The absence of any discernable reality behind the image as it appears on screen leads one to begin to look for some reality beyond the frame. This is what Paul Willemen (2013) does when he focuses on the way "texts relate in some way to the historical dynamics which preside over their production" (121). For Willemen, the index that remains in the digital age is the one that points to "the very display of productive resources that constitute the 'spectacle'" (123). From this perspective, the indexical details that matter most in a digital production like *The Matrix* (1999), to reference a film Willemen explicitly discusses, are those that point to the industry that can produce those effects. Such a focus is not wrong, but neither is it complete. Other indices still exist on the screen, and they do so cinematically, which is to say in a way they can only in the cinema.

Two conditions support the cinematic index herein imagined. The first is motion, or at least the potential for motion. To return to the article from Gunning already mentioned, Gunning turns to Metz's emphasis on motion to check the idea that the cinema ever delivers a reality to the screen. Movies put a world in motion, but this world is never, strictly speaking, real. Gunning argues "in the cinema, we are dealing with realism, not 'reality'" (44). As Gunning explains, motion gives unreal elements life thanks to Metz's "world of imagination," which brings life (45). As above described, Rushton uses Metz's concept of the imagination to create a bridge to reality that Gunning does not accept. One does not need to pick a side on this debate to put both ideas to use. As it relates to Gunning, it hardly matters to this project whether the world on the screen is an instance of reality or realism. In either case, the cinematic index survives. Motion ensures that, and it does so for reasons Gunning articulates: "unlike the literalness of pointing to an actual individual that a narrow adherence to the diminished concept of indexical theory . . . forces on us[,] . . . the cinematic impression of reality affects . . . the fictional world created by the film, and thus escapes the straitjacket of exclusive correspondence or reference to any preexisting reality" (46). Other realities appear to the extent that the "extreme spectator" creates them (47). The reality is not onscreen simply to be received.

Motion alone does not ensure the survival of a more robust cinematic index. After all, the world around would-be spectators moves, and the world is not filled with cinematic indices. This is because questions of truth and accuracy apply in the actual world. These questions can, of course, also apply to cinematic worlds, but they do not necessarily need to do so. In fact, as Gunning and Rushton have already shown, their doing so might cause more problems than they can solve. To avoid these problems, the worlds set in motion satisfy a second condition: they move between the poles of a documentary and animation sensibility, which is to say, most generally, between a desire to tell a "truth" and to do so imaginatively. To be clear, these two poles exist on the same globe, which is to say that they do not mean to mark different worlds as much as different territories. In this way, these poles are like the North and South Poles, which are always on the Earth even as they mark two ends of that globe. The poles of documentary and animation mark two extremes of the cinematic world. Their mutual presence invites spectators to engage and explore rather than simply receive and record the details they entertain. Set at some degree from either pole, the index, set in motion, perpetuates a process that always takes place within a now that begins again, if not anew, each time spectators encounter it. An overview of these two sensibilities—or, given the focus on how movies are experienced and what they set spectators to do, modalities might be the better word—can clarify what is being proposed.

The documentary modality can, itself, move between overly general and specific understandings. Elizabeth Cowie (2011) moves most generally, aligning the documentary with the actuality that dominated the early days of cinema. As Mary Ann Doane (2002) notes, actualities, themselves, were little more than an opportunity to see everyday events, "a baby eating, a train arriving at a station, workers leaving a factory, photographers arriving at a conference, a snowball fight, the demolition of a wall" (22). Any such moment was suitable for projection so long as it was, on the one hand, "filmable," and, on the other, able to deliver some "technological assurance of indexicality," some belief that what was on the screen faithfully represents what was in the world the moment the camera registered it on film (22). Here, again, one finds in the actuality a literal form of rewatching. Filmmakers capture to film whatever it is that occurs in from of the camera. The film strip is projected onto a screen. The screen frames a new reality, but that new reality rarely accounts for the primary appeal of the exhibition.

For Doane, the most important quality of the transfer film facilitated between the world and the screen was the record and performance movies provided of a reality that would otherwise slip unnoticed or unrecognized into the past. After all, spectators cannot be in all places at all times. Neither can they perceive all there is to see about a subject or object through natural perception. A reductive way of seeing emerges too quickly. Diminution sets in. Film offers a response to that tendency, and it does so by indexing the contingency of every moment. Every baby, train, factory worker, conference, snowball fight, demolition is shown to be what it is in some moment, free from both what it has been and what it will be. Each subject and object are brought to the screen just as they are at some particular moment, and with the promise that they can be watched anew each time they are encountered.

Following Cowie, the documentary extends this tradition through the history of cinema. The documentary for Cowie (2011) serves as an "extraction from and organization of reality," one that brings "forward a new reality," which is to say an earlier unrecognized reality (1). This last aspect of the documentary is especially important. In keeping with the emphasis on contingency in Doane, Cowie claims that the documentary means to do more than just record reality. It also means to exhibit contingency. The documentary treats the world as "knowable" and "radically contingent" (3). Regardless of which of these two qualities the documentary emphasizes, or, more properly, the spectator comes to emphasize after encountering it, the performance the documentary delimits makes reality "reviewable, as a present time re-seen in an imagined future" (4). In this way, the documentary works as what Cowie calls a "memory machine, making available present events for future spectator's time of re-viewing, and a present tense—'speaking about the past'—in a 'now time'" (6). One is brought to the edge of the *Kairos* of ongoing adaptation. One is able to delight oneself in "either a mastery of the new and unknown, or a repeated encounter with the impossibility of mastery, of knowledge, and of sense-making" (14). In this way, the documentary is not so unlike other forms of fiction.

No matter how much the documentary is like other forms of fiction, one must admit that spectators rarely engage a documentary the way they engage other forms of fiction. Bill Nichols admits in his *Introduction to Documentary* (2017) that documentaries differ from other forms of fiction if only because they directly "address *the* world in which we live rather than *a* world imagined by the filmmaker" (xi, emphasis in original). This is not to exclude some idea of fiction from the documentary. Nichols leaves space within the documentary for the "performance that we associate with fiction" (xi). The difference is in the relationship a documentary establishes with the subject, the filmmaker, and the audience. Documentaries treat each part of this triad differently than do fictional films. One might say that these differences extend from where a documentary locates its story. Documentaries will "belong to the same historical world" to which the audience belongs (xii). Fictional films can do this as well. Nichols lists *Forrest Gump* (1994), *The Truman Show* (1998), *The Blair Witch Project* (1999), and *The Road to Guantánamo* (2006) as films that do just that, but their sense of belonging will almost always be part of the pretense. In a documentary, this sense of belonging is more than a pretense. It establishes the discursive aim of the project. As Nichols explains, "the sense of an authentic representation of the world . . . can . . . persuade [an audience] to adopt a given perspective or point of view about the world" (xiii). The sense of authenticity extends the documentary whatever sense of authority it has to lend. The very essence of the documentary depends on this sense of authenticity.

Nichols's subsequent explanation names some of the ways documentaries acquire a sense of authenticity. For Nichols, documentaries have three traits: "documentaries are about reality; [they] are about real people; [and they] tell stories about what really happened" (23). In these ways, Nichols suggests that documentaries "rely heavily on the *indexical* capacity of the photographic image and of sound recording to replicate what we take to be the distinctive visual or acoustic qualities of the world" (23). Nichols is referring, of course, to what this project has been calling the impoverished or indefinite index, the literal reality that produces the sign (impoverished) or to which the index points (indefinite). From Nichols's perspective, these two indices would be the same. The reality behind the images in a documentary is what produces the sign, and it is the reality to which the sign points. Still, that is not the only index made available, not even in a documentary. The sign in a documentary has the potential to be intertextual or imaginative. All four expressions of the cinematic index exist. Which one exists most naturally depends on how close one is to each of the two poles. The closer one is to the documentary pole, the more pronounced is the impoverished and indefinite index.

It is worth noting that Nichols allows these less imaginative indices to tolerate various expressions. Nichols, in fact, names six modes of documentary filmmaking: the poetic, the expository, the observational, the participatory, the reflexive, and the performative. Each mode deserves attention, not only as a way to appreciate the documentary but also to provide a basis to appreciate a more general flexibility in the impoverished and indefinite index. The poetic mode works through "associations and patterns . . . [that stress] mood, tone, and affect much more than displays of factual knowledge or acts of rhetorical persuasion" (116). The materials brought to the screen still belong to the world in a tangible way, but these materials are set on the screen to establish a question or problem rather than to provide an answer. The expository mode, on the other hand, "advance[s] an argument" (122). The images placed on the screen tend to serve as evidence supporting the commentator's explicit argument. The voice-over and the images move with "the impression of objectivity," but they are clearly set toward a specific argument (124). This level of specificity is what distinguishes the expository from the reflexive mode. The reflexive mode might have elements that are just as predisposed as those found in the expository mode, but they are introduced to invite reflection rather than acceptance. The tenor of the reflexive mode, in fact, is one of challenge. Nichols explains, "the reflexive mode is the most self-conscious and self-questioning mode of representation. . . . at its best, reflexive documentary prods the viewer to a heightened form of consciousness about his or her relation to the documentary and what it represents" (128).

These first three modes, then, each push the viewer to "take a deeper look" at reality (131). They move according to impression, argument, or reflection.

The last three modes of documentary are more descriptive. The observational mode, for instance, works by letting the camera capture "lived experience spontaneously," trying not to interfere with the reality occurring whether the lens is there or not (133). The goal of the observational documentary is simply to capture life as it exists both in time and space. The participatory mode often maintains the sense of observation, but does so while engaging the life it records. The filmmaker will ask questions and make observations: "what happens in front of the camera becomes an index of the nature of the interaction between filmmaker and subject" (138). The subject of the documentary, therefore, shifts, as the filmmaker's relationship to the subject becomes part of the story. The last mode, the performative mode, extends and exaggerates the subjective aspects of the participatory mode so that "the complexity of our knowledge of the world" is apparent (150). The performative mode parades the subjective and affective qualities of every detail it places on the screen so that "the emotional intensities of situated experience and embodied knowledge" can be perceived (152). In this way, the performative mode invites spectators to a certain feeling rather than a particular argument or even perspective. In each of the more descriptive modes of the documentary, the goal is to construct a world that otherwise might pass by unnoticed.

The benefit of this review of the various modes of the documentary, at least as it relates to the current project, is that it shows that even the impoverished and indefinite indices have a range of expressions rather than the artless responsibility to represent some reality accurately. One might find such representation in only one of these six modes, the observational, in fact. The other five expressions "interfere" with reality in some specific way. The poetic produces patterns and associations. The expository makes an argument. The reflexive creates space for reflection. The participatory engages the world. The performative performs it. In each of these, reality is what it is, but in a particular rather than genuine way. The documentary will provide its reality with a sense of authenticity, but this sense of authenticity will always be postured by the filmmaker. Even the observational mode is a posture. The myth of the transparent eye able to see all as it is without interference must be set aside for a more honest assessment of the cinema. Movies move and they do so in subjective ways. The documentary reminds us of that quality.

The animated documentary, as Paul Ward (2006) warrants, is especially good at reminding audiences that even documentaries use subjective, fantastical, and "non-normative approaches to understanding the world around us" (83). Ward declares that animation's "frame-by-frame production process means that [it] is the most 'interventionist' of modes," but that operating in this mode does not mean one must abandon any correspondence with reality (86). An animated film can very nearly accept the same level of correspondence as a live-action film. Any animation fitting Paul Wells's (1998) imitative mode of animated films, in fact, will have, as Ward offers, a high level of correspondence to the world it animates. Ward lists the *You and Your...* (1955–57) series and *The Sinking of the Lusitania* (1918) as examples of animations working in the imitative mode (85). Both films create images that mean to match to their reality. Still, they are animations, which means their standing as constructions is also always on display. The questions worth asking are: How is an animated documentary being watched? Is it as an animation or as a documentary? One might think that the answers to these questions will have a greater impact on the character of the film than almost anything else. A look at how the sensibilities of the animation relate to the sensibilities of the documentary suggests a different conclusion.

Andrew Selby (2013) celebrates the way "animation permits and encourages the creation of cinematic visual trickery by making unreal events seem real and transporting an audience to new places of discovery" (6). The account matches the early understanding of animated films as Scott Curtis (2019) describes it. Curtis claims early "frame-by-frame animation [films] were ... regarded as ... 'trick films,'" the kind George Méliès made popular, in which "through cinematographic or editing sleight of hand ... the actors could be stopped ... [and] a substitution made ... [so that] it would appear on-screen as an instantaneous, even magical transformation" (19). Curtis declares that animations follow the same principles. Each moment is drawn individually, and then set in magical motion so that it appears as if some moment of continuous action has occurred. The practice realizes the central concept of animation, as articulated by Maureen Furniss (2007), namely, of "bringing objects to life" (1). It also matches the meaning of the Latin verb, *animare*, "to give life to," from which the word "animation" springs. The life of the animated object is, of course, the result of a process rather than some spontaneity. As Selby summarizes it, frames are drawn and set into sequences. These sequences play across a screen in such a way that they appear to move with lifelike precision.

Selby sets this lifelike precision on twelve principles of animation as described by Ollie Johnston and Frank Thomas (1981). The first principle Selby discusses is squash and stretch, which accounts for the "implied weight and flexibility" of every object (11). This principle applies the law of gravity to an object. The second principle is anticipation. Anticipation accounts for the "desire, intention, or need to move" bodies exhibit as they prepare to move (11). The third principle, staging, places an object in a "surrounding environment" (11). The fourth, straight-ahead action and pose-to-pose drawing, "reflect the focus, pace, and concentration of the story being animated" (11). The fifth principle is follow-through and overlapping actions. This principle brings to the screen the laws of physics that determine "that after a body (human or object) has stopped moving, the momentum created by its movement is continued . . . before coming to rest" (11–12). The sixth principle is slow in and slow out, which requires that "a greater number of frames is created at the beginning and the end of a moving sequence" so that the sequence exhibits "acceleration and deceleration" (12). The seventh, arcs, requires animators to set action on arcs that stretch or peak according to speed. Faster actions will stretch, while slower actions will peak. The eighth principle is secondary action. This principle "recognizes that movements seldom happen in isolation," and ensures that all action in the scene is properly synched (12). The ninth principle, timing, recognizes that every action will occur across a certain number of frames. The span of frames will not only indicate the speed at which actions take place, but "wider conditions [too], such as the characters' emotional state and their connection to the plot or other characters" (12). The tenth principle is exaggeration. Exaggeration allows animators "to stretch and distort reality, achieving seemingly impossible feats by amplifying conditions and breaking rules and conventions" (12). The eleventh principle, solid drawing, relates to "anatomy and form" (12). The twelfth and final principle is appeal, which serves as "an embodiment of character traits that touches on an emotional inner core" (12). Taken together, these twelve traits establish a level of believability within the animation. In this way, even animations are not downright detached from reality. In some cases, they extend from the same principles that operate in the real world. They just do so in imaginative ways.

The existence of such a list indicates the very sort of "complementary and oppositional relationship" between animation and live-action films Curtis (2019) describes (11). Animations have long complemented live-action films. In terms of establishing the early appeal of films of either sort, animations appear at a time "when the novelty of early cinema had grown stale"; Curtis reasons that the emergence of "animation promised to restore some of the faded magic" (11–12). One sees the two forms working together as early as the 1920s in characters like the "Fleischers' Koko the Clown [who] moved easily between animated and live-action environments" (12). Examples of movies combining live action and animated sequences pepper every decade of film history. One could construe every film that uses digital technology as a mix of live action and animation. Each instance suggests the collaborative possibilities of the relationship between live action and animation. Curtis cautions, however, that the two forms have "also been somewhat oppositional" (12). Curtis even offers the recurring action in the Koko the Clown sequences as an apt depiction of the tension between the two forms: "if Koko the Clown entered the live-action world, it was often to torment his creator or to escape similar torment" (12). Nearly one hundred years later, one finds animated sequences, especially as they develop through digital technologies, to be tormenting filmmakers again. Cinema's very essence seems to be under attack as it loses a direct connection to some reality. The twelve principles of animation, meant to keep animation in contact with some version of reality, seem to miss their mark.

Julie A. Turnock (2015) provides an interesting correction to the idea that animation somehow necessarily removes one from reality, or, more precisely, some notion of realism. Set within a defense for considering more fully the emergence of the special effects one sees in popular films starting in the late 1960s, Turnock argues that these effects "follow highly stylized forms of realism related to dominant filmmaking aesthetics, replicating an accepted aesthetic *photo*realistically" (10, emphasis in the original). Turnock insists on the inclusion of the term "photo" even as she admits that the period she describes often operates without a lens-based camera, in part, because the term relates to an approach within art history that "describes paintings (and prints) executed to mimic a photographic aesthetic" (10). Turnock contends that those turning to special effects in the late 1960s, and especially by the release of *Star Wars* and *Close Encounters of the Third Kind* in 1977, were imitating the same aesthetic, albeit through different means. Rather than drawing attention to the photographic techniques of setting or framing to play with the photograph, the technique Turnock's filmmakers adopt "depends upon the erasure of the technique by a seamless matching of the special effects material and live-action footage to depict a coherent diegesis" (10). The effects appear *photo*realistic because the tricks used to bring them about remain invisible on screen. One has a realistic animation, or what Turnock calls a plastic reality.

One can imagine a cartoon or a scene that more openly mixes live action and animation appearing as realistic as Turnock's plastic realities. Animations of all sorts can appear real even as they refuse to hide the edges of their unreality. Motion explains one reason this occurs. Spectators will extend some reality to what appears on screen when it moves. The fact that this movement matches the flow of human imagination offers another reason. To return to Münsterberg, even as cinema is still emerging, mimesis is just one aspect of movies; the imagination is another, and perhaps the more critical. The suggestion returns one to Furniss, and to the continuum she constructs between mimesis and abstraction. Mimesis, Furniss (2007) offers, "represents the desire to reproduce natural reality" (5). One might, as Furniss does, align this desire with "live-action," lens-based recordings of the world in front of a camera. Such recordings capture the world as it exists or is made to exist. Abstraction works more generally. It is a "a suggestion of a concept rather than an attempt to explicate [a form] in real life terms" (5). Animations tends to work in abstraction.

Furniss is careful to refuse to set live-action and animation at opposite ends of her "mimesis" and "abstraction" continuum: "everything is relative," she admits (5). A film like Disney's *Snow White and the Seven Dwarfs* (1937) or Norman Ferguson's *The Three Caballeros* (1943) might sit most naturally "somewhere in the middle of this continuum ... while a documentary like *Sleep* (1963) ... would be far to the side of mimesis ... [and] a film like *Hen Hop* (1942) ... would appear ... relatively close to the abstract pole" (5–6). The exact placement might even change slightly as time passes. As Furniss admits, "the placements suggested by [any] description are somewhat arbitrary" (6). The poles of Furniss's continuum are tools rather than descriptors. They mean to isolate a way of seeing a film rather than to discover its character. In this way, the similarities and differences between the two forms can have an equal influence. The present study adopts a similar attitude. The field on which the cinematic index appears arises equally well from any "motion picture production." It emerges as a detail in the plot, which points to any number of realities. It hardly matters if one of those realities relates to an actual world or not. The cinematic index can perform the deictic function of the index with or without such realities. Some reality will always emerge on the screen regardless of whether or not there is a firm reality behind those images, and even whether or not one is operating according to the sensibilities associated with the documentary or the animation. On the screen, the two sensibilities become two sides of the same coin.

Richard Linklater seems especially aware of the shared impulse to participate in the meaning-making process brought to the screen through the documentary and animation modality. His films often quite explicitly sit between the sensibilities of documentary and animation. One might even say that the idea of the documentary and animation serve as two poles in Linklater's films that push and pull spectators toward a specific notion of cinematic reality, one that is consistently being reimagined rather than preserved. Those aware of Linklater's oeuvre might be especially queued to view Linklater's films through these two competing sensibilities. The director is one of the few popular mainstays of contemporary American cinema to have made bona fide documentaries, animations, and feature-length films that openly mix the elements of these genres. Linklater has made two documentaries, *Inning by Inning: A Portrait of a Coach* (2008) and a short, *Live from Shiva's Dance Floor* (2003). More importantly, as David T. Johnson (2012) explains, several other feature-length films feel like documentaries. Johnson esteems *Slacker* (1990) as a movie "with a quasi-documentary sensibility" (21). The film is shot on streets like a documentary with almost no effort to separate the fictional world of the film from the literal world that becomes the film's stage as the film progresses. The soundtrack, in fact, following Johnson, "creates an even greater sense of the reality that exists outside the frame," as Linklater allows the sounds of "cars pass[ing] [and] engines rising" to remain rather than create a tight soundstage (23). The line between the world being documented by the film and the one being brought to life because of it remains razor thin.

Johnson finds this documentary sensibility at play in *Before Sunrise* (1995) as well. In keeping with the attention to detail found in documentaries, Johnson claims that Linklater makes "small gestures . . . more noticeable, such as when Celine looks down as she describes a boy who asked her out at summer camp, or Jesse's starting to sweep [Celine's] hair from her face, then hesitate[s]—because she has looked up, or because that is too familiar, too intimate, for this early moment" (37). One could attribute these small moments to the actors performing them, but Johnson provides a clear reason to let them point to Linklater as well. Their presence documents a movement just as it is being animated, which, in this case, is simply to say as it is being set in motion. It is a subtle moment, but the type of moment that finds frequent expression in Linklater's films. It's the sort of moment that marks Timothy "Speed" Levitch, the subject of Linklater's short documentary *Live from Shiva's Dance Floor*. Throughout the tour of the city, Levitch reveals with even greater precision the thin line between documentary and animation, as he reimagines the meaning and significance of the monuments he encounters.

One example of the ease with which Levitch moves from documenter to animator occurs early in the film when Levitch pauses in front of John Quincy Adams Ward's statue of George Washington as it stands in Wall Street. The statue most directly means to represent George Washington as he takes the oath of office for his presidency; that is its stated objective. Levitch asks his audience to consider another possible representation:

> When I tell you that that's George Washington, as sculpted by John Quincy Ward, taking the oath of office, this will open up an entire floodgate deluge of ideas and principles and history and ideology

and persona. Close off that floodgate for a moment. Look out at that statue and close your eyes. Take a deep breath. And when you open your eyes, let's agree that that's not George Washington. That is just a human being, a man, a soul. He's wearing eighteenth-century regalia. He has good posture, he's almost smiling, and he appears to be holding out his hand. He appears to be waiting for someone to hold his hand. The statue, for me, has clearly just become a declaration of the American need for intimacy, and it has rendered this entire Wall Street simply a parable telling the tale of how much George Washington needs his hand held.

The idea to note in this speech is not that the statue is either a president taking the oath of office or a cry to the American people for some measure of closeness. Within Linklater's cinema, the statue is both. It is the sign John Quincy Adams Ward imagines of a man taking an oath of office, and it is the sign Levitch describes. The statue is at least doubly located in time and purpose. While an iconic or symbolic sign might struggle to support more than one meaning at any one time, the index is free to point in more than one direction. The index is, on balance, an empty sign. It can index multiple realities. If it is working properly, which is to say as an index set between a desire to document and to animate, it will index what it does at any given moment, only to be empty in the next. Such is the notion of the index Peirce describes, and it is the concept of the index in Linklater films.

One could locate this notion of the index within Linklater's notion of reality, which almost always shows reality to still be evolving rather than settled. Johnson attributes this quality to Linklater's unique sense of time. There is an unmistakable presence to Linklater's films, even as his characters are often working to reconcile that present with some past or future. In this way, one might say that Linklater's characters are struck or stung by their past, but they always feel that hit or sting in the present. One might even say there is only the present in Linklater's films. Linklater has his characters explain why that would be the case at least two times. The first example occurs in *Waking Life* (2001). Richard Linklater appears as a pinball player to the film's unnamed protagonist, Main Character (Wiley Wiggins). The pinball player explains a dream he had wherein Yeats's patron, Lady Gregory, discusses the nature of time: "Philip K. Dick is right about time, but he's wrong its 50 A.D.; actually, there's only one instant, and it's right *now*" (emphasis mine). *Waking Life*'s pinball player goes on to explain that time is just human beings saying, "no, to God's invitation . . . [to] be one with eternity." There is only a perpetual no until there is a yes. In between these two responses, there is only now.

The pinball player actually echoes the same idea Linklater pens in an earlier moment in *Waking Life*'s script. The visual and aural likeness of "Speed" Levitch appears in the space a shifting, multicolored, multilayered ink blot occupies on the George Washington Bridge. An animated Levitch stands alone at the center of the frame and begins to pontificate: "on this bridge, Lorca warns, 'life is not a dream . . . beware and beware *and* beware.'" Levitch continues, "and, so many think, because *then* happened, *now* isn't," just as the camera widens to include Main Character in the frame. The inclusion of the unnamed protagonist creates a visual match of sorts between what Levitch is saying and what Linklater shows. The competition Levitch describes between then and now is matched by the competition for attention the two characters enter when both are in the frame. Spectators can only see, in any moment, one character or the other. They cannot keep both in focus. To see both, they need to return to the scene to see it again. Even with a return, though, there is only ever the *wow* of the now Levitch recalls Lorca describing: "didn't I mention the ongoing *wow* is happening right *now*?" Linklater marks the phrase "the ongoing *wow*" with a return to a one-shot and a burst of animation. Levitch, again, stands alone on the screen. The backdrop of the bridge and river is washed out in yellow. Several stars appear on the screen, three of them as stars-within-stars. The whites of Levitch's eyes form large circles that exceed the bounds of the man's eye sockets. The moment visualizes "the ongoing *wow* [that] is happening right *now*," that offers to happen in each now, which is to say in each encounter one has with such a moment. The scene on the bridge anticipates the aforementioned principle the pinball player proposes toward the end of the film: there is only ever a now. Such a view reverses the normal flow of the impoverished and indexical reality. The index in the now exists as a pointer rather than a marker to some reality in the past. The past is overwhelmed by the present, or the two find themselves partnered in a mutually respective dance of time and space.

Linklater returns to this idea again in *Before Sunset* (2004). Jesse (Ethan Hawke), an author at a book signing in a bookstore to support the publication of his book, responds to a question from a journalist about what his next book might be. Jesse begins to outline an idea he has for a book that takes place "within the space of a pop song." The main character would be a depressed man, who lives a good life, but not the life he had always wanted, a life that allowed him to "fight for meaning." The man sits despondently until his five-year-old daughter climbs on top of the table in front of him and begins to dance to the pop song they both hear. Suddenly, the man "looks down, and, all of sudden, he's sixteen . . . the same song is playing on the car radio," and his girlfriend begins dancing on the roof of the car. The man/adolescent recognizes the expression of his daughter in the face of his "high school sweetheart," and the character knows "he's not remembering this dance; he's there, he's there in both moments simultaneously." Jesse continues, "And just, like, for an instant, all his life is folding in on itself, and it's obvious to him that time is a lie . . . it's all happening all the time, and inside every moment is another moment." Jesse's idea for a book spins into the idea articulated by the pinball player in *Waking Life*: time is a lie. The character Jesse imagines as the protagonist for his next book is neither here nor there, absent nor present, true nor false. He is, as Johnson (2012) aptly describes him, neither in a memory nor simply in some present: he is in "two 'nows,' both experienced at once" (1). It is the place Linklater places so many of his characters and, just as importantly, the spectators he asks to consider those characters.

Linklater keeps what normally would be competing realities and competing sensibilities in balance by setting both on the point of index that sits between the push to document and the pull to animate. Symbols and icons cannot keep such things in balance. They close as many accounts as they open, if only because the symbol and the icon are always already bound to the conventions that establish them as a symbol or icon. In the case of the George Washington statute, it symbolizes what it does according to the set of rules shaping it. It looks like what it does according to the policies of representation being adopted. As an index, the statue breaks through both sets of conventions. It points to the time of its creation, to the person who sculpted it, and to the tradition of art in which it exists, just as it also points to other realities. Its placement in a living scene ensures that it remains alive, open to new interpretations. Neither the symbol nor the icon can do that. One must put aside these qualities for the index to work as it can. Linklater shows what it looks like to set aside the symbol and icon, in part, by making each effort to document and to animate so explicit.

One of the ways Linklater emphasizes the indexical qualities of his films is by returning to the same actors over significant amounts of time. *Boyhood* (2014) provides the most extreme example of this practice. Linklater reunites four principal actors, Ellar Coltrane, Lorelei Linklater, Patricia Arquette, and Ethan Hawke once a year for twelve years to tell the story of this particular family, and especially Mason (Ellar Coltrane), as he goes from first grade to high school graduation. As Gregg Kilday (2014) notes, Linklater did not overshoot the film in terms of actual shooting days. While the process did extend across twelve years, there were only "39 filming days" (84). The cast and crew would gather for three or four days each year to shoot one part of the film. The end result is a kind of family album, which starts to tell its own story. In any one particular moment, the audience sees the actors/characters as they looked for one year. The project becomes an index of these lives. Taken as a whole, the film exists, in the words of Coltrane as he reflects on the process with Kilday, as "a vessel for the passage of time ... an exploration ... [of] how times passes and how we perceive it" (87). This same effect would not exist as it does had Linklater followed the more normal practice of aging a character using digital tricks or makeup. An index would exist, but it would, most strictly speaking, index an industry-wide practice rather than the passage of time.

Linklater's *Before* trilogy offers a comparable index of time. The trilogy, which consists of *Before Sunrise*, *Before Sunset*, and *Before Midnight* (2013), stars the same two principals, Julie Delpy and Ethan Hawke, across nearly twenty years. The timing of each film, which are set as they are roughly a decade apart, and the choice to keep this acting duo together as a couple allow the trilogy to realize what Aaron Cutler (2013) accurately describes as the characters "passing time together, and passing through time together" (24). Even more astutely, Cutler writes, "while all films are to some extent simultaneously fiction and documentary, the line becomes especially blurred in the *Before* films' traveling sequences, allowing viewers to watch both the actors and characters role-playing the members of a couple throughout the different stages of their relationship" (24). The characters on screen begin to point to the actors that play them. A gap opens between actor and character, which draws particular attention to the roles these actors and their characters play. In keeping with Cutler's analysis, Jesse (Hawke) and Celine (Delpy) survive as they do because of their ability to "fluidly shift between" roles they might be asked to play (28). Cutler places particular emphasis on the fight at the end of *Before Midnight* that has Celine interrupt a fight with Jessie by converting into a young fan of the author. Jesse plays along, greeting his fan, which is his way of accepting the role Celine's performance assigns him. A moment of humor and play unites the two lovers within a reality that might otherwise displace one or the other, and with it, the relationship. The relationship exists as it does across time because the characters learn to switch between roles as easily as they do. Each performance indexes something other than what the impoverished index indexes. The reality that matters most in the *Before* trilogy, and the one Linklater encourages spectators to index, is the one the two characters, and the spectators with them, come to share. It is an invented reality that emerges from the mutual existence of an impoverished, indefinite, intertextual, and imaginative index.

One sees the same invented reality at play in the other films of the *Before* trilogy. Admittedly, the pull to animate is the opaquer of the two tendencies, which makes especially important Linklater's decision to direct two animations, *Waking Life* and *A Scanner Darkly* (2006). These films do not bring new qualities to his films so much as accentuate the animated qualities already developed in his projects. One clear example of this accentuation in reel time appears in the vignette in *Waking Life* that includes Jesse and Celine as they would be in *Before Sunrise*. Their scene begins with Jesse waking from an afternoon nap to admit that he keeps thinking of something Celine has said. Jesse goes on to mention a moment in the earlier film when Celine talks about seeing her own life as an old woman dying. Jesse reminds Celine of this moment only to have her admit that she still feels "that way sometimes . . . like my waking life is her memories." The conversation turns to the ideas of collective memory and experience. Jesse supplies the thesis of the conversation, if such a thing exists, when he says, "it's like we're all telepathically sharing our experiences." The moment carries a bit of irony as the characters as they appear on screen are brought into several instances of a collective consciousness.

Jesse and Celine participate in the collective consciousness they share with every other character in *Waking Life*, as each body is suddenly animated and set to movements that are at times exaggerated and at other times muted. Johnson's description of a later scene between two women in a coffee shop illustrates this shared quality: "the animation here emphasizes facial features, hair, and clothing with lines and color but does not fill every detail, such as Dawson's hair," which is shaded in such a way that no individual hair can be seen (58). Johnson offers that the choice allows the audience to "complete these images" (59). The inclusion of Jesse and Celine in the midst of a conversation started in another movie would work in the same way. So, too, would the choice to so explicitly relate this moment in the film to the opening moment of Alfred Hitchcock's *Psycho* (1960). That film and this scene both begin with the camera moving through the city before settling on a particular building and through a specific window. Linklater's characters are not meant to enjoy any exclusive claim on the space they occupy, nor are they exclusively their own. They are, in this instance, more naturally intertextual indices that point to a range of realities set within and beyond the frame. Linklater's choice to animate Jesse and Celine admits this preference.

Linklater's second animated film, *A Scanner Darkly*, creates a similar indexical polysemy, although the rotoscoping works differently in *A Scanner Darkly* than it did in *Waking Life*. In *Waking Life*, the technique permits one to move within the logic of a lucid dream. In *A Scanner Darkly*, it emphasizes just how layered everything can be. Every reality in the film is but a surface or a subterfuge. There is no bottom, no firm *there* in what is only ever being represented. The structure of the film does not seem to worry about the absence of a verifiable presence; to the contrary, it seems to delight in this aspect. The uncertainty of what appears on the screen draws one into the frame, where the point of the index can direct one toward a variety of realities. It begins a process of signification, of meaning making, that only the spectator can settle, and then only temporarily. In keeping with the argument Johnson puts forward, "any perception, whether of a film, a memory, a dream, or reality itself, requires an active process of meaning making" (57). This is most especially true in *A Scanner Darkly*, a film where everything is layered, the images on screen, the story being told, even the identities of the characters. All parts of the film are more than what they seem when watched along the surface, which invites the audience to participate in determining the significance of every element.

Linklater reveals this possibility in two distinct ways placed in the scene introducing the main character, Bob Arctor (Keanu Reeves), to the members of Brown Bear Lodge. The words in the script register this possibility in one way. The host (Mitch Baker) of the event introduces the speaker of the event, a man he "will call Fred because that is his code name," as the man sits in a chair on the stage to his left. The host explains why the man appears as he does: "you will notice you can barely see this man because he is wearing what is called a 'scramble suit.' . . . once inside the scramble suit, he cannot be detected." The suit, the host goes on to explain, scrambles his voice, face, and every other identifying mark of the man. The host's words most immediately serve to bring spectators into the story, clarifying particulars of the plot, but they also introduce a person with at least two identities. There is the identity that appears because of the suit, and there is the man who is inside the device. The two are not the same, and Linklater's camera ensures that audiences see that. As the host continues his introduction, Linklater's camera pierces the surface of the scramble suit to reveal the identity being concealed. It stays there long enough to register Bob's voice as he says, "this is terrible." Bob disappears a few seconds later as the host's introduction ends, and Fred stands to give his speech. He does so, at least for Linklater's audience, which knows more than Fred's immediate audience, as two people. The façade the suit creates replaces the "reality" within in it, which, of course is another façade, a matter that carries its own significance, which will be discussed in a moment.

Before discussing Linklater's additional suggestion that there is only one façade after another in *A Scanner Darkly*, several choices made during Fred's speech deserve attention. The first is the decision to let Fred stand and deliver a speech just moments after showing the audience Bob and letting him speak.

The juxtaposition of the subterfuge and the surface undermines the credibility of the surface, which is to say Fred. Fred sounds and appears unnatural. Linklater begins to restore some credibility to his speaker a few lines into the speech when he again cuts to the face beneath the mask just as Bob says, "I'm not going to tell you first what I do as an undercover officer. . . . I'm going to tell you what I am afraid of." The return to Bob's face reminds audiences that there is a man behind these words. A reverse shot, though, calls into question that man's perspective. The camera assumes what would be Bob's point of view from beneath the mask only to reveal how unnatural his view is. The scene in front of him is tinted blue and slightly distorted. Linklater's audience can see Bob's eyes reflecting on the screen of the mask. Bob is quite literally seeing himself in the moment he is also seeing others. The image calls into question Bob's perspective, which also calls into question Fred's authenticity.

This question of Fred's authenticity is undermined further the next time Linklater moves behind the mask and then cuts to a reverse shot from Bob's perspective beneath the mask. Bob's own view begins to interfere with Fred's message. Bob trips over a remark about profits; after a verbal and physical beat in his performance, he says, "Well, it isn't about the profits anyhow, it's something else." Bob then has his own question to ask: "If you were a diabetic, and you didn't have money for insulin, would you steal to get the money or just die?" The question is out of step with the rest of the speech, which is quite obviously promoting a specific perspective. The script clarifies that this impression is accurate when a voice chimes in to say, "I think you better go back to the, you know, prepared text there, Fred." Bob claims he "forgot" the text, but the voice calmly says, "repeat after me, but make it sound casual." After a moment of internal strife over whether to continue speaking or not, Fred resumes his delivery, speaking about the various words the "D" can stand for, in "Substance D," the drug he is combatting: "dumbness and despair and desertion . . . [until] finally, death." The words have been said, but they have been performed poorly. The poor performance makes them suspect, both for Fred's audience in the Brown Bear Lodge, and, certainly, for Linklater's audience.

The role rotoscoping plays in this suspicion emerges during the scene that has Bob remove the scramble suit. Fred returns to the office and enters a room. He removes the head and then body of the suit to uncover Bob, who stands in the likeness of Keanu Reeves. The likeness has iconic and indexical qualities. Iconically, the audience sees the star beneath the character. Indexically, the image reminds audiences that every fictional film has an actor playing a character. The animation the rotoscoping provides adds an additional layer to this mix as if to remind audiences that every fictional character is always layered in at least one or more ways. Under most circumstances, there is at least the layering between actor and character, and of director and character, if not other collaborators and the character. There is also whatever the audience holds in mind about the recognizable performer. In this way, the character in a fictional film is never just a character, not unless audiences force themselves to see it that way. Even then, the character is just one reality set within the image. Every reality brought to the screen entertains a range of realities: those within the frame, the plot, the story, and anything else that informs it. Linklater's choice to use rotoscoping to animate *A Scanner Darkly* admits this reality and it does so along the surface of the film.

Linklater explicitly plays with the alternative idea to what his rotoscoping suggests, namely, that every image has but one meaning, during a test the department administers to Officer Fred a few scenes later. Two medical examiners confirm the man in front of them is Fred and then start what they call a "set-ground test." One of the examiners (Angela Rawna) clarifies the object of the test: "Within the apparently meaningless lines is an object that we all recognize. You are to tell me what that object is and point to it in the total field." A few seconds pass, prompting the second examiner (Chamblee Ferguson) to ask, "Now have you located the familiar object in this line drawing? It should just jump right out at you." Officer Fred identifies a "Coke bottle." The first examiner confirms that "a soda pop bottle is the correct answer." Fred gives the wrong answer to the second card, guessing a sheep where, according to the test, he should have seen a dog. Before being given the correct answer, but after realizing that his first answer was incorrect, Fred wonders if he was close. His question gives the first examiner a chance to clarify that "This is not a Rorschach test, where some abstract blot can be interpreted many ways by many subjects. This has one specific object. . . . It's not interpretative, there are many wrong answers, but there is only one right answer. You either get it or you don't." The test, of course, assumes images work in the exactly opposite direction that the above discussion says they work in this film. Linklater's images are interpretive. There are very few wrong answers, and just as few right answers. There are, instead, a host of possible answers all of which exist somewhere between right and wrong, or, within another set of terms, a documented image and an animated image.

Linklater's screenplay continues to reverse course on the normal indexical argument by having Fred express frustration over the idea that there can only be one right answer to the test he is taking. He refuses to take the test in a serious way, finding in the third image "plastic dog shit, the kind you buy and put in someone's bed." The two examiners mistake the seriousness of his protest and begin to laugh. The first examiner says, "You know, Fred, if you keep your sense of humor like you do, you just might make it after all." Arctor finds no comfort in the examiner's words, which he indicates through an outburst: "Make it. Make what? The team? The girl? Make good? Make do? Make out? Make sense? Make money? Make time? Define your terms." Arctor answers his own challenge by turning to the Latin source of the word "make," which is *facere*. Rather than tracing the etymology of that word, as one normally does when returning to a Latin root, Arctor says what the Latin word reminds him of, typically done, a false Latin word *fuckere*, which he claims means "to fuck." The root is entirely invented. The invention, just as the preference for an associative rather than literal meanings, twice rejects the idea of a test using images with only one right answer. Images entertain more than one reality, as Linklater's animated film continues to make.

One of the more interesting ways Linklater allows his images to entertain more than one reality is through the cycling of identities over one actor. Reeves plays the part of Bob and Fred before becoming Bruce once he arrives at the New Path recovery center toward the end of the film. Reeves's identity in the film is hardly settled. One of the surprises of the film is that Winona Ryder plays Donna and Hank before stepping out from these two personas to reveal her "true identity" as Audrey. Audrey sits with a handler, Mike (Dameon Clarke), to say that she has to "get out" of the organization. She tells Mike, "I can't do this again." Mike tries to reassure Audrey that she is doing good. He claims that God is working "beneath the surface of our reality . . . to transmute evil into good," that he and Audrey can be part of bringing about a new future. The words have one meaning across the surface of the plot. These agents are working to expose the corporate duplicity and corruption that threaten those within the diegetic realm the plot creates. Just above that level is an equally compelling meaning, one where the uncertainties of every reality lead those who perceive such things to continue to engage and explore every representation.

All of this is admittedly rather buried within Linklater's animation in *A Scanner Darkly*. The balance between documentation and animation is enough out of balance that one is only seeing animation. A film more fittingly balanced between the push to document and the pull to animate registers these same suggestions more plainly. One such film is *Bernie* (2011). *Bernie* presents itself as something of a documentary film, but one that is animated, which is to say that it is given a specific life. The title cards at the start of the film reveal the way the film will sit between a documentary and an animation. The first and second cards cooperate to deliver the promise that "what you're fixin to see is . . . A TRUE STORY." The promise to provide a true story suggests what follow might have some documentary qualities. That said, plenty of films are billed as true stories even as they remain fictional retellings. Linklater leans into the suggestion that what follows is something of a documentary by including at least two traits of such films: characters will speak directly to the camera as though they are being interviewed, and, perhaps most importantly, many of these characters are, in fact, local people from Carthage, many of whom knew the "real Bernie" (184). Linklater found these talents through posting online an open call for "Townspeople—Texans who are not professional actors . . . the real deal—funny interesting folks" (184). The presence of people on the screen while outside the timing of the dramatization the film provides lends the film the feel of a documentary.

Despite all of the trappings of a documentary, Linklater ensures that the animated qualities of *Bernie* are never displaced. They are often delivered in the same moments as the documentary elements. For example, the title cards promise to tell a true story, but they do so in two ways that admit that what follows is a performance of a story rather than a documentation of it. The inclusion of the word "fixin," for instance, indicates that what follows means to fit a particular vernacular. The word helps locate the story in Carthage, Texas, which is to say, in East Texas, as one of the townspeople (Sonny Davis) declares early in the plot, the place "where the South begins." The decision to include the word in the first title card prepares the audience for Linklater's highly stylized representation of the story. The second card support this idea. Linklater will only declare that his story is *a* true story. It is not *the* true story. Neither is it the only story to tell. It is, much more modestly, a story, and a stylized one at that.

The third title card introduces the question that runs through the film: "Who is Bernie?" Linklater answers his own question as it relates to the movie by letting the next graphic on the screen be the name Jack Black, the actor playing Bernie. The choice is more than an attempt at humor. It is just as much a confession. Linklater needs his Bernie to be an animated version of a character rather than the real thing. The real Bernie was a murderer. Linklater's is, too, but Linklater's murderer commits an onscreen murder, which is not an actual murder. Moreover, Linklater's Bernie is a performance bent toward humor rather than something more malicious. Linklater privileges these performative qualities in the opening moments of the film, too, as Black moves from simply singing along with the gospel song on his radio to a performance of it, as the song shifts to the moment when "the Master heard [his] despairing cry," and saved him. Linklater will give his audience space to decide their answer to the question of "who is Bernie," but he will do so only after he has suggested his own answer to the question.

The testimonies from the aforementioned townspeople only play into the suggestion Linklater makes. The mix of locals and actors describe Bernie in extremely positive terms. One of the unnamed townspeople (Ann Reeves) describes Bernie as being "so nice, so accommodating, so willing to keep from hurting other people's feelings, he just couldn't tell anybody to piss off." Every other "contributor" to the plot conveys the same sentiment, save that of the District Attorney Danny Buck (Matthew McConaughey), who ultimately prosecutes Bernie the murderer, and Marjorie Nugent's (Shirley MacLaine) financial planner, Lloyd Hornbuckle (Richard Robichaux). Bernie is presented as "just a sweet guy," as his employer, Don Legget (Rick Dial) puts it. His performance, and everyone else's for that matter, portrays a version of the man that can be invented from the *Texas Monthly* story on which the script is based. It is not providing an accurate account of the man, his crime, or the townspeople's reaction to either. Linklater marks the end of his film with a similar admission. At the end of a series of final comments on the "actual story," which include an image of Marjorie Nugent's actual tombstone, a photo of the real Bernie Tiede and Marjorie Nugent, and then a short recording of the actual and somewhat aged Bernie presumably sitting at a table talking to the camera as a graphic appears screen left to report how the real man spends his time in prison. After a few seconds, the handheld camera pans right, enough to cut the actual Bernie from the screen and to reveal that Jack Black sits opposite Bernie. The "Bernie" the audience has witnessed has been part of a cast, and not the actual story. It has been an animation of Bernie explored through a documentary sensibility wanting to remake rather than revere a received story.

Linklater's *Last Flag Flying* (2017) does a similar thing. The film does not have any of the obvious trappings of a documentary or an animated film. It is fictional feature film, albeit one that pays particular attention to indexical arguments, and especially as they relate to trauma. *Last Flag Flying* achieves this focus by always emphasizing the arbitrary and negotiated reality the story creates. These traits are especially salient to anyone who knows Linklater's other films, but there is room for less knowing audiences to see these points of emphasis. The first idea is expressed most clearly through the way the three principal characters, Sal (Bryan Cranston), Mueller (Laurence Fishburne), and "Doc" (Steve Carell) evolve after their time as soldiers in Vietnam, and more especially, their involvement in the accidental killing of one of their own, Jimmy Hightower. The three men very clearly suffer for their role in Jimmy's death, even decades after the event. Their pain is most palpable during a scene late in the film, when Mueller contemptuously asks Sal if he has ever "been ashamed about anything" in his life. Sal responds, "once." The confession catches Doc's attention. He suddenly looks up from the table. Mueller becomes defensive, asking Sal, "Why you looking at me like that?" Sal calmly states, "You know why," before asking, "Did you remember Boston is where . . . he is from?" The pause in the question is, in many ways, the most important part of question, as it shows the difficulty Sal has saying Jimmy's name. Mueller can do no better. He self-righteously proclaims, "I remember he was from Boston." The use of pronoun in this statement is significant. Neither Sal nor Mueller can refer to the fellow American they harmed in Vietnam as anything more than "he" or "him."

Neither can they move from the reality of that night. The best the three men can do is to find a way to cope with what they did. The events of that night push the three men toward three very different lives. The whole of the film illustrates this idea, but Linklater lets Mueller summarize it most economically after Sal claims beer does for him what God does for Mueller. Mueller responds, "I see. I understand. I got God. Doc did his time. You got drunk." The statement explains why each man is the way he is throughout the film, which upon reflection does require explanation. All three men are caricatures of more developed people. They have been flattened by their experiences, and especially one experience they all share. The conversation that follows explains why. These men not only caused the death of their brother in arms, they let him suffer. This point comes out after Sal suggests, "Maybe he got the better of the deal?" Mueller maintains, "He was gonna die anyway." Sal makes clear the dying was never the worst part: "He didn't have to suffer, not like that." Mueller remarks "But he did," which is itself ambiguous. It could mean he did die the way he did, or that he did have to suffer. Doc tires of the discussion and interrupts it by saying the man's name: "Jimmy Hightower. We can't even say his name. We all feel guilty about how he suffered when he was dying, but did it ever occur to you that maybe nobody would have been shot and everybody'd still be alive if we had just been doing our jobs, not fuckin' around?" The remark gets to the center of the shame the three men feel, a point Linklater lets Cranston and Fishburne convey through their performance rather than anything anyone says. The moment shows that the reality that matters to these three men is the one they still have not negotiated.

That negotiation occurs a few scenes later when the three men decide to visit Jimmy's mother to tell them the truth about what happened to her son. Mrs. Hightower (Cicely Tyson) registers the story she had been told just after Sal admits that he went to her house to tell her what happened. Mrs. Hightower interrupts to ask, "Were you . . . were you some of the men he saved . . . I mean . . . were you some of them whose lives Jimmy saved . . . I mean they told me he saved three or four of his buddies before he was killed?" Mrs. Hightower's question opens more than an ethical dilemma for Sal. The dilemma her question would raise has, in fact, already been answered in an earlier scene. Sal learns the true story of what happened to Doc's son in Iraq. Sal is adamant that Doc know the truth about his son's death. Mueller disagrees and begs Sal to let Doc have "his hero." Sal cannot do that. He cannot let Doc "have the lie." One would expect that Sal will be no more content to let Mrs. Hightower have the lie either and, ultimately, he will not be able to give her a lie. He will, however, find a new truth in the story that has shaped three decades of his life. Mrs. Hightower's question creates a space for Jimmy's death to be something other than what it was, a moment of shame. Her question opens space for Sal, Mueller, and Doc to reencounter that night and make of it something new. Linklater captures the significance of this interpretive moment with a reverse shot that cuts from Mrs. Hightower to Sal. The camera tightens around his face and holds for several seconds before he finally answers, "Yes, ma'am, that was us." The answer opens a new space, one that Mueller and Doc readily fill. Mueller chimes in to say, "Jimmy was a great guy." Doc agrees: "Yep, never forget him." Muller continues, "That's why we're here ma'am, uh, we feel we owe him." Sal participates in this new story, saying, "Yeah, we just want to come by to pay our respects." Mueller provides an end to this confession of sorts by telling Mrs. Hightower that Jimmy has always "been in our hearts."

The moment is a near match to the climatic moment in *Saving Mr. Banks*, both in terms of the story arc and how that moment in the arc depends on an index. The index in this moment is the men, whose lives have been touched by the reality their story to Mrs. Hightower is creating. One can see the relief each man feels as they tell some story other than the story they have always told. One could deem this one story false, but such a declaration would bear more falsehood than the story they are telling. There is a sense of truth in every word the men say. Jimmy did save their lives in some sense of saving. The memory of his death is saving them again as they describe that event with his mother. The reality of Jimmy's death stays the same even as the indices extending from it are changing.

The moment differs from the scenario Johnson describes in another Linklater film, *Tape* (2001). As Johnson describes it, Linklater places "at the center of [*Tape*] the trauma of a past event, the effects of that trauma and all three characters, and the truth of what really occurred" (62). The film ultimately frustrates the way these three concerns might intersect by focusing on the "inherently mercurial" nature of truth as it relates first to the past, and then to trauma (62). Johnson likens the resulting scenario to what Linda Williams

(1998) describes—through "Oliver Wendell Holmes's description of a photograph as a 'mirror with a memory'"—what happens when cinema loses its relationship to "reliability and truth": "'what was once a "mirror with memory" can now only reflect another mirror'" (63). Johnson offers that this shift as it is realized in *Tape* "reaches toward an attendance to the present in which the past would inform the current moment without losing any of its inherent complexities, contradictions, or opacity, yet still allow some reflection . . . of the original trauma" (63–64). In this way, the trauma at the center of *Tape* is left open to be reexamined as it is being reexperienced. It means to create space for mourning.

Last Flag Flying provides more than "a mirror with a memory" or a mirror reflecting another mirror. It treats the tragic event from the past that sits at the center of the film, namely, Jimmy's death, as a sign that leads to another sign. Most critically, this sequence of signs is neither symbolic nor iconic. The earlier debate over Doc's son's death empties this sign of its symbolic value. There is in the end no grace in saying Doc's son or Jimmy died a hero. Even the death of heroes can lead to trauma. Nor is the sign realized in the pivotal moment with Mrs. Hightower iconic. None of the men are producing a sign that bears the likeness of the original event. To do so would be to extend the trauma rather than to move through it. It would also yoke one with the demands of representational art, truth, and accuracy, which Linklater is always addressing at one remove. As it relates to this moment, Linklater is not asking his characters to be accurate or to tell a truth. He is creating a space where they can attend to the present moment as the *Kairos* of ongoing adaptation would allow them to do so, which is to say, indexically. The sign that extends from the reality of Jimmy's death they are recounting can signify more than their folly, their guilt, or their shame. In the *now* in which that tragic event is being realized, this sign can signify a moment to remember even if the remembrance works in a new direction. The index can give life rather than take it, and can do so by offering a cinematic reality that means to do something more than deliver a literal reality. Reality as it has been known and experienced in some real experience can be set aside in the cinema, and it can be set aside by virtue of a reconceived index that becomes something more than reality's guarantor.

Chapter 3

TRAUMA

The index has long been taken as the underwriter of any reality that exists in the cinema. For just as long, that reality has long been thought to be some lived reality that existed before the camera. Chapter 2 responds to both parts of this belief with an insistence that the cinematic index means to do more than deliver a fixed reality born in a world that stands in front of the camera. The cinematic index works as all indices do, which is to say that it starts a process pursuant to the consideration of a reality beyond the sign one sees. The cinematic reality invoked need not be an actual, lived reality, nor does it mean to present itself as such; instead, cinematic indices intend to unsettle reality as much as to represent it. They mean to disrupt the meanings and associations, even the shape and form of a verifiable reality that is or was one thing, and they do so in three ways. First, as Tom Gunning (2008) notes, cinematic images move, or at least they have the potential to move, and as they move they offer an impression of reality, rather than a reality. Somewhat ironically, the reality set on a screen is never fully realized as an actual reality, in part because it is moving. The moving image is always progressive, always just out of reach. Its indices point to an impression of reality the spectator searches for rather than sits beneath.

Cinematic indices unsettle reality in a second way, at least initially and if they are moving and serving the narrative. In keeping with Laura Mulvey (2007), the reality brought to the screen is always made arbitrary in the truest sense because its primary obligation, at least in narrative film, is to the narrative. The significance of any item on the screen, in other words, belongs to the narrative. From this perspective, the details remain unspecified until they are set in the narrative and given some specificity. The hold the narrative enjoys is, of course, temporary. It is never fixed. A new way of seeing can open; the significance of an image can be reset and repurposed. As such, the sign of any perceived reality is akin to a garment that one puts on only to take off eventually. This is especially true of the indexical sign, which, to extend the analogy, is always pointing to a dressing room filled with various garments rather than a specific piece of apparel. No garment is *the* reality. There is a different garment for each occasion.

The very presence of this variety highlights the third way cinematic indices intend to unsettle rather than establish a fixed reality. In keeping with the argument developed over the first half of this book, the cinematic index will unseat reality through one of the four types of indices. It will, as the impoverished index, retrieve some reality inferred but not set on screen. This retrieval will always be incomplete. The reality before the camera will remain in its past as it was in the past. That same reality becomes something else after the camera leaves. In the exact moment the reality existed in front of the camera, it was not what it will be, but only what it was. Once seized by the camera and set on screen, that reality gains a sense of *there*, which becomes a moment between some past and some future. It is a time not yet determined. In this way, even the impoverished index entices audiences to search out the possibilities of the moment it brings to screen, and to do so anew in each encounter.

The indefinite index, the second type of cinematic index that can unseat reality, works similarly to the impoverished index. It, too, points to a reality that exists before the camera. The difference is where its attention lies. The indefinite index limits the possibilities of the impoverished index in the way an indefinite pronoun like *somebody* or *everybody* does. Such pronouns reference something, but without the specificity of definite pronouns, which operate best when they refer to an already acknowledged noun. Indefinite pronouns work more generally. Their meaning exists regardless of whether they are connected to some more specific noun or not. The sentence "Somebody needs to close the door" does not worry about who it is that will ultimately close the door. It simply begs for anyone who falls within the category of *somebody* to perform a desired action. The indefinite cinematic index works in just this way, in part by referring to its own status as a sign at least as much as a reference to some earlier reality. It emphasizes the various possibilities of its referent rather than any specific reference. In this way, it is smoke or a knock that refers to all fires or every hand, a reality that begs to be considered even above the fire or hand that produced it. The indefinite cinematic index stays in the frame longer than the other cinematic indices. It exists to be considered rather than simply to refer to something beyond it. It is quite explicitly a sign that has been produced by some other sign, a sign that can lead to still other signs, but that also stands on its own, at least to the extent that any sign stands on its own.

The last two types of cinematic indices, the intertextual and the imaginative indices, shift attention from specific forms that exist in front of the camera or even in the frame to suggest realities that do not exist during the moment of registration or production. The intertextual and imaginative indices point forward to realities that can only ever be constructed by the spectator. Both indices resist the aspect of retrieval by pointing to realities that do not exist until spectators build them through their imagination. The intertextual index becomes a mold containing more than one reality. It is a footprint that reveals not just a specific foot, but a specific period in time when some specific boot would be worn, or some specific ground would be trod. The intertextual index tempts the spectator to work with associations and within networks. It suggests relationships that can be sought and explored. Like all indices, the intertextual index bears some existential connection to the reality that produces it. It does not, however, try to define that reality; it points forward rather than backward. It admits that some pairing or set of realities cooperate to form a joint reality. The imaginative index does something similar but deals as much in the reimagination of a reality as the admission of it. The imaginative index reconstitutes some accepted reality. It adds to or subtracts from that reality. It (re)imagines as much as it accepts. It is a little girl reimaging a scene with (rather than without) her father or a group of men finding honor (rather than shame) in a memory. The imaginative index creates space to see some earlier reality in a new way through the process of ongoing adaptation that rewatching can invite.

In all four instances, the cinematic index will work more loosely than film scholars have typically theorized. The impoverished and indefinite indices, for example, will deliver some reality to the screen, but without insisting on the particulars of that reality. The particulars belong to icons and symbols. Icons and symbols recover what indices only ever suggest. The impoverished and indefinite indices may limit the range of contingencies the reality they bring to the screen will entertain, but even those limits will eventually relax, which means that even the impoverished and indefinite indices can surprise those who see them again. They can reveal different aspects of the reality they seize. All indices are, after all, an approximation. Every encounter offers spectators the chance to see something again and anew. No index captures the reality that is, was, and forevermore will be. Every index is but a suggestion, an opportunity to reconsider what has been. The intertextual and imaginative indices most especially exploit this aspect of the index, and, in so doing, most especially realize the process of signification Peirce imagines the sign, and especially the index, performing. The intertextual index can operate like any other intertextual referent, pointing toward two or more realities at once. The imaginative index can lead spectators to yet-to-be-known realities, realities only they can shape. Regardless of which form the cinematic index takes, it is always a sign that refuses to be an end point. It is always a sign that points toward a reality yet to be realized. It is a process rather than a site. To ignore or bypass the process the cinematic index initiates can leave one within displaced nostalgia or ongoing trauma, something the typical discussion of the index within film studies recognizes.

Mary Ann Doane (2002) captures the ways in which the index can lead to displaced nostalgia when talking about what Fredric Jameson describes as a "mesmerizing lost reality" (19). The whole of Doane's approach, which treats the index as an archive, demonstrates the way the "cinema emerges from and contributes to the archival impulse of the nineteenth century," all of which leads to the "pathos of archival desire" (23). Doane admits that the index "is free to convey anything and everything," even as she also indicates that what the cinematic index most often conveys is "that anything and everything is filmable" (25). Doane's index, then, ultimately points toward the lens-based camera that captures a reality that would otherwise be lost in time and space. This is certainly one part of the index the lens-based camera delivers, but it does not need to be the only or even most enduring index in the cinema. As Doane's intent is not to capture the whole of the index, her view is certainly not wrong. But it is extremely focused; it considers one instance and only one aspect of the index this project deems either the diminished index Gunning describes or the closely related impoverished index. For those who emphasize the impoverished index, the act of filming becomes what Doane describes as "the narrativization of chance, the historization of the present" (107). This description relates the index to what Jameson explains when he writes that Lawrence Kasdan's *Body Heat* (1981) "endows present reality and the openness of present history with the spell and distance of a glossy image" (21). From this view, the present is always constrained by a past that is always beyond reach. The past becomes accessible as little more than a glossy image that is itself caught between a *here* and a *there*, which is to say that it is neither entirely past nor present. Rather, it exists in a time that is born through a kind of conditional statement: the time on the screen exists if the time before it also exists. In this way, the time on the screen becomes a marker of a time that is any time but *now*. The index becomes an instance of displaced nostalgia, of a *then* that leaves out of reach whatever it denotes.

Displaced nostalgia is one outcome of a limited notion of the index. Laura Mulvey (2007) isolates a second, which most concisely can be referred to as an instance of ongoing trauma. Mulvey argues that the indexical sign left by the lens-based photograph or film enjoys "a privileged relation to time, to the moment and duration of its inscription ... which inscribes ... an unprecedented reality into its representation of the past" (9). Mulvey compares the image captured on the photo-strip to "the memory left in the unconscious by an incident lost to the consciousness. Both have the attributes of the indexical sign, the mark of trauma or the mark of light, and both need to be deciphered retrospectively across delayed time" (9). Mulvey's comment openly treats the index as a mark of trauma. Her succeeding remarks explain why: the index serves as the "trace of the past in the present ... or a fact, that is preserved in but also bears witness to the elusive nature of reality and its representations.... the reality of the photograph as index becomes entwined with the problem of time" (10). For Mulvey, the index becomes an indefinite marker of the past, one that posits a definite past but that also leaves that past in the past. This placement creates a reality that can be observed but cannot be manipulated. It is there to be recognized, and to be accepted as a time that is out of time in significant ways. The index for Mulvey has the form of the past but the consciousness of the present, which makes it something of a phantom, an object doubly loaded with but standing outside of time.

Set within and without time, the index Mulvey describes operates as something like a shade of time. This shadow arises most keenly when the image is stopped. Mulvey argues that the still image brings to the screen a reality that would otherwise be twice lost: the reality would first be lost in time, set within a past that cannot be recovered; and it would be lost beneath the narrative. This narrative loss is especially interesting if only because it admits that a cinematic index can accept realities beyond those that produced it. From Mulvey's view, the reality causing the cinematic index can be washed away by the narrative. Mulvey explains that when the moving image is stopped, spectators are confronted with "stillness and repetition" that uncovers realities the narrative would otherwise mask (170). The spectator becomes empowered to commit "an act of violence against the cohesion of the story, the aesthetic integrity that holds it together, and the vision of its creator" (171). Mulvey claims that spectators can set all of this aside to investigate other realities by pausing the image. In the absence of constant motion, the spectator is suddenly free to look beyond authorial intent to see what she is able to see. Mulvey brings the discussion of the index to the edge of the intertextual and imaginative index, only to stay within the grip of the indefinite index, in the hold of an image of the past that maintains its authority even as it challenges so many other points of authority. For Mulvey, "the time of the camera, its embalmed time, comes to the surface, shifting from a narrative 'now' to 'then.' ... the time of the index displaces the time of the fiction" (173). It is this "time of the index" that bears the mark of trauma.

Mulvey admits that the index she imagines exhibits an unmistakable trauma. For Mulvey, the index bears this mark of trauma because it captures a duality of time and reality that cannot be reconciled. Mulvey remarks that "the index is a reminder that at the heart of the medium these celluloid images are not replicas but are an actual, literal inscription of [an actor's] living movements," and of a version of the world that no longer exists (175–76). These realities cannot be set aside as easily as can a story, an aesthetic, or an artistic vision. They bear for Mulvey a truth and an accuracy about death that spectators must acknowledge, if only because the cinematic index materializes attitudes about life and death in one gesture. For Mulvey, the cinema is always considering divisions between life and death. A spectator's ability to stop a scene and to return to it later admits both sides of this materialization: "in the act of halting the flow of film, then returning it to movement and vitality, the possessive spectator inherits the long-standing fascination with the human body's mutation [in the cinema] from animate to inanimate and vice versa" (176). This transfer between the animate and the inanimate and back again occurs on the screen, but only after it has occurred at the moment of registration. In this way, Mulvey maintains that the stilled image recovers not contingency and multiplicity but the time of registration. One can explore this moment indefinitely, but the boundaries of the exploration will be set by the moment of registration rather than the spectator. These boundaries remain until the image is set in motion again, and the image begins to serve the narrative again. As such, there is no lasting sense of *now* in Mulvey's account. There is only the *then* provided, first in the moment of registration, and second by the narrative. For Mulvey, some *then* displaces every *now*.

The intertextual and imaginative index proposed within this study returns a sense of *now* even to Mulvey's *then*, which is to say to some moment in time that has been traumatized by that sense of time. The cinematic index preserves the now-ness of every now: the now of every encounter, the now embedded in each moment of registration, and the now that lingers in between each of those two moments. One can see each now, but only when one conceives of rewatching in the broadest sense, only when one the *Kairos* of ongoing adaptation guides the encounter of the index. Mulvey provides a way in to this requisite concept of rewatching, but she frames rewatching in ways that serve her specific interests. Every return for Mulvey is set within the moment of registration rather than an instance of observation. Drawing on Bazin's words in his ontology essay, Mulvey claims "the more often a sequence is viewed, the more it becomes an extended 'emanation of an intractable reality'" (189). The return, in other words, reveals the original moment rather than leading to any other moment. The reality that first impresses the image on the screen becomes the only reality that matters, in part because what is delivered in the replaying of the moment accounts for the primary appeal of the cinema Mulvey describes. The image set in the moment of registration becomes a reflection "on the representation of time . . . as it relates to . . . the inevitability of death" (189, 191). Mulvey reasons a return to a moment lost in the world, offering spectators the pleasure of postponing death, or at least avoiding "the finality of an ending" (193). Mulvey's image surrenders its ability to live beyond the frame of time the moment of registration builds around it.

The four cinematic indices discussed herein move beyond the moment of registration and encourage spectators to move with them. This movement can directly relate to the attitude toward trauma an image encourages from spectators. All four indices encourage spectators to return to some original moment either to reconsider or remake that moment. When set upon the point of the index, these returns refuse to fall into displaced nostalgia or ongoing trauma. They are involved in the ongoing adaptation of every representation, which, when approached as an index, will always move from sign to sign, index to index. This movement starts a process that works beyond the idea of an original and a copy, between some reality that exists and some representation of that reality. As it relates to time, this movement frustrates the sense of *here* and *there* that so much discussion about trauma and the index tends to encourage. The index-to-index movement the *Kairos* of ongoing adaptation occasions will always happen in a now, in an encounter, that breaks from the typical division between past and present. The image and the spectator are brought into the same sense of time and space, a time and space that rejects displaced nostalgia and that promises to move through trauma.

This is the space Pamela (Emma Thompson) occupies in John Lee Hancock's *Saving Mr. Banks* (2013). Pamela reimagines her past as it relates to the guilt she feels about her supposed complicity in her father's death. She finds a way to forgive herself and her father. The act redeems the father and the daughter who remembers him, something Hancock brings to the surface of the film in the final moments. The indexical quality of the first scene changes, as a traumatic memory is replaced through an instance of adaptation. The memory is repopulated to include the father. Sal (Bryan Cranston), Mueller (Laurence Fishburne), and Doc (Steve Carell) eventually experience something similar in Richard Linklater's *Last Flag Flying* (2017). The three men, who have been traumatized by a past experience that has played a familiar refrain over their lives, come to experience a new story in the presence of the fallen soldier's mother. Suddenly, one sign leads to other signs. It leads to something other than a complicity that results in a catastrophe. The men begin to adapt the story of that experience, to imagine it not only as an instance of shame and guilt, but a moment of respect and honor for the man who died that night. This shift occurs in a now rather than in the past. The past remains even as it comes to signify something new.

An index of any sort can generate something like what the four cinematic indices on offer here yield. Only the cinema, however, can show the process at work. Real life does not offer demonstrations of the process of ongoing adaptation the cinema set on the point of an index can demonstrate. Neither can real life exist in the reality the cinema creates as it exists between a push to document and a pull to animate. Such a reality encourages engagement, as every detail becomes a proposal rather than a reality. The pathos of archival desire Doane describes gives way to a *Kairos* of ongoing adaptation, which accepts the challenge Amy Herzog (2000) says awaits theorists, who need "to see film not as a means of representation, but as an assemblage of images in flux" (16). The cinematic image is in flux, not because it lacks specificity but because any specificity turns out to be a possibility rather than an accurate representation. As a possibility, the image sets aside questions of accuracy or inaccuracy, truth or untruth. The indexical cinematic image forgoes such binaries. It is always a *this-is-here-now* rather than a *this-is* (or *was*).

The difference between a *this-is-here-now* and a *this-is* (or *was*) highlights the way in which the cinematic index does more than underwrite a reality. It invites one to reimagine a reality, to remake it, and to do so each time one encounters it. Every act of perception is, after all, limited. Just as importantly, every reality is more compressed than any single viewing can accommodate. Every encounter will only see some part of the whole. Cinema plays on that fact; it invites rewatching in every sense of the word. It offers spectators the chance to see a reality before the camera, in the frame, in relationship to other realities, and even realities they otherwise would never see. Indices set in motion on the screen exist in their frame but are never bound by it. Imaginative spectators can move beyond the frame, and they can do so at the point of the index, so long as the index itself is not traumatized or taken as the mark of some trauma.

Gaining distance from a traumatized index is more difficult than it might seem at first. Nancy K. Miller and Jason Tougaw (2002) offer one reason why: "if every age has its symptoms, ours appears to be the age of trauma" (1). The editors continue, "trauma has become a portmanteau that covers a multitude of different injuries," as well as a way to capture and hold public attention (1–2). Books and movies frequently feature characters experiencing some trauma, so much so, in fact, that Miller and Tougaw suggest "narratives of illness, sexual abuse, torture, or the death of loved ones have come to rival the classic, heroic adventure as a test of limits that offers the reader [or spectator] the suspicious thrill of borrowed emotion" (2). From Miller and Tougaw's perspective, the great adventure of today is to endure beyond one's emotional limits. Miller and Tougaw determine that such stories appeal to audiences because they throw off a sense of the normal or everyday. Moments of trauma allow one to test assumptions that would otherwise go untested. Trauma, following Miller and Tougaw, fractures every assumption so that the very act of representation as it relates to trauma will be tested. How does one represent the horrors of trauma, especially a collective trauma? Can such traumas be represented? Should they be? Regardless of how one answers these questions, one must deal with the fact that such things are represented and, to the point Miller and Tougaw most astutely raise, this occurs regularly. Miller and Tougaw estimate that the frequency of representations of "extreme experiences" indicates an "almost compulsory" impulse to "document the disaster" (11). This need to document the disaster often stands against a push to animate, remake, or reimagine the trauma. In this way, the cinematic index becomes traumatized, set within the original trauma rather than working through it.

The tendency of stories featuring trauma to traumatize the index results in what Janet Walker designates a trauma cinema. As Walker (2001) explains, a cycle of films that can be called "trauma cinema [emerges by] the 1980s and 1990s" that mimics contemporary understandings of traumatic memory (214). These films set "vivid bodily and visual sensation over 'verbal narrative and context' by . . . [adopting] non-linearity, fragmentation, nonsynchronous sound, repetition, rapid editing and strange angles" (214). They operate in what Walker deems a "realist mode," only to use the trauma at the center of their story as an excuse to create "disorientation and moral ambiguity" (215). Walker offers *Apocalypse Now* (1979), *Platoon* (1986), and *Saving Private Ryan* (1998) as three popular examples. Walker argues that all three films, like all the films that would adopt the characteristics of trauma cinema, intentionally fail to deliver a true account of what happened. They convey a fractured account of some reality that would be impossible to construct or to verify. As such, these films become as much a representation of trauma as an instance of it, at least as the audiences comes to experience it. These films certainly do little to show any working through of trauma. In some cases, they might even come to celebrate trauma.

This celebration extends from what Janet Walker (2005) refers to as the "traumatic paradox," which accounts for the way the repeated performance of trauma can "trigger fantasies[,] . . . misperceptions, and interpretations created by the real events but not realistically representative of them" (7). Attention settles on trauma itself, not on any movement through trauma. One might take M. Night Shyamalan's *Split* (2016) as an example of what might follow. Shyamalan's film comes very close to celebrating trauma, and it does so in several ways. The film tells the story of Kevin (James McAvoy), a man suffering from dissociative identity disorder, who commits a series of crimes to satiate the demands of his twenty-fourth personality, "The Beast." The film begins with one of the personalities, David, kidnapping three teenage girls from a mall parking lot. David takes the three girls to his home where he tries to hold them until "The Beast" is ready for them. The film is immediately grounded in two perceived strands of trauma. There is the trauma that Kevin suffers as a consequence of his mental illness. There is also the trauma Kevin/David inflicts on the three girls. Shyamalan includes a third strand of trauma in his story by having one of the hostages, Casey (Anya Taylor-Joy), be the victim of sexual abuse, a point revealed through flashback at key moments in the film. These flashbacks and the trauma they reveal become particularly important, especially as it relates to how Shyamalan's film could be seen as a celebration of trauma, but it will only be most fully understood when set within the whole of Shyamalan's plot, which can be shown to lean toward celebrating trauma in at least three ways.

For one thing, Kevin's psychiatrist, Dr. Karen Fletcher (Betty Buckley), twice proposes that her patients might have, by virtue of their traumatic experiences, unlocked something extraordinary about the human mind. The first occurrence arises in Fletcher's apartment as she talks with a neighbor. Fletcher offers, "We look at people who've been shattered and different as *less than*. What if they are *more than* us?" The neighbor resists this idea, but Fletcher defends her position. Fletcher is shown a few scenes later advocating the same thesis in a lecture on dissociative identity disorder to a panel of colleagues. After marveling about the ways in which one personality in a group of personalities in the same body can express their individuality "with different IQs . . . different physical strengths," Dr. Fletcher asks, "Have these individuals, through their suffering, unlocked the potential of the brain? Is this the ultimate doorway to all things we call unknown? Is this where our sense of the supernatural comes from?" Fletcher's professional questions extend from the same personal belief she advances with her neighbor, namely, that those who experience trauma may be on a path to a more evolved existence.

Fletcher does soften this suggestion a bit during a dramatic confrontation with Kevin, who appears to her as Dennis, but not in way that undermines her original idea. The good doctor goes to see her patient, sensing that Dennis is involved in something horrific. She learns during her discussion with her patient that Dennis actually believes in the reality of The Beast. This twenty-fourth personality is, in other words, more than a fantasy. It is as real as the others. Dennis claims that Fletcher will understand the true significance of The Beast as a more highly evolved human expression. Dennis explains,

"When you said that this situation was extraordinary, I knew you can maybe understand.... The Beast is real. He has just emerged. You were right about everything.... He believes that we are extraordinary, that we don't represent a mistake but our potential." When Fletcher's face flinches at this suggestion, Dennis declares, "You say the same things." Dr. Fletcher looks dumbfounded. She insists, "He can't be real. There must be limits to what a human being can become." The doctor's words work in at least two directions. Most literally, they reject Dennis's claims. The reason they reject them, however, leads to the real insight in this conversation. Fletcher argues that The Beast must not be real because "there must be limits to what human beings can become." In other words, Fletcher's hesitation is less about the horrors her idea supports than it is about the limits of her own imagination. The Beast's presence does not unsettle her. The Beast's existence confirms her view that trauma can advance humanity. Following Fletcher's logic, she might be prevented from seeing the fullness of The Beast because she has been spared from the trauma her patient faces. Only those who have endured the horrors of trauma can evolve to the level of The Beast. Dr. Fletcher's position leaves The Beast as something to celebrate rather than to cure.

One could relate all of this to the misgivings of a character rather than a presumption of the story except that the subtext of *Split* also celebrates trauma. The most dramatic moment of the film occurs when The Beast confronts Casey, who has retreated into a jail cell to try to escape the predator. The superhuman being begins to pull apart the bars of Casey's cell. He is sure to kill her until he sees the scars on her shoulders and belly. Seeing the evidence of her abuse, The Beast declares, "You are different from the rest. Your heart is pure! Rejoice! The broken are the more evolved. Rejoice." He then recedes into the dark. The audience knows more about Casey's abuse than The Beast can see in this moment. As already mentioned, Shyamalan shows Casey's story of sexual abuse at the hands of her Uncle John (Brad William Henke) during a series of flashbacks. In one flashback, Uncle John commands a then five-year-old Casey (Izzie Coffey) to "pretend [they're] animals again." When the little girl refuses, the uncle threatens to tell her dad that she is not "being nice." The threat motivates Casey to comply. She begins to walk around the rock that hides Uncle John from the camera while sounds of the pedophile's howling fill the soundtrack. After Casey walks a few paces, the camera shows Uncle John on all fours, stripped down to his underwear. He commands Casey to do the same with the reminder, "Animals don't wear clothes."

As the little girl starts to undress, the screen cuts to an idyllic scene with a flowing stream bathed in sunlight, then to Uncle John, now fully dressed, walking toward the campsite. Somewhat surprisingly, the camera finds Casey in his path holding a shotgun. She raises the barrel on her assailant. The film cuts to an extreme point-of-view shot so that the audience is literally looking with Casey down the barrel on Uncle John. Images of the uncle, Casey's eye, and her finger resting against the trigger flash in quick succession. One expects the gun to go off at any moment. Instead, Uncle John overpowers Casey (again) and grabs the weapon from her hands. The little girl stands still, panting as the relative empties the shells from the gun. The next frame returns the action to the present day and to the now adolescent Casey as she is leaning against a wall crying. The positioning of the shot is ambiguous enough to suggest that the image could double as a depiction of the kinds of assault Casey has suffered while her Uncle raped her. In this way, the plot mentions the trauma Casey has suffered in order to explain The Beast's decision to spare Casey in a way he did not spare the other two girls. The Beast declares Casey pure in heart. He offers her abuse has made her whole, an idea that extends rather than qualifies Dr. Fletcher's argument. The Beast's statements return the audience to Dr. Fletcher's proposal that traumatic suffering leads to a more highly evolved human being.

This position is an unsettling one. Trauma more often leads to trauma than to a more highly evolved human being. More typical stories of trauma admit this point. Maureen Turim's (2001) discussion of Sidney Lumet's *The Pawnbroker* (1965) provides an interesting example, especially as it relates to more contemporary stories of trauma. The film's antihero, Sol Nazerman (Rod Steiger), experiences his existence as a pawnshop operator in New York during the 1960s through his experience in a concentration camp during the Holocaust. Every moment of Sol's "present calls [his] past to [his] attention" (209). The film's choice of presentation aptly illustrates this fractured and displaced reality. Turim notes the way Lumet visualizes Nazerman's trauma through "staccato crosscutting of past and present . . . that show . . . a man haunted by images [from his past] that slice into his daily existence against his will and outside his control" (209). The demonstration follows what Turim terms a "poesis of trauma . . . [wherein] trauma invades, troubles, and even forecloses by asserting the unresolved pain of events that cumulatively have overwhelmed a subject's ability to cope" (209). Sol does not return to his past; rather, the past returns to him. In fact, there is no present, strictly speaking; there is only the past and, perhaps most importantly, Nazerman's inability to act in that original moment or the long line of moments that extend from it. Nazerman declares in a pivotal moment of reflection, "There is nothing I could do. Nothing. Strange, I could do nothing. No, there was nothing I could do." Taken out of context, these claims might be taken as a kind of acceptance, but Turim explicates them in another way: "monumental traumas of history cause such personal wounds, repeatedly, one on top of another, each conjoining with some larger historically-based symbolism of one's helplessness, one's guilt, one's disenfranchisement" (209–10). Turim further explains that the original utterance, wherein Nazerman twice offers that he did not die, and four times says there was nothing he could do, demonstrate the "haunting return inherent in the traumatic" (210). The experience of trauma becomes an instance of closure, but a very particular type of closure. The trauma Turim describes refuses resolution, in part because it turns a memory into a crime scene that can never be disturbed. The details become fixed in the way icons and symbols become fixed. The original event becomes a site to honor through repetition rather than a detail to reimagine through ongoing adaptation.

The difference between films that remain stuck in some trauma and those that find a way to move through it are especially important to this study. Those films that remain stuck in their trauma tend to rely on icons or symbols or the diminished forms of the index, while those that move through it would seem to do so on the point of a more sophisticated index. A quick comparison between two films, Kenneth Lonergan's *Manchester by the Sea* (2016) and Michel Gondry's *Eternal Sunshine of the Spotless Mind* (2004), marks the difference between these two responses. The main character of Lonergan's film, Lee (Casey Affleck), is quite openly a wounded individual who is wholly unable to escape his trauma. This point is explicitly made in the final moments of the film when Lee explains to his orphaned teenage nephew, Patrick (Lucas Hedges), that he must move back to Boston rather than remain in Manchester Bay to act as Patrick's guardian. Lee concedes to Patrick, "I can't beat it. I can't beat it. I'm sorry." Spectators are hardly surprised by this final admission. While the story has been arranged in such a way that one can hope for some turn in the character that would allow Lee to evolve beyond his trauma, Lonergan's plot, and especially the writer's use of flashbacks, suggest that such a turn is unlikely. One sees this unlikelihood from the opening moments of the film, too, especially when one returns to the opening after having seen the whole of the film. The opening offers Lee and his audience a sense of past, or at least a before, that Lumet refuses Nazerman. As it relates to Lee, the opening scene captures Lee, a younger Patrick (Ben O'Brien), and Lee's brother, Joe (Kyle Chandler), as they ride together in a commercial boat. The scene is very nearly idyllic. The occupants of the boat enjoy one another. The waters remain relatively calm. The sun sharpens the various colors dancing on the water and dotting the shore.

The most striking aspect of the scene, especially to those rewatching it, is the playful attitude Lee exhibits in it. This Lee is not the Lee that will fill so many other scenes in Lonergan's film. Lee jokes with his young nephew, Patrick, about how lucky the boy is to have him as his uncle. He asks the boy who he would want to have with him if he could only keep one person in his world. Patrick answers his father, but Lee tells him he should be careful what he chooses. The whole scene stands in sharp contrast to the character the audience will come to know as the film progresses. Lonergan introduces that contrast in the very next set of images. The jump in time quite literally places Lee in a new world. The sunlit bay is replaced by the wet and cold of a Boston winter. The weatherworn character shovels snow in one shot before enduring a series of mechanical conversations and tasks for tenants in the scenes that follow. In each moment, Lee is expressionless. He simply completes the next task, stopping a leaky faucet, working on a fan, plunging a toilet, and, finally, arguing with an adversarial woman. Lee is a shell of the character depicted on the boat in the opening scene. His playfulness has been replaced by indifference.

Lonergan explains this shift in Lee through crosscuts that bring the gloomier present Lee experiences into contact with a series of events spectators can see as a time in between the opening moment of the film and the one long moment Lee comes to occupy. The most interesting aspect of these early cuts is the way they would seem to serve the narrative and the narrator rather than the character. While the cuts can be seen as memories, following the logic of the film, they seem more inclined to serve the whims of a narrator. Each cut does, in the end, serve to develop the emotional context of the story rather than to explain the character. For example, upon hearing about the hospitalization of his brother, Lee begins to drive to Manchester Bay. During the drive, the plot cuts to another day in Lee's life, one that had him riding again in his brother's boat. The scene establishes the relationship Lee and Joe had more than anything else, which, in this moment, elicits an emotional response rather than explores one. Lee would appear as emotionless in this moment as he does in so many others. The same sort of thing occurs a few moments later when Lee is riding down an elevator to see his brother's dead body in the basement. The plot leaves the elevator to show the moment when Lee learns with his brother's family that Joe has congestive heart disease. The scene creates an emotional connection between the audience and the onscreen action, but it does not try to place those emotions in the character as much as in the audience. Lee is unmistakably emotionless.

The two cuts in time that occur after Lee leaves the hospital work in a similar way. Both develop the context of the story more than they develop

Lee. In the first scene, the audience sees Lee driving to the hockey rink to retrieve his nephew. The plot cuts to what would be a third day on Joe's boat. Lee and Joe joke with Patrick about the dangers of drawing sharks to them. The scene encourages the audience to begin to predict the kind of exchange Lee will have with his nephew when he gets to the hockey rink. A subsequent cut brings the action back to the present where the camera remains until Lee sees a church and accompanying cemetery. The sight pulls Lee back to the same day found in the earlier memory, only Lee is no longer with Joe and Patrick; instead, he is returning home to his own family, to his wife Randi (Michelle Williams), and to their two daughters and infant son. Lee gives each child a hug and a kiss. He jokes and flirts with his wife, who is just as playful as her husband. This extended flashback does begin to divulge a bit more about Lee than the three earlier flashbacks, but even here, the moment from the past would seem to develop the story more than the character. It marks a time before the tragedy that sits at the center of the film and the experience that follows that moment. None of the flashbacks develop Lee as much as they shape the story Lonergan wants to tell. Lonergan's central character is surprisingly undeveloped.

More accurately, Lee is entirely inhibited by a moment he cannot escape. Lonergan brings that moment to the screen during the scene wherein Lee learns that Joe named Lee as Patrick's guardian. Lee immediately protests: "I can't be his guardian . . . I mean I can't." The protest is not unlike Nazerman's declaration that there was/is nothing he could do. The moment in Lonergan's film bears a potential to act that Lumet never allows. This potential extends, in part, from the earlier flashbacks, which at least registered a time before the tragedy and trauma Lee experiences. For Nazerman, there is no before. There is only one moment in time. The same one moment arises for Lee, and Lonergan shows it through a flashback that follows Lee's declaration that he cannot be Patrick's guardian. The first cut carries the plot to the scene of a house party that has Lee playing Ping-Pong and partying with a group of friends. Randi bursts into the room to break up the party. Lonergan shows the ways in which this past moment invades Lee's present by intermixing the images from what would be Lee's present with the sounds from Lee's past. As Lee sits in the lawyer's office, the sounds of his friends leaving the party fill the soundtrack. The screen shows one time while the soundtrack plays from another. Eventually, Lonergan's script shows Lee walking to and from a convenience store to find his house fully ablaze. His wife's screams are the only thing that match the sound of the fire. She pleads with the firefighters to save her children, but it is obviously too late for anyone to be saved. As the plot continues to show the story in the past, Lee watches the next morning while firefighters remove the bodies of his children in body bags. Lonergan's intercuts indicate why Lee cannot be Patrick's guardian: he is too traumatized by the past to be fully in the present.

The question that develops as the film moves from this moment is to what extent can Lee rise above his experience. Lonergan does offer some moments that suggest his character might progress. The moment that invites the most hope occurs after Lee sells Joe's rifles to pay for a new motor for the boat Patrick so desperately wants to keep. The boat features in so many of the moments before the tragedy brought to the screen earlier in the plot that one might expect a new outing to mark a new beginning for Lee. The scene that occurs just after the motor is replaced even begins in a way that would encourage this expectation. Patrick takes his girlfriend for a ride on the boat. Lee sits on the back rail watching the two teenagers interact with one another. The resulting image is a near visual match to an earlier shot of Lee on Joe's boat. In a different story, such a moment might signal some return to an earlier self (if such returns are ever possible) or at least some development that would allow Lee to approximate that version of his earlier self. But Lonergan's film ultimately tells the story of a character stuck in trauma. No such (re)turn will be permitted. Lonergan establishes this point by creating within his script a chance encounter between Lee and Randi on the street. Lee is clearly made uncomfortable by the happenstance. He tries to leave, but Randi convinces him to stay. The ex-wife apologizes for the things she said to Lee after they lost their children. Lee tries to tell her she does not need to apologize, but Randi continues to say what she feels she must. She eventually says to Lee, "You can't just die." Lee finally finds the only words he has to say: "There's nothin' there. There's nothin' there." The remark brings Lee to the place of Nazerman. The traumatic past has fully invaded the present so that there is only that past, which, more accurately, becomes one long present.

Lonergan provides a visual for what Lee's long present looks like. The camera cycles through a series of shots that establish a typical day for Lee. One moment shows him warming a sauce on the stove. The next shows the broadcast of a basketball game on the television. A third cut captures Lee asleep on the sofa. The camera frames Lee in a tight medium shot that is disrupted by the voice of a little girl who twice says, "Daddy." Lee slowly wakes and turns his head to his right as the camera pans and widens and Lee's two daughters are revealed on to be with Lee on the couch. Lee responds to the little girl's call only to hear her say, "can't you see we're burning?" Lee corrects the little girl as the camera pulls back, and the sound of a smoke alarm enters the soundtrack: "No, honey, you're not burning." A hard cut visually brings the audience and the character back into Lee's actual present. The room is full of smoke. Lee dashes to the kitchen to find the pot on the stove smoking. One could conclude that the smell of smoke brings Lee back to his children, but Lonergan's plot just as easily justifies the idea that Lee never leaves this thought. His children are always burning in some sense. He can respond to this knowledge as calmly as he likes, but he cannot lessen its power over him. He cannot move through or beyond his trauma. It is simply there to be experienced. This is the truth the film ends with as it relates to both the main character and the audience. Both can only witness a trauma that invades every aspect of the story.

The whole of Lonergan's story is reduced to "an event," namely, the night Lee loses his children in the fire. This is the sense of loss Thomas Elsaesser (2001) describes will occur in cinema. For Elsaesser, cinematic trauma will often refuse any sense of referentiality so that the story on the screen "can no longer be placed . . . in a particular time or place, but whose time-space-place-referentiality is nonetheless posited, in fact, doubled and displaced in relation to an 'event'" (200). The emergence of *the event* collapses all other realities. The event itself becomes mono-referential, reducing the significance of every detail to one common denominator. As such, the event denies the normal sense of inside or outside. There is only an inside, which Elsaesser claims demands a "(persistent, obsessive) return" (197). Each return brings one closer to the original event. As Elsaesser explains, "repetition becomes part of creating in the spectator not just 'prosthetic memory' but prosthetic trauma . . . [which] deliberately or inadvertently set[s] up a gap between the (visual, somatic) impact of an event or image and the (media's) ability to make sense of it" (197). Elsaesser insists that "even the category of witnessing . . . collapses . . . [because] trauma is experienced through its forgetting, its repeated forgetting," which eventually leads "to the absence of all signs of it" (199). This is the place Lee reaches. He is ultimately in a place where "nothin'[s] there." Following the logic Elsaesser develops, nothing is there except trauma.

Following the logic of this book, cinematic portrayals of trauma can deliver more than trauma, especially when the spectator emphasizes the indexical qualities of the image. The cinematic index always points beyond the event even as it points to it. In keeping with all indices, the recovery or realization of this reality beyond the index can only materialize through the work of the active spectator (or the active character who operates within the story as a spectator). No one within screen studies has founded a concept of the active spectator on a revised notion of the index, but Susannah Radstone (2007) does provide the logic for such a foundation. Working from Elsaesser's notion of recovered referentiality, Radstone regards trauma theory's willingness to explore the site that opens between a concept of some actuality and an effort to represent that actuality, even inaccurately, as a major service to the humanities. If nothing else, trauma studies finds a way to rehabilitate the subject at the center or on the edges of a personal or collective tragedy. In keeping with Radstone, it is "the event rather than the subject [that] emerges [from some trauma] as unpredictable or ungovernable," and it is the subject who "confer[s], negotiate[s,] and mediate[s]" every experience (18). A traumatic experience may not be properly remembered, but it can be reconstituted through what Radstone terms "belated acknowledgement," which creates space for "processes of dialogic meaning making between testifier and witness" (20). In other words, even though the event cannot be recovered, those who testify or witness the event can bring some meaning to it and from it. Following the argument of this book, these meanings will work on the point of the index.

One can view Michel Gondry's *Eternal Sunshine of the Spotless Mind* as a film that seems especially aware of the possibility Radstone describes and this project champions. The main character in *Eternal Sunshine*, Joel (Jim Carrey), exists at the beginning of Gondry's plot in a state similar to the one Lonergan assigns Lee. Unlike Lee, however, Joel does not end there. He recovers himself and a life with his girlfriend, Clementine (Kate Winslet). Together, the two characters move through the trauma Joel faces, reimagining key moments from his past in the ways Pamela does in *Saving Mr. Banks* and the men do in *Last Flag Flying*, which is to say imaginatively, and on the point of an index that points to a reality these characters negotiate rather than recall or accept.

Gondry's plot suggests his story will be one of negotiation from the first moments of the film. Joel wakes from his sleep, but he seems to do so with plenty of uncertainty. He looks at the room and his pajamas as if they are foreign to him. A cut carries the plot to the parking lot as Joel walks to his car only to find it damaged from some accident he clearly does not recall having had. The next cut brings the plot to the platform along the route of a train. Joel stands with a host of other morning commuters waiting for their shuttle to carry them to work. Even before Joel's inner dialogue begins to play on the soundtrack, it is clear that Joel feels out of place despite the fact that he is going through what is almost assuredly his normal routine. In these ways, the reality on the screen exists but without the authority of a more typical reality. Joel's reality is one that exists to be searched through rather than settled into.

The next segment of the opening sequence continues to mark the difference between searching through and settling into by having Joel admit the confusion implied in the three opening scenes. In the aforementioned voiceover, Joel acknowledges that he wakes up feeling "out of sorts." He explains the strange actions that play on the screen as he suddenly runs from one platform to another to catch at the last moment a train to Montauk rather than the one that would take him to work. The events that follow that train ride each reveal the fact that Joel is in the midst of some existential crisis that extends from his feeling invisible, irrelevant, and insecure. Joel calls in sick to work only to have the person on the other end seemingly not know who he is. He walks the shore in Montauk while mocking himself for making the impromptu decision to go to Montauk in the middle of winter. He sits on some steps along the beach to write in his journal to find that a page has been ripped out. A drawing appears on the opposite page, which confirms the way this character the plot is introducing feels. A man sits with a scared look on his face and his knees pulled to his chest in the corner of a basement. In the voiceover that continues to reveal Joel's thoughts, the character comments, "it appears this is my first entry in two years," which creates questions for the character and the spectator rather than confirming something about him.

The inner dialogue explicitly turns to these questions as the opening sequence continues. Joel sees Clementine on the beach, only he clearly does not know her in this moment. The audience can assume she is a stranger to him. The lines that follow would confirm that suspicion. Joel expresses a desire to "meet someone new." The images show that will not happen, not in this moment, for the reasons Joel admits in the next line: "I guess my chances of that happening are somewhat diminished, seeing that I am incapable of making eye contact with a woman I don't know." Joel's claim that he is "incapable" of even a basic gesture builds the case that he is a man suffering some trauma, even if that trauma extends from the fact that he exists. This idea is registered a second time when the two characters coincidentally find themselves in the same coffee shop at opposite tables. Joel watches Clementine from a distance until she notices him and offers him a smile, at which point he wonders, "Why do I fall in love with every woman I see who shows me the least bit of attention?" The question becomes more than an admission of some awkwardness. It becomes something of a guiding question throughout the film, one that the film will ultimately answer in stereotypical psychological fashion during a scene where the mother ignores her son as he pleads for her attention. In this way, *Eternal Sunshine* will move along Joel's traumas even as it never simply accepts those traumas as definite realities. They are always starting points rather than defining points.

In truth, the whole of the nearly eighteen-minute opening prologue of sorts offers itself as the same sort of reality. It becomes something of a baseline without a through line, which is to say something of an unconfirmed reality. Everything unfolds plainly enough, but without the frame that would present a fixed story. Clementine rises to confront Joel on the train and the two go through an awkward set of exchanges that keep them from connecting. When they arrive at their mutual station, Joel looks back for Clementine, but he does not have the courage to wait for her. He does stop his car when he sees her walking along the sidewalk, and offers her a ride, which leads to a sort of accelerated courtship. Joel goes to Clementine's apartment for drinks. They agree to have a nighttime picnic on a frozen lake the next night. He drives her back to her apartment the next morning, only to agree to wait for her as she goes to get her toothbrush so that she can go to his apartment to sleep. While waiting in the car for her, what appears to be a passer-by knocks on Joel's car window to ask the question the Joel in the earlier moments of the film might have asked himself: "What are you doing here?" Joel has no idea what to make of the question. He rolls up his window and keeps looking in the mirror on his door as if to try to see something that can explain what just happened. The image dissolves to black and, when it returns, the camera holds a tight frame around a different Joel, one who is clutching the steering wheel and crying as he drives his car along a road at night. He is quite clearly in a different time and place, emotionally and physically.

The abrupt shift in time and space is but the first of a series of abrupt shifts the film makes. The plot is set in the night before the opening scene, as Joel is having his memory erased to forget Clementine. The premise allows the plot to travel wherever and whenever Joel's memory goes. Even before that procedure begins, the film establishes that these trips to a memory mean to negotiate rather than recognize what occurs. They are searching out an answer. For example, in a scene that the audience will come to understand occurred three days before the day on which the movie begins, Joel complains to his friends about not being able to connect with Clementine. He tries to call her, but her number is disconnected. He goes to see her at work, but he finds her looking at him as if she does not know him. The camera cuts to the scene Joel describes, which allows the audience to see Joel in the moment he is describing. He is forced to watch as his would-be girlfriend looks at him as though she does not recognize him, and, worse, as she kisses another man as he stands and watches in disbelief and confusion. Disheartened, Joel turns to leave the store. The lights literally go out on his memory as the overhead lights darken and the site of the scene seamlessly changes from the store to Joel's friends' apartment again. Joel stands out of breath, holding the gift he planned to give Clementine as an apology. He turns to sit on the stairs asking, "Why? Why would she do that to me?" One of Joel's friends, Rob (David Cross), decides to give Joel an explanation. He shows Joel a letter from a company that explains what has happened: "Clementine Kruczynski has had Joel Barish erased from her memory. Please never mention their relationship to her again." As Joel looks at the card, Clementine's name disappears. It becomes clear that Joel is going through the same procedure.

The premise arranges an interesting competition between forgetting and remembering. The former involves ignoring or, more radically, erasing a memory, in the way Clementine ignores Joel in the above scene after having had him erased from her memory. As Joel and the audience will learn, Dr. Mierzwiak (Tom Wilkinson) has made this option a more practical possibility by developing a procedure that erases painful memories from a person's mind. He tells Joel that he can help him forget Clementine. Joel just needs to "go home and collect everything you own that has some association with Clementine." As the doctor gives his directives, the screen presents images of letters, games, photographs, presents, entries in Joel's journal, mugs, knickknacks, a host of things that brings Clementine to Joel's mind. Joel gives each of these items to the technician, Stan (Mark Ruffalo), who re-presents them to Joel to get "an emotional read" on the items and to create a mental map of Joel's brain that can be used to perform the erasure. Interestingly, the script overlays the moments these images are being presented with the moments they are being erased, so that past and present are in this moment the same. The images show the past. The soundtrack shows the present. A sharp line between past and present is blurred. Interestingly, Joel maintains a sense of *now* throughout the entire ordeal, which allows him to engage rather than just recall his memories. Over time, Joel begins to resist the procedure to remember Clementine.

The plot makes clear that Joel will need to confront his past, even a distant past before he knew Clementine, to be able to keep hold of his memories of her. He will, in other words, need to renegotiate his past. This renegotiation starts as an acknowledgment of what transpired in the past. Joel's renegotiation cannot begin with forgetting. Charlie Kaufman's script makes this prerequisite plain by having Joel provide a commentary to his memory. For example, Joel has a memory of getting in his car to try and convince Clementine to return to his house with him. The memory is not just a memory, though; it is also a present, as Joel says things he could not have said in the original moment. Joel tells Clementine, for instance, "I'm erasing you and I am happy. You did it to me first." Joel is left in a loop, but it is a loop that is at least aware of itself. This awareness turns into an ability to escape the memory, to leave the map Stan had earlier created. In an effort to save Clementine in his mind, Joel carries Clementine to places he never would have been with her, places the "eraser guys" Stan and Patrick would not know to look. The most interesting thing about this plan as it relates to the indexical argument this book advances is the way in which these memories eventually point to new realities. Kaufman's script provides a wonderful picture of what this looks like during a scene that has Joel and Clementine sitting in a car beyond the fence of a drive-in movie theater. They can see the screen, but they cannot hear the words, so they are free to create their own dialogue. *Eternal Sunshine* allows the characters to do the same thing with their memories. The characters see the action, but they do not hear the dialogue, which allows them to inscribe those moments in new ways.

The most dramatic remaking takes place when Joel takes Clementine to his most shameful moment. The camera cuts to a moment in Joel's elementary school days. A group of kids stand around a wagon. Little Joel (Ryan Whitney) kneels on one side of the wagon with a hammer in his hands. A team of bullies urge him to hit the bird. The voice of the adult Joel says the words the little boy almost certainly said: "I can't. I gotta go home. I'll do it later." The boys continue their taunting, screaming "come on you big sissy, hit it, hurry up." Ultimately, little Joel obliges them. He swings his hammer at the body of the dead bird. The camera cuts to a treetop where another bird flies away. The next cut returns the memory, only now Jim Carrey is in the place of the little boy. Kate Winslet, dressed in the outfit a little girl sitting to the side of the event was wearing, comes to his rescue. Joel sobs here just as he is found sobbing in the shift in time at the start of the film. The next cut replaces the adult actors with the child actors again, only to have the adult actors replace the children a few seconds later. The memory is quite clearly a mix of past and present, all of which occurs in a now that has Clementine's character with Joel in the past moment of shame. Her presence allows Joel to confront that memory and speak to it, to renegotiate it. Joel confesses, "I'm so ashamed." Clementine tells him, "It's okay, you were a little kid." The "okay" is the difference in the scene. It clearly did not exist until Joel comes to accept what he did through a renegotiation of a past memory.

The moment encapsulates what so much of *Eternal Sunshine* dramatizes. The lines between past and present are disrupted so that there is only the now. Through a present encounter, the past and present intermingle so that both can be remade by their contact with each other. This reimagining is what *Manchester by the Sea* refuses to offer its character, even if it brings Lee to the place where such reimagination could occur. Lee, however, is unable to confront his past, and, thereby, unable to negotiate it. He is simply trapped by it. Joel and Clementine, by contrast, remake their past. They see in their past indexical signs that keep the memory open rather than fixed.

The characters see contingency where Lee sees certainty. The past remains for Joel and Clementine, as do the indexical markers of that past, but those indices and that past are stories to be adapted rather than merely accepted. The indices of the past can serve specific plots as they do in Kaufman's narrative, but they can serve other stories, too, and that is the point Kaufman's film ultimately makes.

Gondry's film presents an interesting challenge to the normal representations of trauma. *Eternal Sunshine* is clearly focused on a trauma, but it reaches an equilibrium films that would fit Walker's category of trauma cinema never realize. The trauma itself becomes a site of negotiation rather than an excuse to overwhelm the character or the spectator. The turn realizes the opportunity E. Ann Kaplan and Ban Wang (2004) describe when they claim that "the visual media" can become "a matrix of understanding and of experiencing a world out of joint" (17).

The cinematic projection of trauma can lead to recognition, negotiation, and reconfiguration. These responses do not need to lead to some instance of healing. Recognition can, after all, prompt anxiety as much as tranquility. Negotiation can be as frustrating as it is freeing. Reconfiguration can result in collapse as well as creation. More positive responses can also occur. This is what happens in Gondry's film. Joel reimagines his past and his present. He presumably finds a way through his trauma, and he does so by returning to "the event." As Radstone remarks, trauma theory, as it is discussed within the humanities, frequently focuses on "the event," which is most generally regarded as the instance or instances at which some trauma was encountered. "The event" functions as a kind of originary moment. It is an occurrence that reproduces those who experience it, at least until they begin to reproduce it. This is what Joel begins to do; in so doing, he begins to remake what had been a traumatic past and a traumatized present. By the end of *Eternal Sunshine*, there is only the "OK" that Joel offers Clementine at the end of their plot, the perpetual *now* wherein the process of ongoing adaptation begins to unfold.

Such a moment could be taken as the kind of moment that is only possible in fiction. A true story, so the argument would go, would need to stick to the facts. The general attitude is most succinctly captured in the opening claim made in the graphic that begins Joel and Ethan Coen's *Fargo* (1996): "This is a true story. The events depicted in this film took place in Minnesota in 1987. At the request of the survivors, the names have been changed. Out of respect for the dead, the rest has been told exactly as it occurred." The claim the statement makes is fictitious. The story the Coen brothers' *Fargo* tells never took place in any lived space in Minnesota in 1987. It does, however, deliver a truth about the accepted responsibility "true stories" have: to tell their tales with as much accuracy as possible out of respect for the dead. In this way, a "true story" becomes something of a memorial. This need is especially pronounced when the story centers on a national event, and especially a trauma. Cinematic stories based on real-world traumas, events like the Holocaust or 9/11, would seem to owe the victims of those horrors a repetition of the facts. Following the insights of those in trauma studies, such repetition can extend the trauma rather than simply depict it. The films can begin to participate in the traumatic event.

In keeping with Radstone, interpreters do not have to treat the images traumatic stories circulate as mediated or deferred representations of some actual event. Radstone offers that one of trauma theory's primary contributions has been to reveal that the relation between representation and "actuality" is always tenuous at best, something invented rather than preserved. The relations a text creates to a traumatic event may act like a trace, but that does not mean that the trail this trace travels arose naturally. It is more likely an invention. The fact that popularly conceived traumas will begin to accept particular images, if not a way to fit those images into a narrative, reveals the ways in which these trails develop over time. A familiar image, say the floating papers shown so many times during the reporting of 9/11, might begin to acquire some privileged representational status as more and more reports of that story include that image. Such an image will arrive, in any narrative it finds itself in, with a pre-loaded point of significance. The repeated viewing of the same event can begin to power what Cathy Caruth (1996) calls a "traumatic neurosis . . . [which] emerges as the reenactment of an event that one cannot simply leave behind" (2). From Caruth's view, images of falling paper, to continue that example, capture some piece of the trauma that viewers cannot discard. The image begins to bring them back to "the event," rather than to offer a way for those who see it to move through their original experience.

To return to Radstone, traumatic stories can work in the opposite direction, too. They can become part of a recovery rather than just a continuation of the original event. This study contends that this possibility is best realized when spectators treat whatever image is set on screen as an index rather than an icon or a symbol. In the language of Elsaesser, movies can begin to move spectators through trauma when the images they deliver are treated less as an instance of "recovered memory" and more as an opportunity to recover some referentiality through interpretation (201). The difference between these two responses is substantial. The former works to make an event visible so that it can be seen and recognized. To work as a memory is to surrender to symbols and icons. Elsaesser estimates that the recovery of a memory will tend to make the event itself more indecipherable, as, by its nature, it is beyond the grasp and comprehension of those who experience. Every depiction will reveal that fact again, especially when the event is being shown to tell or represent some truth. The event will be made visible, but spectators will not have a way to confront it. They will have no way to "beat it," to use the words of Lonergan's character. They will have no way to say okay to it, to speak in the language Gondry's character comes to speak.

The form of watching Elsaesser offers as an alternative involves a more active response. Spectators begin to remake, reconstitute, and reimagine the images they see because the referentiality of any image has only been suggested, and only so that the spectator can search for it. It depends less on the accurate or truthful representation of an event and more on the opportunity any instance of representation gives one to re-present a representation. To seize upon this opportunity, spectators must wrestle the text from the past. They must bring the past into a now where it can move to the whims of the *Kairos* of ongoing adaptation that arises anew in every encounter. Each encounter exists in an undeniable sense of now. The cinema can tell stories of the past and the future, but those stories will always be performed for the spectator in a current moment. Any instance of interpretation will occur in that moment, in the now. Any sense of referentiality, even a sense reconstituted from some understanding of the past, can only be experienced in that moment, and even then only temporarily. Those same images can be reexperienced in the next encounter.

Elsaesser's discussion directly relates to the larger argument that some films participate in the traumas they present, and some films offer their characters as an example of a way to move through a trauma. This is the difference described above between films like *Manchester by the Sea* and *Eternal Sunshine of the Spotless Mind*. An examination of three 9/11 films—Paul Greengrass's *United 93* (2006), Oliver Stone's *World Trade Center* (2006), and Stephen Daldry's *Extremely Loud and Incredibly Close* (2011)—explores the ways in which films based on national traumas can sit along the same divide. All three of these films focus on the events of 9/11, even if they do so differently. To return to Peter Wollen's way of distinguishing between iconic, symbolic, and indexical filmmaking, one could say that Greengrass means his film to move iconically, Stone means his film to move symbolically, while Daldry means his film to move indexically. This is not to say that these three films are only iconic, symbolic, or indexical; rather, it is to acknowledge that each film can favor one aspect of the sign over another. Greengrass allows audiences to remember, to participate in the likeness of the original event. Stone invites audiences to feel a sense of national pride in the face of tragedy.

Daldry shows audiences how to move through the trauma that emerges because of an initial experience. The sharpest difference between the three films arises in the performance of authenticity. Greengrass and Stone favor a resolute authenticity. In keeping with Kaufman's implied insistence that one must remember a past to remake it, Daldry's film does not refuse authenticity entirely, but it does ultimately favor inventive play on the point of the index above being accurate. In other words, it ultimately goes the way of Pamela in *Saving Mr. Banks* and the three soldiers in *Last Flag Flying*. Daldry allows his main character, Oskar (Thomas Horn), to remake a memory in the way the characters in these two films begin to remake their memories, and, in so doing, to begin to move through their trauma.

United 93 was widely praised for its desire to present itself with some authenticity. One can complicate the idea of authenticity in Greengrass's film, as Duncan Greenlaw (2010) does using Jacques Derrida's distinction "between 'doing justice' and 'giving justice'" and Walter Benjamin's divisions "between auratic and non-auratic conceptions of art and between involuntary and voluntary memory" (3). Greenlaw ultimately presents a strong argument for the ways in which Greengrass's *Bloody Sunday* (2002) and *United 93* "read the notion of authenticity against itself, not as a term of identity that ensures direct correspondence between cinematic sign and its referent, but instead as a term that describes the disjunction between them" (5). Greenlaw's argument is persuasive, but it does not displace the experience a great many audiences have watching *United 93*. The film appears authentic. Its presentation is persuasive.

Those who know that the film casts a number of people who experienced 9/11 to play themselves only guarantees some viewers will leave the theater feeling like they have witnessed an authentic retelling. Other cinematic devices provide an impression of authenticity, too. For example, Greengrass's soundtrack often carries nothing but the sounds that one would hear if they were in the places Greengrass's camera settles. This is especially true in the early parts of the film when the soundtrack overhears the conversations soon-to-be-passengers have on their cell phones or the voices over the public announcer system. The soundtrack has the same sort of faithfulness to authentic sounds when the camera cuts to the airstrip as the plane goes through its preflight checks. All that is heard are the sounds from the engine, the other planes, the luggage carts, the trucks, and the people talking. Greengrass keeps the soundtrack exceptionally bare, which creates the feeling of being in the actual moment.

The narrative promotes the same having-been-there feeling. The images capture all the types of characters one might find in a story of a tragic plane flight—workers dealing with frustrations they will never get to settle, loved ones making plans for an arrival they will not experience, the passenger who almost saves his life by missing the flight, but Greengrass's script does not pause on any of these stories. They only flash across the screen, providing glimpses of some of the stories those who spoke about such things after the event said about that day. Greengrass provides his audience an omniscient view, one they could not have had as an actual passenger, but he does not delve into any of these stories. They are simply there to be recalled. Greengrass prefers to let the travelers simply board the plane and take their seats. Some of the passengers engage in casual conversation, but either the camera leaves those conversations before the characters exchange much more than the pleasantries or the respondent only returns a quick comment. Audiences are unlikely to feel any strong sense of connection with any of the characters, individually. The passengers themselves emerge as a group rather than individuals. Any connection is with the group rather than the individuals. This choice serves the impression of authenticity Greengrass's film favors.

Greengrass elects to let the narrative tension in his film emerge from the same push for authenticity. The film uses what the audience knows to heighten the tension and a sense of tragedy. For example, Greengrass lingers just long enough on the door closing for United Flight 93 that audiences likely feel the finality of that door closing. A cut to Boston Air Traffic Control Center and a dramatization of the silence from American Flight 11, one of the other planes involved in the terrorist attack, intensify what would otherwise be a tedious representation of a takeoff. The crosscutting between the delayed takeoff of United Flight 93 and the realizations those in the Boston Air Traffic Control have about American Flight 11 match the deadline scenario so many films adopt. Some terrible event is just about to happen unless it can be stopped in time. Of course, Greengrass's audience already knows that this particular deadline will be missed. Those in Boston will not ground United Flight 93 quick enough. It will take off, and it will meet a heroic even if tragic end. Armed with this knowledge, the choice to craft the narrative as if some possibility exists to stop this tragedy from occurring only heightens the emotional response to what follows. The choice drapes a sense of tragedy over each step in the preflight routine. The flight attendants' assurances that "everything is fine, just a *normal* delay," only exaggerate the sense of tragedy the audience would be feeling. The fact that Greengrass achieves this heightened sense of tension and tragic feel with what appears to be virtually no cinematic tricks—no music on the soundtrack, no accelerated cuts, no attempt to build any sense of sentimentality—creates a sense of authenticity that turns what appears on screen into something of a recovered memory rather than an opportunity to recover, or, more properly, to extend the referentiality of the images set on screen.

This sense of authenticity continues when the military is brought into the story. The camera carries the viewer to Northeast Air Defense Command Center just moments after Boston "pulls the tapes" from the cockpit of American Flight 11, certain they have a hijacking. The military is involved in a military exercise along the Eastern Seaboard at the time of the call, so the second person to hear the report assumes that this news is part of the exercise rather than anything actually occurring. Major Dawn Deskins (Karen Kirkpatrick) reports the "real-world situation" to a commanding officer, Colonel Robert Marr (Gregg Henry). The military begins to try to ascertain what is happening. A cut first to Boston Air Traffic Control and then to United Flight 93 returns the viewer to the primary subject of Greengrass's film, with at least some hope that someone will realize what is happening soon enough to keep any more planes from taking off. The pilot comes on the intercom to announce "the progress" they have made during the time they were off screen; United Flight 93 has moved from fifteen to four in the holding pattern. Greengrass cuts to the two sites he has established as complementary places for his story to deliver the news that the hijacking of American Flight 11 is legitimate. The command center chief, Ben Sliney (as himself), alerts his team that the flight has "turned south," and he asks his team to let New York know about this occurrence, thinking the hijackers might be looking to land at a New York airport. All of these conversations appear to occur just as they might have occurred, which creates the "approach toward authenticity" Greenlaw begrudges (18). Audiences are likely to feel they are part of the story, witness to what happens around them rather than observers of what happens in front of them on a screen.

This is not to say that Greengrass's film does not create some cinematic moments. Greengrass does include some movie moments in his film, moments of action that are the sorts of thing that only happen in the movies. Such moments are relatively rare. One example occurs just before United Flight 93 lifts for takeoff. The pilot shares the "good news" that the flight has been cleared for takeoff. The crew begins their preparations. The passengers are relieved that their delay has ended. Nearly every viewer recognizes the irony of the good news they are experiencing. The script heightens a sense of frustration some in the audience might feel by inserting just before takeoff the realization that the tapes from American Flight 11 speak of more than one plane: "it's planes, planes, plural, definitely." The next cut carries the plot back to United Flight 93 as it aligns itself on the runway. The moment would play like a chase scene except that Greengrass continues to measure every move.

The camera remains steady. The soundtrack continues to deliver sounds and noises within the diegesis. There is no music until the plane begins to accelerate, and then it is far enough in the background that one hardly notices it. The camera cuts to a number of the passengers as the plane gathers speed. A subsequent cut moves outside the plane as United Flight 93 is airborne. For one of the first times in the film, the music fills the soundtrack as if to emphasize the significance of this moment. The narrative elements have already been arranged to underscore the implication of this instant. More than that, the audience already knows what the characters do not, which creates all the weight one needs to wish the plane would have remained grounded.

United 93 uses what the audience knows to create a sense of suspense in much the way it uses what the audience knows to create its sense of tension and tragedy. This trick is on display when the action shifts to New York Air Traffic Control Center. The call comes in to have that center track American Flight 11. The audience knows that there is another flight New York Air Traffic Control should be tracking, United Flight 175. That news arrives to the New York center moments later. The script emphasizes what the characters in the scene do not know, which contrasts with what the audience does know. The news from United Flight 175 is nothing more than a suspicious behavior and a recording that involves someone telling the passengers to stay in their seat. No one in the New York center knows what to make of that information; nor do they know anything more about American Flight 11. One of the air traffic controllers mistakenly suspects the plane is going into "Newark or Kennedy," only to admit in the next breath, "I don't know." Greengrass pits what the characters do not know against what the audiences does know, which, among other things, decreases the likelihood that the audience is going to identify with any of these characters. The characters' lack of appeal creates a certain resistance to any identification. Greengrass creates some moments where empathy might be extended to some characters, like the moment when American Flight 11 "just disappears." The air traffic controller, Curt Applegate (as himself) tells his supervisor, "Paul" (Peter Pellicane), that the plane "just disappeared" in a way that makes the frustration he feels palpable. But a quick cut to some other part of the story prevents one from lingering with this character for long, which minimizes the opportunity one has to identify with this character in a way that pulls the audience from their own experience.

A second instance of the plot using what the audience knows is going to happen to create some sense of suspense occurs after United Flight 93 reaches its cruising altitude and the pilot announces that the travelers are free to move about the cabin. The camera holds on one of the flight attendants as she moves up the cabin and into first class. The audience waits for the men who will be the hijackers to start their attack. The camera cuts to those men who have already been identified as the hijackers only to leave them in their seat. The plot returns to the concern it earlier had regarding United Flight 175. Greengrass extends the sense of anticipation the audience feels about when the hijackers on United Flight 93 will attack by overlaying that anxiety with the events in some other part of the story. This choice becomes another way Greengrass ensures that the emotions the audience likely feels at this point in the plot belong to the audience rather than any of the characters. The audience sees the anxiety the air traffic controllers feel as they realize that United Flight 175 "is another hijacking," but the viewers are likely to remain with the story they know will take over the plot at some point in the movie. A certain amount of detachment emerges toward other parts of the story. Greengrass heightens this sense of detachment, too, by ultimately showing the "disappearance" of United Flight 175 indirectly. The whole scene plays out on a monitor, which would seem to diminish the drama, or at least shift it. Rather than show the travelers' response as they realized something was very wrong, or show the plane hitting the building, Greengrass prefers to show the crash on the monitor. The blip on the screen, the target as it is called in the film, is there until it is not. This trick would seem to avoid showing audiences the image of the plane hitting the building that almost everyone in the audience had already seen dozens of times. One could argue, however, that the choice to show the crash as a blip on the screen allows the audience to see that scene in the way they remember it, rather than to compete with that memory. The choice literally recovers a memory in this case.

The events that follow this moment perform a similar trick, albeit in reverse. Rather than refuse a visual the audience can provide, Greengrass gives a visual to stories audiences would have heard occurred. Initially, this reversal allows Greengrass to show the way the terrorists might have acted ahead of their takeover. The group of men begin to grow impatient with Ziad (Khalid Abdalla), the terrorist who pilots the plane after the takeover. Somewhat oddly, the audience is likely to have the same growing impatience as the terrorists. Greengrass's script teases this impatience by having one of the men rise from his seat as though the takeover is about to begin only to go to the toilet instead. When the man exits the toilet, he turns to Ziad to say, "We have to do it now." Ziad gives no response. Another member of the team puts similar pressure on Ziad later in the script. He sits beside Ziad to ask why he is waiting. Ziad says, "It's not the right time." The audience can only speculate if this is a ploy or his real thought. He seems conflicted in a way the others are not. This sense is further developed as the terrorist plot starts without Ziad's consent. A member of the group goes to the toilet to strap himself with explosives. Greengrass continues to delay the actual takeover for as long as he can. The plot cuts from the man in the toilet to a series of shots of travelers. Some of the images capture Americans engaging in casual conversation or simply getting their food and beverages. Other images focus on the members of the terrorist group. One man prays; the other stares straight ahead. Ziad sits motionless. The man in the toilet arms himself with the explosives. Another series of cuts throughout the cabin occurs before a fourth man on the team rises from his seat and holds one of the flight attendants with a knife. The man armed with explosives begins to shout and cuts the throat of the man in the seat in front of him. Ziad commands the flight attendant to open the cockpit door and he sits in the seat of the copilot. Control center hears the pilot telling the man to "get out of here," as the plot matches the transcripts from the takeover.

The plot continues to match unofficial transcripts of the takeover as it continues. The camera focuses on individual passengers as they make phone calls that reveal to them the extent to which they are caught in a larger plot. The passengers realize that they are probably on "a suicide mission," and determine "to do something." One of the passengers asks the flight attendant to collect anything that can be used as a weapon. As some of the passengers organize, the remaining travelers make calls to loved ones to say goodbyes. Greengrass again avoids the full emotional impact of these moments. Greengrass could have overheard more of these conversations. He did, after all, have transcripts of the calls available to him. He utilized the transcripts from the command centers to create actual dialogue. Greengrass chooses to present the travelers during their final moments in the way he did when he first introduced them. He cuts from person to person, never lingering on any one character longer than he must. Greengrass focuses on the way passengers share their phones with those who do not have one and other more global aspects of the story. His intent is clear: Greengrass wants to represent the travelers as brave heroes, to memorialize this group of Americans in a particular way, rather than to focus on the travelers as individuals. This focus continues during the final minutes of the film. The camera suddenly begins to lose its hold on the action. The shots are clear enough to convey that the passengers overcome the two terrorists in the aisles and break into the cockpit, but not clear enough to see who does what or the outcome of their action. Interestingly, during the moments the camera begins to fail the audience, the soundtrack swells with the kinds of melodramatic music one would expect during a moment like the one on screen. The aural qualities of the film provide a clarity of emotion, detached from any of the individuals, but very much present, that departs from Greengrass's strategy in other parts of the film. The camera continues to struggle to frame the action until the plane points straight down and the ground comes into view and remains on the screen for a few seconds. The plane hits the ground. The screen goes black. The music begins to fade. A moment of silence follows just before a dedication appears.

A series of title cards appears that provides some sense of closure to the film. The first card reads, "Of the four aircraft hijacked that day, United 93 was the only one that did not reach its target. It crashed near Shanksville, Pennsylvania at 10:03am. No one survived." The next card amplifies the impression the earlier sequences provided that authorities did not recognize the reality they were in soon enough to respond to that reality: "Military commanders were not notified that United 93 had been hijacked until four minutes after it had crashed. The nearest fighter jets were 100 miles away." The next card implicates the Office of the President in the failure to perceive what was happening soon enough: "At 10:18am the President authorizes the military to engage hijacked aircraft. Fearing an accidental shoot down, military commanders chose not to pass the order to the pilots in the air." The antepenultimate title card, "By 12:06pm every civilian airliner over America had been forced to land. Amidst an unprecedented military mobilization, US airspace was closed until further notice," further emphasizes how much behind the action the official responses were to hijackers' plot. Each card reinforces the reality that the film itself had already established. The last card does the same: "Dedicated to the memory of all of those who lost their lives on September 11, 2001."

Greengrass's film moves with an air of authenticity that makes it nearly impossible to amend, adjust, or adapt any of the details. Spectators are asked to see the images for what they were on the day they occurred. The whole of the film exists as a document to be understood but not necessarily interpreted. The characters occupy space in that document, but their stories do not engage the emotions of the audience. They are not on screen to be felt as much as to be recognized and recognized in a particular way. In these ways, Greengrass's film might extend the trauma 9/11 enacted rather than providing some way through it. The sense of trauma becomes more pronounced but not necessarily more malleable. One does not leave the theater with some new sense; rather, one leaves with a confirmed sense that what has been said, what there is to be known, has been disclosed. One turns to Greengrass's film for the same reason one would return to it, namely, to get the record right. Greengrass leaves virtually no space for the audience to extend that record or to remake it in imaginative ways. To remake it would be to dishonor it, or so the film would have one believe. In this way, Greengrass surrounds the audience with some reality from 9/11 without providing them a way through it.

Oliver Stone does something similar in *World Trade Center*, although one might more accurately say Stone leaves viewers under the images he presents. The film details the story of two Port Authority Police officers, John McLoughlin (Nicolas Cage) and Will Jimeno (Michael Peña), who were trapped under the debris after the towers collapsed. Stone's film shares some traits with Greengrass's. Stone's film begins with a title card that reads "These events are based on the accounts of the surviving participants." The claim gives the story that follows a certain authority it would not have without it. It also allows some of the more fantastic details to try to fit the shock of the day rather than play to some movie formula. Stone also relies on familiar images or occurrences to fill in gaps his story might otherwise have. Papers fall from the sky. People fall from buildings. The smoke pours out of the towers. Each of these images likely assumes an authority a straight fiction film would not since they are the images that were constantly circulated during live coverage of the tragedies. The prominent use of news reports has a similar effect. Not only are the familiar images shown on television sets throughout the movie but the soundtrack is often filled with the voices of Tom Brokaw, Katie Couric, and others. The opening claim, the details and arranged scenes, and the prominent use of news broadcasts all serve as something of an homage to the actual events of 9/11.

These elements are set alongside what many would deem strictly cinematic elements. The way the characters speak about McLoughlin, for instance, frames him as the kind of movie hero one might find in roles Cage plays in movies like *National Treasure* (2004), *Gone in Sixty Seconds* (2000), or *Con Air* (1997). Lieutenant Kassimatis (Nick Damici) explains to the younger officers riding in the bus from the Port Authority Bus Terminal to the buildings after the first plane hits Tower One that Sergeant McLoughlin was "one of the guys who came up with a plan after the attack in '93. Anybody knows what to do down there, it's him." A sequence soon after the group of men arrives downtown plays to this sense that McLoughlin might have some meaningful response, too. The men look in horror at the scene in front of them. One of the men expresses what most in the group must be feeling after seeing a person fall from the top of the building: "Nothing's gonna help them.... how you gonna save people that high up? It's impossible." Another officer looks across the street, sees McLoughlin approaching them, and yells, "Sarge!" A cut establishes a long shot that watches as McLoughlin runs up the street toward the men. The moment is just the kind of image one might find in the types of films above listed. The visual image certainly suggests that "Sarge" will have an answer to the officer's questions. The audience already knows that no one will have a response to this developing crisis that will continue to worsen throughout the day. They have already heard McLoughlin say that there is "no plan" for what they are facing. Still, audiences are likely to have some hope that McLoughlin and his team will be able to save a few people before their tragic story begins. The first tower collapses just after McLoughlin and his men have gathered enough air tanks to feel like they can begin a successful rescue. Most of McLoughlin's team is killed immediately. Only three men survive. One of those, Dom (Jay Hernandez), gets pinned by a falling piece of concrete when Tower Two collapses, and decides to shoot himself rather than wait to bleed out. Stone turns any hope the audience might have felt for something positive against them almost as quickly as he creates that hope.

Stone does, however, frame McLoughlin as the only person who has any insight of what to do. When the first tower falls, McLoughlin sees what is happening in front of him and shouts through a slow-motion sequence of images "the elevator shaft" in an effort to give his team the best chance for survival. A 180-degree cut assumes a position just behind where McLoughlin stood that allows the audience to see what the sergeant had seen. The sequence of who sees what and when reveals the choice Stone will make throughout his film to set his audience within the experience of McLoughlin and his subordinate, Will. In this way, Stone sets his audience in some space between movie-reality and actual-reality. For example, Stone chooses to frame the men's attempt to escape the worst part of the collapse by diving into the elevator shaft in the way one might frame a scene in a film like *The Day After Tomorrow* (2004), which details the world coming apart. He refuses to follow the documentary-like approach Greengrass maintained. In this in-between space, Stone exploits cinema's ability to cut between stories to explore the depths of tragedy involved in the story he tells. His plot often cuts to details from the personal lives of the two men his story considers. The purpose, it would seem, is to make the story more tragic. For instance, as it relates to John, the plot typically inserts moments involving his son, JJ (Anthony Piccininni), who becomes the one character in the story to refuse to accept that his father has been lost. An early exchange between John's wife, Donna (Maria Bello), and JJ shows the son asking about whether or not Dad will be home to celebrate the child's birthday. The mom evades the question, choosing instead to inform JJ that his dad intends to take him to a Yankees playoff game. The information creates in the viewer the same feelings they might feel listening to the Greengrass's travelers talk about work plans that they may or may not be able to realize. One is left to wonder how many plans like this did not come off following 9/11, which increases the weight of the tragedy Stone asks his audience to witness.

Stone rarely creates space in the flashbacks he sets in his plot for audiences to remake what they have seen. The assumption is that to do so would be to dishonor the actual testimony Stone claims at the beginning of his film to be following. Each insert favors a strong sense of sentimentality over exploration or the kind of spectatorial identification that pulls viewers from the emotions they might have already felt having witnessed the trauma firsthand. The inserts meant to explain what would make Will's death so tragic work in the same way. This is presumably the intent of the introduction of Will's wife, Allison (Maggie Gyllenhaal), which twice marks the fact that the young wife is pregnant. Later narrative inserts play on this point, too. During what might be explained as a flashback motivated by Will's story of his five-months-pregnant wife, the camera frames Will and Allison in bed talking about what to name their second child. Will wants to name the child Alyssa. Allison wants Olivia. The couple do not settle the debate in that moment. The plot returns to Will and John, and the two men presumably continue the discussion that was taking place just before the flashback. Will writes a note to his wife, "I heart U A." A cut returns the audience to the Jimeno residence. Allison comes down the stairs to announce that she is going to name the baby Alyssa: "It's what Will wanted," she explains. When the action returns to the rubble, Will asks John to announce "over the radio that [he requests his] daughter be named Olivia," and he asks that John have them tell "Allison that [he loves] her, and that she should name [his daughter] Olivia." John obliges Will. He makes the announcement. The narrative sequences cooperate to produce a heartbreaking sense of tragedy.

The flashbacks as a whole consistently generate an appreciable sense of tragedy. Flashbacks are frequently used in stories of trauma, as Janet Walker admits (see above), to mirror the fractures trauma creates. Stone uses flashback differently. The flashbacks actually begin to create a sense of coherence, which also begins to account for the ways in which Stone's film becomes a record and performance of 9/11 rather than a film allowing audiences to move through that experience. This sense of coherence is particularly strong across the flashbacks associated with John. After watching John tell Will about his four kids, and that the couple had their last child "late," the plot cuts to the day Donna discovers she is pregnant. John sits on the edge of the bed clearly concerned about what the future will hold if she is pregnant. John seems just as concerned only to play the part of the loving husband when the pregnancy test reports that the couple is pregnant. Another flashback a few scenes later establishes the extent to which John is also a loving father.

Donna watches as John teaches JJ how to cut a board. The patient father tells his son "not to force it." John looks up and sees Donna and smiles. A third flashback continues to develop the small pleasures the couple takes in one another and their family. Donna hears John working on the roof while she is in their bedroom. John strikes his thumb with a hammer and Donna leans out the window to tease him. Again, the couple smile at each other. These memories confirm the point John and Donna will discover in an imaginative discussion late in John's ordeal. John wonders if he loved Donna "good, like [he] was supposed to." Donna responds the couple "had it . . . in the moments." The audience knows she is telling the truth. Stone's flashbacks have focused on those moments that have shown what the couple enjoyed together. They also explain what motivates John to hold on to his life throughout what gets revealed to be an agonizing experience. Again, Stone implies this function throughout the film before confirming it with an explicit statement when John sees Donna in the hospital. The husband admits what the audience already knows: "You kept me alive." Stone's flashbacks have already suggested this point. John's explicit statement ensures that the audience does not miss this point or the emotional experience these points have caused in the character.

 Stone's final focus matches the formative approach throughout his plot. Stone consistently marks the emotional response his viewers should be having by creating emotional moments that are likely to overwhelm spectators rather than provide them an opportunity to explore the nuances of what they are seeing or feeling. This point is particularly on display during John and Will's discussion over the regret they feel for costing others their lives. Will regrets Rodrigues (Armando Riesco) pushing the cart of air tanks for him, which put him in the place Will would have occupied when the first building collapsed and killed most of the men. He regrets having begged Dom to try to free him when the character could have saved himself had Will let him go. John bemoans bringing the men into the building: "What good did we do?" Will tries to help John feel better: "We wanted to go in. Kassimatis said you were the best. You were the guy who knew everything down here. . . . nothing was gonna stop [us] from trying to help. We figured we might as well follow the best guy in." John thanks Will for his words just before another round of rubble falls around them. As that wave washes over them, John and Will begin to pray. Will offers a prayer of thanksgiving for his wife and daughter. John prays the words of the Lord's Prayer. The sequence comes to an end when John utters the lines, "forgive us our trespasses as we forgive those who trespass against us." Both prayers give viewers a reason to honor the men on screen, just as their regret gives audiences a reason to honor them. Stone's point is clear: these men deserve all the honor society can give them. The argument certainly holds for almost any who see it, but it also ensures that viewers remain inside the trauma rather than above it. The job of the viewer is merely to recognize the story that took place, not to move through it. In this way, Stone's film is strongly prefocused toward not only how one is to see these characters, but how one is to receive them as well.

Stone continues to create a strongly prefocused film that erases any uncertainty about what his characters represent as the plot moves toward John and Will's rescue. The above described scene that involves the men's praying ends with a brightly lit scene that gives way to a stereotypical-looking Jesus, who happens to carry a bottle of water with him. The image lingers on the screen for a few seconds before disappearing into a brightly lit circle of light. Stone uses this circle of light as a motif throughout the remainder of the film that associates certain people with some concept of Jesus. The stylistic choice expands the connotative circle for Jesus by including, first, Dave Karnes (Michael Shannon), the Marine who earlier responded to God's calling to go to the site, and later defies everyone's orders to see if he can find some survivors. His flashlight appears to answer the foreshadowing the earlier light predicts when it finds Will's face, and he promises to stay with Will until he is rescued: "We're not leaving you, buddy. We're Marines. You are our mission." A similar light appears later when John is pulled from the site. When the light fades and the scene becomes visible, an overwhelming number of people are shown aligned along a trail that has been carved to carry the survivors to more level ground. Each person becomes a visual extension of the first image of Christ who was shown reaching out to Will and/or John, depending on who saw the image.

The final voice-over delivered by John at the end of the film makes explicit the visual argument the Christ-as-light motif suggests throughout the film: "9/11 showed us what humans are capable of. The evil, yeah, sure. But it also brought out a goodness we forgot could exist. People taking care of each other for no other reason that it was the right thing to do. . . . It's important for us to talk about that good, to remember." The inclusion of this terminal speech aligns nearly everything that occurs before it into a well-constructed visual and rhetorical argument about 9/11, which turns Stone's *World Trade Center* into something of a moving memorial. It remembers the "2749 people died at the World Trade Center . . . including citizens from 87 countries." It makes sure that each of the 343 New York City firemen, 84 Port Authority employees, and 23 New York City police lives lost responding to the collective trauma are registered. It also reminds viewers how few people were actually pulled from the rubble: "Only 20 people were pulled out alive. Will and John were numbers 18 and 19." Other title cards let audiences know that those who were saved from the rubble faced a long road to recovery: "Will had 8 surgeries in 13 days. John was put into a medically-induced coma for 6 weeks to allow for 27 surgeries." Stone seems especially interested in exploring the extent to which the traumas started on 9/11 continue to be felt long after that day. The final title card makes this interest transparent: Stone dedicates his film to "the fallen men and women of the Port Authority Police Department . . . and for all those who fought, died, and were wounded that day." This last phrase does what the film does, namely, stretches the trauma beyond the events at the site of the World Trade Center. There were people wounded across America and other parts of the world on 9/11. Stone seems to want to honor those wounds as much as anything else.

Daldry's *Extremely Loud and Incredibly Close* takes a different approach to 9/11. The film begins with the familiar only to extend the story beyond the original traumas registered on September 11, 2001. The film begins, in fact, with an extreme closeup of what audiences would immediately recognize as a reference to the images of people falling from the towers. The camera captures one shoe and then another, a leg, and then a shoulder and the side of a man's face as he presumably falls through the sky. The vertical lines of these images begin to give way to another image, the face of Daldry's hero, nine-year-old Oskar Schell, whose father, Thomas (Tom Hanks) died in the towers on 9/11. The audience would not know this backstory in this opening moment unless they also knew Foer's novel on which the film is based. In either case, the cinematography captures equally well for those who know the novel and for those who do not that this image of a man falling from the sky, be it the little boy's father or not, has fractured something in the boy. Daldry's film shows this by mixing the images of the man falling with the face of the boy in the closet. The face of the boy eventually overwhelms the images of the man falling. Oskar's face remains heavily shadowed as his opening voice-over begins, and the audience learns of his idea for "skyscrapers for dead people that were built." The idea, itself, is more ambiguous than it appears, and this ambiguity is more useful than it might seem at first glance. One could contend the idea for skyscrapers for dead people might be little more than an extension of what skyscrapers have come to represent for Oskar, namely, death. His father does die in a skyscraper, or, if what is implied in the opening images is true, falling from the sky. With this knowledge in place, one could understand Oskar's idea as a literal projection of the metaphor already in his mind. At the same time, the idea could be seen as an adaptation of the world as it is currently constructed. The current world will one day face the problem Oskar perceives: "One day, there isn't going to be room to bury people anymore." The young boy's idea might be a legitimate response from a nine-year-old perspective to that problem. His idea works more as a reworking of the world than a sign of trauma. Most accurately, the idea is probably both, and a succinct representation of Oskar's placement in some space between trauma and adaptation at the beginning of the film.

Daldry's film remains in this place between trauma and adaption, too, both as it relates to Oskar and to the audience that watches his story. The film assigns Oskar and the audience a space between either reexperiencing the trauma of 9/11 or beginning to move from one's initial experience of those events. The difference between reexperiencing the trauma or moving beyond it depends, at least for Oskar, on the character's ability to identify with the characters he meets and to participate in the ongoing adaptation of the images he imagines related to 9/11. Spectators' ability to experience something other than ongoing trauma depends on these same two abilities. To move through the traumatic experiences associated with 9/11, they, too, must begin to identify with emotions and stories beyond their own experience and to become willing to participate in the ongoing adaptation of the stories that only begin on 9/11.

Daldry explicitly admits the reward Oskar can experience by learning to identify with others and by beginning to participate in the ongoing adaptation of his own trauma. The plot of the film registers the need for both lessons in Oskar's life. In terms of his need to identify with others, Oskar admits in a voice-over that his father, Thomas, would invent expeditions so that his son "would have to talk to people, which [his dad] knew he had a hard time doing." The search for New York's missing sixth borough is the prime example, but the game Oskar imagines his father arranged for him to find the lock that fits the key he left him also illustrates the need for Oskar to identify with others. When combined with the ideas of spectatorial identification, one might consider both "reconnaissance expeditions" a kind of recreation of the act of watching a film, especially a film that details trauma. Each new character, each new scenario forces audiences "to talk to people" in stories they might otherwise struggle to see and hear. Spectatorial identification can pull one into new relationships, first with fictional characters and then with oneself. Oskar's need to adapt—or, in the language of this book, to rewatch his memories of 9/11 in a range of ways—develops more slowly but no less observably.

Daldry's film reveals the benefits of spectatorial identification and ongoing adaptation at the end of Oskar's journey to find the lock that matches the key he suspects his father has left for him. The revelation scene at the end of the movie shared by Oskar and his mother (Sandra Bullock) brings this aspect of the story to the film's surface. Oskar admits to his mother a common denominator about the "472 people named Black" he encountered: "So many of them had lost something or someone, mom." His mom's response, "Just like us," is interesting if only because it resonates with the simulation construction of identification, which brings into focus the extent to which her comment is at once accurate and inaccurate. The losses each person suffered were, in a general sense, like their losses; but they were also different, and this difference is especially important as it relates to trauma studies, and adaptation studies as well. The differences provide a point of departure from individual trauma, because a return to the well-known details associated with 9/11 provides spectators a chance to renegotiate these images, which is to say to move beyond the trauma these details generated. Every encounter with a person who shares in the experience a traumatized person tries to keep as his own creates space for some renegotiation of one's own experience to take place.

Extremely Loud and Incredibly Close reveals what this renegotiation looks like in two flashbacks that play during Oskar's discussion with Mr. William Black (Jeffrey Wright), the rightful owner of the key Oskar believes his father has left him. Mr. Black recounts how he had unknowingly passed the key to Oskar's father, Thomas, at an estate sale when he gave Thomas a blue vase. While Mr. Black talks, the camera returns to the exchange, or at least some version of it. Mr. Black's voice-over narration contradicts the certainty of the images, which suggests that what Mr. Black is saying may or may not be the actual event as it happened. A gap opens between what happens in some real time and some real space and how one remembers those events to have taken place. The conflict between the narration and the image locates the flashback in the present. The moment seems to respond to the *Kairos* of ongoing adaptation rather than some desire to give an accurate testimony. Daldry's choice allows the moments in the past to be nothing more or less than plot points meant to convey a particular sense of a story, a story that might change in some ways the next time it is told, depending on who is telling it and to whom. Such is the nature of stories.

These same points are on display again during a second flashback played during Mr. Black's conversation with Oskar. Mr. Black relates the story of how he tried to relocate the key by hanging signs asking the man with the blue vase from the estate sale to contact him. Given that his attempts were occurring one week after 9/11, though, his advertisement had to compete with thousands of signs posted by families and friends trying to locate loved ones. As before, a voice-over plays over visuals that affirm what Mr. Black says. This affirmation gives way a moment later when Mr. Black passes Oskar and his mother as they hang a poster for Thomas. The camera suddenly stops following Mr. Black. It holds on Oskar as if to suggest the person having this flashback has suddenly shifted from Mr. Black to Oskar. The "memory," which becomes something other than a memory, suddenly belongs to Oskar. The subsequent events in this sequence support the idea that what began as Mr. Black's memory becomes Oskar's when Oskar turns and sees Mr. Black standing a few paces from him. Oskar presumably watches as Mr. Black spins in place before Oskar's mother says it is time to leave. Oskar's memory of one event expands in a way it would not have without his meeting, his having identified, with Mr. Black. The scene begins to accept a different indexical quality. Rather than being a sign that has been made by some literal contact with the past, the memory of sorts become a sign of the ongoing adaptation Oskar begins to perform. Oskar has returned to an early memory, as did Mr. Black before him, to reconstitute it, adapt it.

Of course, this adaptive return to an index can be off-putting to some. Some spectators may not yet be willing to identify with other stories from 9/11, to extend the story of those events beyond the day they occurred, or to adapt the images, mental or otherwise, associated with that event. These spectators have their own stories and images. They have the accepted representation of those realities. Such spectators might prefer another memorialization of 9/11, the sort *United 93* or *World Trade Center* delivers. Daldry's film very clearly tries to move beyond such an impulse. His film refuses to be authentic to the accepted or even accurate version of the tragedy it considers in the way Greengrass's film appears authentic or Stone's film ultimately becomes didactic. Daldry creates an open image of an event that begins in one place only to find another. He places that shift in the indices of his film, especially as they relate to flashbacks, which become, more accurately, instances of ongoing adaptation in some present, rather than a strict return to some past. The pasts in these moments are neither despotic nor decisive. They exist to be reconsidered and adapted. They exist in this way because the signs themselves emphasize their indexical status over their status as symbols or icons. Each image points to a reality that exists beyond the image actually set in the frame. These images, and the trauma they suggest, refuse to remain traumatized. They open themselves to a process of adaptation that finds a way through trauma.

Chapter 4

ADAPTATION

Bessel A. van der Kolk and Alexander C. McFarlane (1996) claim that "some people have adapted to terrible life events with flexibility and creativity, while others have become fixated on the trauma and gone on to lead traumatized and traumatizing existences" (3). At its most basic, the comment imagines one of two outcomes: ongoing trauma or ongoing adaptation. One has plenty of reasons to reject this binary just as one might reject most any such binary. There are, however, good reasons to consider it, especially as it relates to the idea of rewatching herein described or the set of complex cinematic indices on which that rewatching occurs. The index itself, at least as it is most typically discussed in film studies, ensures a certain kind of ongoing trauma. The diminished index is both traumatized and traumatizing. It is a sign that exists outside of space and time. It pulls spectators into a similar place, a place that is neither *there* nor *here*. To return to the language of van der Kolk and McFarlane, the diminished index participates in a more general "tyranny of the past [that] interferes with the ability to pay attention to both new and familiar situations" (4). The diminished index haunts those who see it, leading to Doane's pathos of archival desire but circumventing the *Kairos* of ongoing adaptation rewatching on the point of the cinematic index can invite.

One sees examples of this divide in the films discussed in the previous chapter. Two of those films, Greengrass's *United 93* (2006) and Stone's *World Trade Center* (2006), return audiences to some aspect of 9/11 but neither move audiences beyond that day. Nor do they mean to do so, presumably. These films move with sanctimony toward the original event. Audiences have the chance to experience that day all over again as they watch either film. In keeping with what most interests van der Kolk and McFarlane, namely, the news media, the images Greengrass and Stone place on the screen are in some ways akin to a news story. They can cause spectators to face again "the full brunt of the [original] experience" (8). Such confrontations, van der Kolk and McFarlane argue, often frustrate one's ability to process trauma, which can only ever begin when a subject finds some "personal meaning" within a trauma (9). The authors argue that personal meaning arises best when subjects, in this case spectators, discover a new sense of the event, see a new detail, or find a new way to (re)organize their original experience. They must, in short, come to adapt the event in some personal manner.

This is the process Stephen Daldry's *Extremely Loud and Incredibly Close* (2011) models. In that film, the main character, Oskar (Thomas Horn), begins to see his original experience in new ways. He sees new faces and new stories in the midst of his recollections of his initial trauma. What becomes most important about Daldry's film, at least as it relates to this study, is the way these new relations are represented indexically. Oskar does not invent an entire new reality; rather, he sees an old reality in a new way. His initial experience gives way to new experiences. In this way, Oskar's experience and Daldry's visual representation of that experience performs the process of ongoing adaptation the more complex set of indices invite. The performance permits spectators to enter a similar process. The act shows spectators how to watch and rewatch a film on the point of a cinematic index set within a cinematic reality. The signs circulating on the screen might extend from a more definite type of reality, but, as indices, they point to new realities, other signs, in just the way an index is always already pointing to another index. Once perceived, the presence of the cinematic index starts a process rather than marks a moment to recall.

This process of ongoing adaptation brings the discussion back to the binary between ongoing trauma and ongoing adaptation offered in the statement at the start of this chapter. The process being imagined, occurring on the point of a more complex set of cinematic indices, stands in direct contrast to the more accepted view of traumatic representations as they are understood within the humanities. The typical account of trauma within the humanities offers that the presence of some trauma explains why creative and ongoing adaptation cannot occur. McFarlane and van der Kolk (1996) claim that this is especially true of media representation of collective and historical traumas. Representations of traumas that have been shared in some actual experience tend to depend on a well-established set of facts. Subsequent portrayals repeatedly circulate the same details in the name of authenticity. The plots for these representations tend to be broken and full of gaps, as if to model how trauma works. The whole ordeal becomes a kind of telling-trauma-like-it-is that grants the representation an authority it would not otherwise have and, at the same time, rebuffs attempts to revise the story in some creative way. Creative revisions, in fact, get cast as an act of irreverence. Such a view treats representations of traumatic events as fixed memorials rather than the living document they can be (and will be, given enough time and space from the original event).

In keeping with Judith Lewis Herman (1992), even these fixed memorials can lead to a living document. The fixed memorials often exist for a surprising reason, namely, for "forgetting" (8). The representation of a specific trauma exists, in other words, so that audiences can forget the trauma they endured. One might list *United 93* (2006) and *World Trade Center* (2006) as two such representations. The two films function, in turn, as a kind of iconic or symbolic memorial. They name an otherwise overwhelming experience with such precision that one need not return to it again. The narrative documents what occurred, which means the audience can understand it. This act of documentation names the experience in such a way that it does not need to be reencountered. There is, in other words, no reason to adapt the experience further. Such a text, of course, stands in direct contrast to the ongoing process of adaptation the most robust notion of the cinematic index can support. The more complex set of indices leave open the possibility of revision, and they do so by reimagining the event and the experience one might have with it or because of it.

When separated from the need or desire to reify an event, the cinematic index can cause spectators to reimagine their traumatic experiences. It can encourage audiences to remake actual experiences in just the way Richard Rushton suggests fictional realities can always remake lived experiences. Such an argument depends on a looser notion of reality, or at least a looser evaluation of the reality cinema brings forward. As chapter 2 makes plain, film theorists have explored this looser cinematic reality in important ways. So, too, have trauma theorists, and especially Ruth Leys (2000). Leys identifies the ways in which most renderings of trauma, and particularly those within the humanities, tend to treat trauma as a real event that literally leaves an imprint of itself on the psyche. Leys relegates this view of trauma within a mimetic camp and argues for an alternative anti-mimetic camp opposite the more accepted mimetic view. The former depends on a fixed, internal reality, the latter on an external reality that, while imposing, exists alongside a still cogent subject. Unlike the mimetic view of trauma that assumes some event has entirely overwhelmed a subject, the anti-mimetic view of trauma allows for autonomous subjects who still possesses agency to negotiate the reality set before them. In other words, Leys finds a way for a process of ongoing adaptation from within a trauma that occurs alongside rather than over an individual.

Leys's parsing of two attitudes toward trauma creates space for a process of ongoing adaptation on the point of a complex cinematic index that otherwise might not exist. Leys imagines active spectators who maintain some autonomy from the images they watch. Their imaginative response to a complex rather than diminished cinematic index can turn the cinema into something more than simply a record of past realities. The cinema can become a way to work through trauma. A fuller discussion of Leys's criticism of the mimetic attitude toward trauma as it is discussed within the humanities and the anti-mimetic attitude that finds a way to reimagine that trauma provides a clear way to see that possibility for the cinema.

While never declaring the mimetic or the anti-mimetic the right attitude toward trauma, Leys does level sharp criticism against the two scholars she considers most responsible for a mimetic view of trauma, at least as it exists within the humanities: van der Kolk and Cathy Caruth. Leys claims that both the practitioner, van der Kolk, and the theorist, Caruth, treat trauma as a literal imprint in the brain of an otherwise external reality. Leys argues that such an understanding depends on two questionable claims: "(1) an empirical claim, according to which traumatic symptoms, such as traumatic dreams and flashbacks, are *veridical* memories or representations of the traumatic event; and (2) . . . those same symptoms are *literal* replicas or repetitions of the trauma . . . [that] stand outside the trauma" (229). Leys explains that while these two assumptions have become the starting point for most discussions of trauma in the humanities, they do bear some clear problems. Most significantly, the approach toward trauma van der Kolk and Caruth help establish treats the traumatic event both as "a completely literal record of the truth . . . and a temporal gap or aporia . . . such that [trauma] is always experienced *too late* for knowledge and representation" (231). Without saying so, Leys finds van der Kolk and Caruth landing in the same place the leading theorists on the cinematic index tend to land, in an unreconcilable contest between an unreachable *there* that turns the present into an inaccessible *here*. Leys provides a way through this contest, and she does so in a way that can further develop the *Kairos* of ongoing adaptation that occurs on the point of the index. To appreciate the ways in which Leys's approach to trauma might develop the concept of the *Kairos* of ongoing adaptation, one does well to work through her critique of, in turn, van der Kolk and Caruth.

Leys recounts the way in which van der Kolk's early discussions of trauma assumed that the dreams of combat veterans suffering trauma "were exact replicas of [their] combat experience" (237). Leys explains, "van der Kolk and his colleagues . . . [argue that] the traumatic nightmare is a unique phenomenon . . . [in relation to other anxiety dreams] precisely because [traumatic nightmares are] an accurate replica of the traumatic experience" (237). Leys claims there is plenty of evidence to contradict van der Kolk's position, yet the idea that traumatic memories are somehow accurate records of a past event has gained wide acceptance throughout the humanities. One finds evidence of this acceptance in the discussions of the cinematic index already recounted here, and most especially in Laura Mulvey (2006). Leys implicitly relates Mulvey to van der Kolk by discussing the attitude van der Kolk takes toward trauma in very nearly the same language Mulvey uses to discuss the index. Both scholars treat the index as an indicator of some past that depends on some likeness to the reality that produced it. For Mulvey, the index points to a reality before the camera. For van der Kolk, the dream replays the original trauma. In both cases, Leys argues that the scholars are discussing an icon rather than an index because both are making some likeness the defining characteristic of the resulting image. In short, the cinematic image and the traumatic nightmare deliver an icon rather than strict index.

Leys extends the criticism against iconic representations of trauma by offering that such representations are "automatic, corporeal, and nonautobiographical in character.... [they] cannot be feigned or suggested" (246). The lens-based image Mulvey imagines and the traumatic nightmare van der Kolk considers are, in the end, presented as literal representations or reenactments of an actual event. Leys unequivocally challenges such a claim, offering that van der Kolk's "ideas about the nature of icons and images are mistaken" (249). The ideas the practitioner parades rely on the assumption that "pictures and visual images ... [are] inherently nonsymbolic ... [and] that there exists a fundamental opposition between pictures and visual images ... and verbal representations" (249). Leys rejects both assumptions. Iconic signs *can* be symbolic, and, by logical extension, they can also be indexical. In keeping with Peirce, every type of sign is also a sign, which is a way to say that it can also be every type of sign. An icon can be more than icon, for example. As such, every representation plays to more than the demands of iconicity. To ignore those demands is to misunderstand the character and content of the sign itself.

Leys insists that the signs within any traumatic memory can represent more than the literal occurrence of that event. Every representation can, in other words, be more than a record or a reenactment of the initial episode. Leys contends that this possibility directly challenges van der Kolk's claim that traumatic nightmares or memories deliver an accurate representation of anything. Leys believes that van der Kolk's confidence in the traumatic memory as the representation of reality par excellence turns the initial depiction into a "sacred object or 'icon' that it would be 'sacrilege' to misappropriate or tamper with in any way" (253). The underlying attitude toward trauma van der Kolk adopts, then, ensnares one in an endless cycle of trauma. From Leys's perspective, traumatic nightmares and memories should not be taken as any more accurate than any other type of nightmare or memory. Leys offers that any other position establishes a false construct that treats the traumatic memory as an accurate depiction of a traumatic event that must be distorted if not falsified each time it is represented. Such is the way memories work. One can speculate that this is also how spectators encounter representations of trauma when they do so on the point of the index rather than a shape or likeness of the symbol or icon. This possibility exists even if the standard practice is to treat the representation itself as a true impression of a past event, one that can only be misrepresented if altered.

Leys addresses this idea most directly in her criticism of Cathy Caruth's widely accepted position on trauma. Leys argues that Caruth's opinion ultimately succumbs to the same issues that threaten van der Kolk's argument. Most specifically, Leys faults Caruth for treating trauma as a "*literal* registration of the traumatic event that, dissociated from normal mental processes of cognition, cannot be known or represented" (266). The trauma Leys sees Caurth describing can only return to the subject and only belatedly. Leys suggests that Caruth's approach more neatly matches Paul de Man's performative theory of language than it does any established tradition within trauma studies. Caruth's attitude toward trauma more accurately matches de Man's views on performative language, in which words can only be "perform[ed], reenact[ed], or reexperience[ed] . . . in the forms of flashbacks, dreams, and related symptoms" (267). From this view, trauma can be seen as a loop that ensnares subjects so that the original event can only be reexperienced again and again and just as it was initially experienced. No recollection of the event ever properly breaks from the reality that has been firmly established through the repeated performance of that experience. Leys explains that such a view treats traumatic memories as an actual experience rather than a representation. The remembrance of any experience can only operate according to the rules established in the initial experience. The recalled experience operates "simultaneously as an ineluctable process of infection and as involving an ethical obligation on the part of the listener" that enculturates audiences into a history of trauma that "must not, indeed cannot, be cured but simply transmitted, passed on" (269). Reception becomes an ongoing extension of trauma when left within this history of trauma. One is left with nothing more but the pathos of the literal, as the title of Leys's chapter on Caruth makes plain.

Leys contends that Caruth sidesteps the more concerning aspects of this position by treating trauma as a "*critical concept*" rather than a term that possesses a particular genealogy. Leys argues that Caruth tolerates this shift because it satisfies the scholar's commitment to a "performative theory of language" (275). Caruth turns to the ideas within trauma theory she does, Leys offers, and especially those passages she quotes from Freud, to uncover the "*thematizations* . . . of certain privileged figures and tropes," rather than careful readings of the earlier theorist's work (279). Leys points to Caruth's discussion of nightmares as one example of such treatment. Caruth grounds her view of traumatic memories in a reading of Freud that Leys claims simply does not exist. In an extended note, Leys explains how Freud never claims what Caruth says he claims, namely that "traumatic neurosis becomes the paradigm not only of all neurosis but more broadly for what shapes every individual life" (273). Leys alleges that this claim depends on a generalization of Freud rather than an actual argument. From Leys's perspective, Caruth too quickly aligns Freud with those who consider the traumatic memory to be "a literal memory of the traumatic event" (274). Leys insists that Freud never states this idea; to the contrary, Leys states that for Freud trauma is never the literal repetition of an actual event. Freud always allows for some displacement and condensation. There is, in other words, some adjustment of the memory rather than a simple replaying of it. The acts of displacement and condensation make every memory unstable in ways Leys claims Caruth ignores.

Leys ultimately prefers an unstable view of trauma and the way it has been studied over the last hundred years to the one she finds in either van der Kolk or Caruth (298). She claims that trauma itself alternates between a view in which the traumatic image can be trusted and one in which it cannot. The former operates from the mimetic view of trauma, which holds that the trauma is literally realized within the mind of the traumatized. The external world makes a reliable and inexorable imprint in the mind. Even as an event disrupts normal forms of cognition, the mimetic view holds that trauma exists as an external event that makes a definite impression on the mind of the one who experiences it. This impression will exist in the mind of the sufferer even as the sufferer remains unable to access it or articulate it properly. It can be performed or repeated, but never engaged, not without some type of recovery—the kind of recovery hypnosis provides, for example. The counter to this idea moves within an anti-mimetic climate that leaves the traumatic event itself outside the subject. Such a placement allows if not necessitates that the trauma be engaged, adjusted, and interpreted like any other sight or experience. Rather than impressing some reality on the mind, Leys explains that the anti-mimetic attitude argues that there always remains a "fully constituted subject" no matter what "befalls" that person (299). The original event, the trauma, can be remembered. It can also be reconstituted and remade when it is recalled; in fact, it is meant to be refashioned.

The recognition of two traumatic traditions, the mimetic and the anti-mimetic, does not neutralize the value of the divide van der Kolk and McFarlane mark in the quote at the top of this chapter: "some people have adapted to terrible life events with flexibility and creativity, while others have become fixated on the trauma and gone on to lead traumatized and traumatizing existences." Leys' criticism can invigorate rather than frustrate this statement. Truth be told, one can come to adapt a terrible event through either attitude. Neither the mimetic nor the anti-mimetic attitude naturally leads to adaption or trauma. One can, in other words, reexperience literal experiences even when they are understood from a mimetic perspective. Imitation can, after all, lead to adaptation. Repetition can lead to accidental alteration, the kinds of alterations that push or pull a text or an experience in some unexpected direction. A reminder that repetition is but one response does, however, wrestle movies depicting trauma from the constraints they might otherwise feel to recall an event in a particular way. Those who dramatize a trauma or watch such dramatizations can do something other than memorialize the event they depict or see depicted. Another option is to provide a looser adaptation, one that begins to set the trauma in motion rather than holding it in a fixed frame. The choice to imitate or not may only really matter when there is technically not a choice on offer. The inability to choose to imitate or not is trauma. The decision to imitate, just as the decision to refuse to imitate, are both adaptive choices. From this view, Gus Van Sant's 1998 remake of Alfred Hitchcock's *Psycho* (1960) is an adaptation both when it matches Hitchcock and when it does not, a perspective Fernando Canet (2018) aptly articulates.

The traumatized mind still suffering from trauma does not have a choice of whether to imitate or not. Those minds suffer what E. Ann Kaplan and Ban Wang (2004) describe as an "irredeemable breakdown in the psyche, representation, and language" (4). The mind suffering trauma must imitate the traumatic event, replaying it repeatedly and without variation. The trauma comes to possess those who suffer it, and, just as concerningly for Kaplan and Wang, it "may push trauma into the mystified circle of the occult, something untouchable and unreachable" (8). Such placement frustrates any opportunity for adaptation. Some theoretical arguments even reinforce such fixity, and they do so across a culture consumed by trauma even as that culture consumes stories of trauma.

Kaplan and Wang work to cross the gap trauma theorists sometimes manufacture between trauma and adaptation by shifting attention away from how a traumatic event marks an individual to consider the means by which movies about trauma can mark the viewer. Kaplan and Wang identify four positions. Two of the positions separate the spectator from the trauma in one degree or another. The first of these two positions simply introduces spectators to some trauma. Kaplan and Wang regard melodrama to be given to this type of depiction of trauma. The authors offer Hitchcock's *Spellbound* (1945) or *Marnie* (1964) as examples. The traumas in melodramas like these tend to feature "a discrete past event, locatable, representable, and curable" (9). The introduction of these past events means to reinforce the idea that the trauma has been cured. The second of these two positions turns the spectator into a voyeur. Spectators watch stories of various "catastrophes such as airplane crashes, deaths of famous people, ethnic wars" in the way one would watch a live action news report (10). The film places the spectator in a position to see the event even if they can do nothing more than observe it. The event does, after all, move on the screen rather than in the real world. From these first two positions, the spectator is there to see trauma as an external reality.

The other two positions Kaplan and Wang describe bring the spectator into the trauma in some way. The first of these two positions brings the spectator to the shock of trauma. Spectators are "vicariously traumatized" as the representation tries to bring them into the trauma (9). Kaplan and Wang offer David Cronenberg's *The Brood* (1979) and *The Fly* (1986) as two specific examples. They also more generally mention "some Holocaust films." The implication is that some Holocaust films work to produce the sensation of trauma rather than simply show it. The second of the positions that bring spectators into trauma works differently. It moves spectators from being mere observers or experiencers of a trauma to witnesses. Kaplan and Wang list Maya Deren's *Meshes of the Afternoon* (1943), Alain Resnais's *Night and Fog* (1956) and *Hiroshima, mon amour* (1959), and Andrew Cymek's *Night Cries* (2015) as examples of films that want spectators to witness the onscreen trauma rather than suffer the horrors their films depict. Each of these films works to turn spectators into part of the defense against such catastrophes from ever happening again. They become part of the solution to trauma.

Kaplan and Wang claim that this last position is made possible only when moviemakers avoid a mistake: "it is a mistake to think that investment in the abysmal, unrepresentable quality of trauma is the only way to be fair to the traumatized and injured, or the proper way to remain open-ended and to defy metaphysical, sensationalist or ideological closure" (12). Kaplan and Wang wager that the better way is to treat traumatic stories as "an episode in a longer chain of structural mutations in modern systems that have accumulated a record of violence, suffering, and misery" (12). They are representations or, more accurately, signs, "indexes to the still unfolding traumas of a history—the history of modernity—that has become synonymous with trauma and shocks" (12). To refuse to do anything more than imitate or copy these indices is to go the way of the most limited view of the impoverished index, which might only record some past reality that was, and to set that reality, at least for one fleeting moment, *there*. It is to deny the imagination space to do the work it can do to move one through trauma. In keeping with Kaplan and Wang, "these acts . . . are imaginary, because given the depleted and exhausted cultural resources, little but the imagination is readily available for the reinvention of new narratives, new social forms" (13). In keeping with the argument of this book, these new narratives and new social forms can find their beginning in the various expressions of the cinematic index, which can only operate as a link, an episode, in a longer chain of signification.

Admittedly, for the cinematic index to spur the spectator in the way it can, it must gain some distance from the restrictive perspective a belief in the originary moment will often promote. One can find a way to achieve this distance by turning to the discussion of the "original" within adaptation studies. As Dudley Andrew's (1985/2012) essay admits, a belief in the original plays an important role in early film adaptations. Andrew estimates that "well over half of all commercial films have come from literary originals" (66). Among other things, the adapted story will already have a ready-made audience. Financiers can protect their investment by circulating stories that people already enjoy or respect. The adaptation can borrow from the already established successes of its predecessor. Andrew explains, "the adaptation hopes to win an audience by the prestige [or presumed popularity] of its borrowed title or subject" (67). One could rightly list the steady succession of adaptations of canonical and popular literary texts as examples of this type of borrowing. Films based on Shakespeare or Dickens, on the one hand, or Stephen King or J. K. Rowling, on the other, all hope to lean into the status and acceptance of the texts they adapt. In certain cases, a general borrowing turns into what Andrew deems "intersecting," which occurs when an adapted text tries to preserve "the uniqueness of the original text" as much as possible (67). Andrew cites Robert Bresson's *Diary of a Country Priest* (1951) and André Bazin's praise of that film as the quintessential example of intersection: "Bazin . . . claimed that in this instance we are presented not with an adaptation so much as a refraction of the original" (67). In this mode, an adaptation not only needs to admit its source to secure an audience, but it also needs to meet its obligation to that source by presenting the original "as it was."

Andrew bemoans the discussion scholars have at the service of this second obligation. He suggests such patronage leads to "the most frequent and tiresome discussion of adaptation . . . [which] concerns fidelity and transmission" (68). What begins as an occurrence for financial reasons turns into a matter of critical importance. The adapted text begins to exist beneath the tyranny of the original. The significance of the original begins to operate with the same inescapable authority of the event in the attitudes toward trauma Leys challenges. Andrew turns to E. H. Gombrich's discussion to highlight this attitude at its most extreme. From the position Andrew sees Gombrich fashioning, adaptation becomes something of a game of "matching" (69). By following the matches that exist between the adapted and adapting texts, one can isolate the constraints found in competing systems of meaning. Andrew concedes that such an interest can highlight meaningful attributes about adaptations and other types of texts, but he does not accept that the correspondences between an adapting and an adapted text are the only or even the most interesting aspect of an adaptation. The mode of adaptation any single adaptation exhibits is often more interesting, because the way an adaptation works, or how an audience comes to experience it, tends to invite more engaging discussions than does whether an adaptation is or is not the original. A focus on mode searches for, among other things, the function of a text, which can more properly highlight the indexical qualities of a text and the process of ongoing adaptation those qualities can occasion anew in every encounter. These indexical qualities exist when a text keeps to an original and when it does not. Those who see these indexical qualities can follow the point of either cinematic index, as the one leads back to the original, and the other leads to a reality not yet imagined or represented in either text.

The current epoch seems inclined to gloss either indexical point. Scholars are more attuned to icons and symbols. Even those who discuss the index tend to find themselves stumbling into discussions of icons and symbols. A turn toward the side of adaptation studies that focuses on process over product, on what it means to be adapting a text rather than to encounter an adapted text, can draw scholars back to a fuller discussion of the indexical. Adaptation theorists have already addressed some of the most frequent obstacles to seeing something more than iconic and symbolic signs. They have done so by measuring the role of the original alongside the adaptation, by working to overcome the wider preference for the written word to the visual image, and by describing the process adaptations enter and invite spectators to enter. Each of these clarifications, especially when contrasted alongside the insights of trauma studies, can rehabilitate indexical thinking, and highlight the ways in which rewatching on the point of the cinematic index can occur.

The form of rewatching being imagined here is something different from a simple return to a text. A simple return might be more akin to reexperiencing a film than rewatching it. The term *rewatching* is the preferred term here because it includes the word *watching*, which is taken as something more active than experiential. A sharper contrast between trauma and adaptation, here taken as a literary device meant to denote an active process of reading or watching a text, can clarify the full force of rewatching. One of the first ways to contrast trauma studies and adaptation studies is to consider the ways in which the discussion of "the event" within trauma studies is not unlike the early discussions of "the original" within adaptation studies. Both considerations make some allowance to cast the event and the original as an originary moment, one that threatens to determine all moments after it. Both consider the extent to which what follows the original event can only ever be an accurate or inaccurate copy of that moment. The discussion within adaptation studies has progressed a bit more on this front than the one in trauma studies. This forward movement is of interest, and especially so once the earlier comments on the original and the priorities used to justify that concept have been explored.

As almost any introduction to adaptation studies will note, the early years of the field were almost always set to measure the film against the book, the eventual expression to the original one. Robert Stam (2005) begins his discussion of the conversation by admitting an undeniable preference for the text being adapted, especially when that text is a film. The adapted text routinely needed to be defended against what was taken as obvious forms of "'infidelity,' 'betrayal,' 'deformation,' 'violation,' 'bastardization,' 'vulgarization,' and 'desecration'" (3). From Stam's view, these charges often stem from a prioritization of the literary and written word over the filmic and visual. The written word conveyed in literature is just more original. The visual image expressed in film is only derivative, either of the world it steals or, in the case of an adaptation, the text it vandalizes. Stam attributes several scholarly miscalculations to this view. Scholars, Stam suggests, tend to treat "the older arts [as] necessarily better arts"; the older arts have the chance to "accrue prestige over time" (4). They also think in dichotomies, so that two things must compete against one another. The old competes against the new. The visual competes against the written. What comes will have to secure its place alongside what has been. Such is the way of scholarly thinking, and that way of thinking both establishes an idea of the original and sets the original above anything that follows it.

Stam offers that there also exists a general "hostility . . . [toward] the visual arts" that keeps a film from standing over or even alongside a literary text. Stam relates this hostility to two attitudes, iconoclasm and logophilia. As it relates to iconoclasm, Stam summarizes the long-running argument against signification that depends on "illusion" (5). It is Plato's cave in all its expressions, confident that there exists an ideal form and a copy. The copy must be rejected so that the original is not tarnished. The same idea undergirds those who "exalt . . . the written word as the privileged medium of communication" (6). Such valorization regards anything but the written word as lesser than. The visual can be too "fleshy," too "obscene" (6). It plays against the tenants of puritanical decency. Stam list three other reasons for an accepted hostility toward films. Films are thought to accept mindless consumption. They are enjoyed by the masses rather than the elite. As such, cinematic adaptations are thought to be parasitic: "they burrow into the body of the source text and steal its vitality" (7). The film can never be better than the book, in part, because the film is never the book. It is a film, and, as Stam shows, there are any number of misgivings about film and other forms of visual art.

As Stam goes on to explain, these misgivings toward film only add to a more general misgiving toward copies. The original is always preferred to the copy even if the original is also a copy of something. Stam suggests: "the 'original' always turns out to be partially 'copied' from something earlier: the *Odyssey* goes back to anonymous oral formulaic stories, *Don Quixote* goes back to chivalric romances, *Robinson Crusoe* goes back to travel journalism, and so on ad infinitum" (8). The point Stam wants to establish is that there hardly exists a true original. There are but expressions. Some are favored, others are not. The reasons for these preferences become more interesting than the preferences themselves. Why, for instance, does society continue to push the idea of an original even though it knows that such a thing hardly ever exists? Why must some texts be elevated while others are subjugated? Stam shows that the birth of the "posts," post-structuralism, post-modernism, post-most anything, should unseat such treatment: "all signifying practices . . . [are] worthy of the same careful scrutiny. . . . the very category of the literary as an unstable, open-ended configuration . . . [should make] for a more tolerant view" of expressions earlier stripped of their literary value (8–9). In the age of the "posts," every expression has some literary capacity. It is the task of the interlocutor to uncover that capacity.

Walter Benjamin's essay, "The Task of the Translator" (1921/1969), expresses some of the responsibilities those wanting to consider the literary qualities of a text must accept. Benjamin's essay may seem like a strange text to introduce into this discussion. Benjamin begins his essay favoring some of the very things Stam tries to undermine. Benjamin believes in the original. He boasts of the way art exists regardless of whether it is ever engaged or not. Benjamin delivers his opening statements with a distinction between translation and translatability already in mind. Translation, Benjamin explains, "is a form" that accepts the "laws . . . within the original" (254). It means to carry that which exists in one place to another. This is something altogether different from translatability, which deals not in carrying forward one life from one place to another, but rather in the "afterlife" of a text (254). "The history of the great works of art," Benjamin explains, "tells us about their descent from prior models, their realization in the age of the artist, and what in principle should be their eternal afterlife in succeeding generations" (255). The translations that extend from translatability realize their own "fame . . . they do not so much serve the works [they translate] as owe their existence to [them]" (255). They testify to the embryo, which exists as a partial beginning rather than a fully developed form. Benjamin argues that any text that possesses translatability can also exist as an embryo rather than a mature expression. Mature expressions, after all, have said what they mean to say. Their form is as certain as the linguistic markers that fill that form. Embryos are more uncertain, or, more properly, indeterminate.

Benjamin challenges that the task of the translator is to exhibit the indeterminacy of the original. The translator is to bring the original into its afterlife, which is to ensure it "undergoes a change" that matches changes in language, taste, or historical perspective (256). These changes do not deny the original its essence. They pursue it by bringing one expression of a text into concert with another. Collectively, the co-presence of the two texts, or mutual presence of multiple texts, realizes the "totality" of the text that cannot be recovered in any one expression (257). This idea leads Benjamin to contend "that all translation is only a somewhat provisional way of coming to terms with the foreignness of languages" (257). The translation pushes "the original . . . into higher and purer linguistic air" (257). The task of the translator, Benjamin concludes, is to find the "echo of the original," to outline a path through the forest that the original did not take, in fact, could not take, located as it was in its own linguistic and cultural contexts. The translator moves beyond those specific limitations by bringing the text into a new set of limitations, every bit as limiting but nonetheless new. The novelty of those contexts brings forward new dimensions of the original, making the translation an original reflection of the version of the text that was initial rather than singular. The translator can only be faithful to the initial text by being unfaithful to the limits that initially shaped it: "fidelity in the translation of individual words can almost never fully reproduce the sense they have in the original" (259). The new words will redress the words that were, refashioning them to another time and place.

Translators will realize Benjamin's ideal when they imitate "the original's way of meaning" rather than any specific detail from the original (260). The translation is to remain "transparent . . . not cover[ing] the original," but shining a light on it, by "liberat[ing] the language imprisoned in a work in [the] re-creation of that work" (260–61). An adaptation can perform this same task. Without any reference to Benjamin, Lesley Stern (2000) shows how an adaptation can perform the work of a translator. Stern's discussion of *Clueless* (1995) as *Emma*, the character Jane Austen writes, and *Emma* (1815), the novel Austen places that character in, shows the way a cinematic adaptation can bring the adapted text into a new light and liberate it from its original linguistic and cultural limits. As Stern explains, "by reading *Emma* through the lens of a contemporary genre—the teen movie—and by rendering this teen world through a predominantly feminine consciousness, [Amy Heckerling] has exercised the sort of fictionally ethnographic exploration epitomized by Austen" (223). From Stern's view, Heckerling asks the same questions Austen asks even if she uses different words in the process. Austen and Heckerling alike exhibit "an utterly engaging impulse—an impulse at once utopian and comic—to remake or refashion the world" (225). The commonality pulls the two texts together in a way a literal translation of Austen for the late twentieth century never could. A literal translation would feel foreign and out of place in the new context. Heckerling's film feels at home in its context and with Austen's text. In Benjamin's language, the film uncovers the translatability of initial text, and brings it into a new realm. The two texts together convey a totality that neither could deliver on its own.

Another example of a discussion within adaptation studies of the adapted and adapting text conveying a totality that neither can achieve on their own appears in Robert Stam's essay "Revisionist Adaptation" (2017). Stam focuses on various adaptations "that dramatically transform and revitalize their source texts through provocative changes in locale, epoch, casting, genre, perspective, performance modes, or production processes" (239). Some examples Stam offers include *West Side Story*, a reset of *Romeo and Juliet*, which first finds the form that interests Stam in a 1957 Broadway musical, and later in a 1961 movie directed by Robert Wise and Jerome Robbins. Stam also mentions Tim Blake Nelson's *O* (2001), a retelling of *Othello*, and Michael Almereyda's *Hamlet* (2000), which changes the realm of Shakespeare's play from a castle to a corporation. These and other productions Stam mentions exhibit a "communalization of textual transmission" that Stam grounds in Gérard Genette's five categories of transtextuality: intertextuality, paratextuality, metatextuality, architextuality, and hypertextuality. Stam claims that any of these five types of transtextuality can lift a text beyond

> the fetishism of a single text and the sacralization of the solitary author-genius . . . [by] appealing to a broad relationality between texts and other texts (the intertext), between texts and surrounding

discourses (paratext), and between genres of discourse (architext), while also extending the concept to refer to the critique of anterior texts (metatext), and to the posterior revisionist adaptation of texts (hypertext). (241)

Every instance of transtextuality moves both the earlier text and the text being encountered into "networks of socially shared meaning" where neither text must stand entirely alone. The richness of any text is developed with attention to what is within and what is beyond the specific details within its frame.

The process Stam describes can realize the priorities Benjamin assigns the translator. As Stam states, "the update of a novel is obliged to discard historically obsolete laws" (245). Stam means this sentence literally; he is specifically referring to laws like those that once existed to prevent "women from inheriting estates" (245). His discussion supports a more general interpretation of his initial statement: the update of a text is obliged to discard every type of law that time and space render obsolete. Moving a text through time will force one sort of update as the world shifts into different patterns. The same thing occurs when a text crosses cultural boundaries. The customs and practices taken for granted in one place are replaced by other customs and practices to match the cultural milieu of the text updating an earlier text. Stam mentions Gurinder Chadha's *Bride and Prejudice* (2004) as one example. The text updates Austen's *Pride and Prejudice* in a variety of ways, all to serve the shift from Austen's early nineteenth-century England to twenty-first-century India and America. Stam contends that Chandha's film and those like it can serve as "ideological barometers that register the shifts in social/discursive atmosphere," and that they do so in a polyvocal and dissensual" manner (247). They speak with and against the earlier text and everything that supported that text. They speak together to bring together the otherwise "competing languages and discourses that refract and interpret the world" (245). The task of the adaptor begins to align with the task of Benjamin's translator, which leads to the task the point of the index assigns the spectator.

Deborah Cartmell and Imelda Whelehan (2010) begin to develop this aspect of adaptation as they discuss the "impure cinema," a cinema that intermingles with literary sources rather than accepting the role of passive transmitter of the reality before the camera (2). Cartmell and Whelehan refer to Benjamin's belief that cinematic adaptations of literary sources have "a democratising effect" even if they do not develop that idea through Benjamin's own words (48). They implicitly show how adaptations that refuse to stay in one text realize both Benjamin's idea of the democratizing effect of adaptations and the task in front of those who elect to create such adaptations. Cartmell and Whelehan offer Chris Columbus's *Harry Potter and the Sorcerer's Stone* (2001) as a film that "tries too hard to *be* the book" and fails because of it (75). As Cartmell and Whelehan explain, a film adaptation should not be a reenactment of the book, a pure presentation of what appears on the page; rather, it must intermix the original with the conventions of medium in the period in which it is released. Cartmell and Whelehan offer Peter Jackson's *Lord of the Rings: The Fellowship of the Ring* (2001) as an example of the more successful formula. Jackson's film received a much more favorable reception, in part, Cartmell and Whelehan argue, "because it adapted the novel to Hollywood conventions ... [even as] Columbus felt the need to preserve the book as much as possible" (76–77). The principal idea is that Jackson's film fares better than Columbus's because it becomes impure, a mixture of some source text and the conditions in which it will be viewed.

One can rather safely argue that all film viewing enters this same sort of mixed space, regardless of whether a text is being adapted or not. This space exists for no other reason than that the story set on the screen exists in one space while the audience comes to it from another. So long as the spectator does not surrender completely to the external event occurring on the screen, allowing it to make a literal impression on their mind as they perceive it, then one can assume that the spectator is always in the process of making the cinema impure, in the above sense of the word. The images are a mixture of the event itself and the observation of that event. This quality emerges most easily when the literary qualities of the cinema are emphasized, which is to highlight the arbitrary qualities of every image rather than something belonging to literature. This arbitrary status can only ever really be explored, and, when received as an index, it will best be explored on the point of the index.

The task herein imagined assumes cinema possesses a kind of literary value, at least as it relates to two qualities. Cinema should arrange the world it creates in a particular way, even as it accepts that other arrangements are also possible. Every arrangement is, to some extent, arbitrary in the strictest sense. The structure brought to the screen is purposeful rather than spontaneous, but that structure is not inherently true. It could be rearranged. Just as importantly, the details within this arrangement should be open to more than one meaning. The film can have its preferred or its criterially prefocused meaning, to use Noël Carroll's (2008) term for describing the way an element in a text can be "so structured that the description and depictions of the pertinent objects of our attention clearly and decisively satisfy the criteria for the emotional state intended by the creators"; but even criterially prefocused details can be set free from their initial focus (159). Spectators will consider other meanings; they may even privilege other meanings. As such, the details in every film can become arbitrary even if they intend to be otherwise. In keeping with the argument of this book, the details of a film will become more arbitrary the more they are set on the point of the cinematic index, if only because such points lead to other indices. The cinematic index is never fixed nor final. It marks the start of a process rather than the end of referent.

David Bordwell's four levels of meaning, which consist of referential, explicit, implicit, and symptomatic meaning, provide a tidy way to discuss these qualities of the cinema. The presence of symptomatic meaning, which regards meaning as a symptom of the society that produces a text, either originally or through interpretation, ensures a cinematic text has literary value in the sense being developed here. The above form of literary value requires the spectator to have a certain kind of active literacy. Spectators who experience a film without engaging it may ignore the literary value of cinematic text even as it exists in front of them. The widely held belief that popular film promotes a mindless activity could lull some spectators into overlooking the literary qualities of cinema. In fact, some might believe that cinema can only ever borrow the literary quality it realizes by leaning into literary sources. Adaptation studies might even unintentionally play into this idea.

Adaptation scholars have long looked at the cinema because it adapted a literary source text. The intent has been to measure the relationship the two mediums enjoy because some adaptor chooses to bring some literary work to the screen. Considering the leading titles of monographs and anthologies within adaptation studies over the years, one sees just how consistently this idea has been promoted within adaptation studies: George Bluestone, *Novel into Film* (1957/2003); Morris Beja, *Film and Literature* (1979); Keith Cohen, *Film and Fiction* (1979); William Klein and Gillian Parker, *The English Novel and the Movies* (1981); Joy Gould Boyum, *Double Exposure: Fiction into Film* (1985); Neil Sinyard, *Filming Literature: The Art of Screen Adaptation* (1986); Linda Seger, *The Art of Adaptation: Turning Fact and Fiction into Film* (1992); Brian McFarlane, *Novel into Film: An Introduction to the Theory of Adaptation* (1996); Deborah Cartmell and Imelda Whelehan, *Adaptations: From Text to Screen, Screen to Text* (1999) and *The Cambridge Companion to Literature on Screen* (2007); Deborah Cartmell, I. Q. Hunter, Heidi Kaye, and Imelda Whelehan, *Classics in Film and Fiction* (2000); Ginette Vincendeau, *Film/Literature/Heritage* (2000); Deborah Cartmell, I. Q. Hunter, and Imelda Whelehan, *Retrovisions: Reinventing the Past in Film and Fiction* (2001); Sarah Cardwell, *Adaptation Revisited: Television and the Classic Novel*

(2002); Kamilla Elliott, *Rethinking the Novel/Film Debate* (2003); Robert Stam, *Literature Through Film: Realism, Magic, and the Art of Adaptation* (2004); Robert Stam and Alessandro Raengo, *A Companion to Literature and Film* (2004) and *Literature and Film: A Guide to Theory and Practice* (2005); John Tibbetts and James M. Welsh, *The Encyclopedia of Novels into Films* (2005); Mireia Aragay, *Books in Motion: Adaptation, Intertextuality, Authorship* (2006); Linda Chair, *Literature into Film: Theory and Practical Approaches* (2006); James M. Welsh and Peter Lev, *The Literature/Film Reader* (2007); Christine Geraghty, *Now a Major Motion Picture: Film Adaptations of Literature and Drama* (2007); Timothy Corrigan, *Film and Literature: An Introduction and Reader* (2011); Deborah Cartmell, *The Blackwell Companion to Literature, Film and Adaptation* (2012); Kiene Brillenburg Wurth, *Between Page and Screen: Remaking Literature through Cinema and Cyberspace* (2012); Gordon E. Slethaug, *Adaptation Theory and Criticism: Postmodern Literature and Cinema in the USA* (2014); and Jan Baetens, *Novelization: From Film to Novel* (2018). This list provides an interesting working bibliography, but, even more than that, it tells a story of a particular focus within adaptation studies that considers film as an instance of adaptation to the extent that the screen holds some text that was born on the page.

This focus on film treats the medium as an end point to a process that begins with a novel or some other piece of literature and ends on the silver screen. One might be tempted to conclude that the two expressions share some natural kinship. Kamilla Elliott (2003) provides one of the most insightful critiques of that conclusion. For Elliott, the relationship novels and films have shared is tenuous at best. As the fourth chapter of Elliott's monograph makes plain, "Cinematic Novels/Literary Cinema," scholarly discourse regularly blurs the lines between the novel and cinema, treating the two forms as "sister arts" (29). Elliott attributes this tendency to two commonly held (mis)beliefs. The first is that the nineteenth-century novel is often thought to surrender itself to the same "realist, empirical, visual representational style" to which the cinema surrenders (122). Both mediums try to be realistic, to give their interlocutor the world as it would really appear if they were in front of the piece of the world being staged. The only way the two art forms break from reality is through their use of space, which leads to the second commonly held assumption, namely, that the novel and film share a preference for "shifting back and forth between groups of characters and of cutting between various points of view within a scene" (122). Scholars link the nineteenth-century novel and early film through these two shared traits, and they routinely argue that the novel somehow leads into cinema just as the cinema leads back to the novel. Elliott questions both conclusions. She insists that literary and cinema scholars alike do not always applaud these presumed parallels. For many, a filmed version of a novel is different enough from the novel that the relationship between the two texts is mostly titular. At the same time, film scholars balk at films that rely on novels for their form and function. Such films often forfeit their standing as film.

As the above list of titles suggests, adaptation scholars have done little to lessen the sting of either criticism. They may, in fact, unintentionally exaggerate it, at least by turning to film only to discuss its relationship to some earlier text. Such a result is unfortunate for many reasons, but the main reason is that it fails to account for the ways in which a film is, first, always already an instance of adaptation, and, second, always already inviting audiences to participate in the ongoing adaptation initiated by the images on screen. Julie Grossman (2015) provides a wonderful corrective to both missteps. Grossman looks to disrupt how one relates a source text and an adapted text by changing the metaphor for the relationship between the two texts. Rather than thinking of "the preexisting text as the authority, like a controlling parent," Grossman challenges adaptation scholars to examine the "independent lines of inquiry and ingenious expressions of art . . . [literary] descendants [can] explore" (18). These independent lines can spark an exploration that not only extends from the adaptation, but to the preexisting text as well. That "home," as Grossman describes it, can, in turn, be reoriented by the adapted text to reveal the source text as "a construct that may disguise an extensive series of previous works" in the "original" (21). The adaptation becomes something like a new notation that throws the earlier construct into a new context. Such a shift returns those who see it to a process of ongoing adaptation that starts anew in every now, every encounter the text that is never fully realized.

The cinematic index being discussed in these pages can also return one to the process of ongoing adaptation, and it can do so by inviting spectators to rewatch rather than merely to reexperience the images or story set on screen. This rewatching matches Benjamin's translator and Stam's adaptor. Even the impoverished index, which provides a return to some literal reality that existed before the camera, allows rewatching rather than reexperiencing. The reality set on the screen by the camera means to be repurposed if only to fit the narrative a narrative film develops. This is as true of Gance's famed mountain and clouds in *La Roue* (1922) as it is of any element in a digital film. The mountain and clouds are *there* as they were by some stroke of good fortune, but the moment they appear on the screen they are also brought *here*. They remain here, too, if only by virtue of the *Kairos* of ongoing adaptation. They are ready to be observed and inspected, to be appreciated or adjusted, and all according to the whims of the person who watches them.

The same opportunity arises with the indefinite index. The moment they are placed on screen, the mountain and clouds become *some* set of mountains and clouds, *every* set of mountains and clouds. They invite the spectator to consider the categories of mountains and clouds rather than any individual mountain or cloud. Each image points to any number of actual or imagined mountains or clouds, and they do so on the point of the indefinite index Gance's clouds and mountains constitute the moment they are set in motion on the screen. The intertextual and imaginative indices operate similarly. They invite the spectator to track the trails the initial point of the index admits exist somewhere down the path paved by the index. The intertextual and imaginative indices expect the spectator to traverse these trails with a sense of agency and purpose that can only exist with the spectator and only for the time in which the spectator engages them.

All indices being described in this study have the potential to become sites of play and exploration, adaptation and appropriation. Such sites open most properly when, as Elsie Walker and David T. Johnson (2005) write, "anxiety about preservation is undone by a spirit of exploration" (3). For adaptation scholars, this undoing occurs when adaptors—those who produce adaptations or who watch them—do so without an obligation to preserve the adapted text. For trauma theorists, it means reconstituting the validity of "the event." Neither "the original" nor "the event" captures anything essential about the reality they behold. Both initial realities capture details that can be carried forward, adjusted, or altogether set aside. They do not have to remain as they were to have meaning or significance. Spectators will always decide how to preserve, perform, or morph those details in whatever way they see fit. In some cases, the spectator will decide to preserve certain details, and that choice will have its own temporary value. As Kenneth Longden (2018) notes, the choice to bring forward a story assumes a kind of agency within the details that provide the "reasons" to bring a story forward at all (15). The sense of agency that matters most to this study, however, is the agency that belongs to the spectator. The spectator can be brought into the process of adaptation that an adaptation performs even if it exists to do something other than to provide a performance of ongoing adaptation.

Laurence Raw (2013) attends to the difference between these reasons to exist. Raw argues that adaptation studies need to look not only at "the ways in which texts have been transformed, but [also] the ways in which readers, audiences, and critics have responded to [those transformations] at different points in time and space" (3). David Wyatt (1986) provides an interesting example of the kinds of transformations Raw wants adaptation studies to consider. Wyatt admits at the beginning of his essay that readers "take what we need from the books we need, and what we need changes" (106). He suggests that the meaning of a book might most properly be "located . . . [in] our return to it" (106). Wyatt's essay offers an example of how that might work through a recounting of his own decade-long interaction with Robert Penn Warren's *A Place to Come To* (1977). Wyatt recounts how what he sees in the story changes over the decade that passes. Initially, Wyatt admits to seeing the events that tell a story of "the lost father and the lost home" as the "novel's major incidents" (2). A decade later he wonders how he "overlook the story of Jed's wives" and the "romance about remarriage" Warren is telling (107). The novel, of course, stays the same on the page, but Wyatt shares how he, the reader, changes over the decade. He describes how his return to Warren's novel can mark those changes.

To show that the returns rereading provides are not bound to one text, Wyatt narrates another long encounter with a text, James Agee's *A Death in the Family* (1957). Wyatt describes reading the novel "as a son, not as a father," and he measures the impact that position has on his focus as a reader (111). When read from the position of a son, key passages seemed to be about grand themes of life and death. Years later, after becoming a father, Wyatt sees how those same passages can speak to "the pain of parenthood" (111). Wyatt shares how other passages spoke to another pain, the pain of loss, something he was not ready to see before he was ready to process the losses in his life. Wyatt's point is not to provide a memoir of his life and emotions through the texts he reads; rather, it is to describe what it means to reread a text, and how a commitment to rereading can compel one to engage in an activity "defined by the lack of a foreseeable end" (112). Readers can, after all, reread indefinitely, and they probably should so long as a text remains alive to them. The reason is buried in Raw's appeal to the Silk Road metaphor. The repeated encounters with a text can pave roads that will reveal, as Raw says it, the "*continuous* process in which individuals continually have to adjust themselves to new ideas and new materials" (3, emphasis mine). A return to a text uncovers the various paths a reader takes, or at least the paths that are open for them to take. Since no one can take more than one path at a time, every return encourages a subsequent return to travel a path not yet taken, or, perhaps, to see a path one could not see earlier.

Cinematic adaptations might be particularly good at revealing and traveling various paths in a story. They certainly become good markers of the journeys one takes. Linda Hutcheon (2013) suggests that one of the things that makes adaptations particularly useful is the way they track the kinds of connections between texts one story can have with another, and one reader can have with a text they reencounter. Adaptations are especially good at marking these relationships, in part, because they "openly announce" the relationship they have with other texts (3). Each mark exists as a "repetition [and] variation" of an earlier text (4). An adaptation bears these marks whether or not a spectator knows the text being adapted. These marks can be discovered even if they are initially missed. Moreover, not knowing the text being adapted does not keep even those who do not know that text from realizing that the text in front of them, the adaptation, is an adaptation of something. Such knowledge returns spectators to the cinematic reality that has always existed for spectators, one in which what appears has been adapted from something else, that has come to be documented and animated in some specific way. Hutcheon reasons that the interlocutor who knows that the significance of this documenting and animating might be most appreciated by the spectator who knows both the text being encountered and the text(s) that text is adapting. Hutcheon suggests the adapted text being directly experienced can possess what Roland Barthes describes as "a plural 'stereophony of echoes, citations, and references'" (Barthes 1977/2010, 160, quoted in Hutcheon, 6). This experience satisfies a desire to "retell the same story over and over in different ways" (9). Each difference marks the difference described in the last chapter between trauma and adaptation. In trauma, there is only retelling the same story. With adaptation, there is "repetition with variation," there is a process rather than simply a product or a prompt (8). It is, as Hutcheon contends, "the process of making the adapted material one's own" (20). It is a process readers and writers alike can enter.

Thomas Leitch (2007) develops a fuller discussion of the process of ongoing creation an adaptation can afford. Leitch works against attitudes toward texts that treat texts as commodities to be bought and sold, and, ultimately, consumed in and by a market. He prefers a more literate attitude toward texts, one that emphasizes the active and ongoing response readers and spectators can have with texts. Leitch explains "texts remain alive only to the extent that they can be rewritten and that to experience a text in all its power requires each reader to rewrite it" (12–13). Leitch lists "the whole process of film adaptation . . . [as] an obvious practical demonstration" of readers rewriting a text (13). He treats adaptations not as "transcriptions of canonical classics or attempts to create new classics, rather as illustrations of the incessant process of rewriting as critical reading" (16). The point Leitch establishes across these two passages is that reading is writing, and that writing is reading. The two acts cooperate to express an active literacy that has always been just beneath the surface of the cinematic adaptation, an adaptation that invites those who see it to "become active producers of the text they might otherwise be content simply to read [or watch]" (18). Open adaptations demonstrate this process. They show readers becoming writers. Spectators can become something similar.

To participate in this active process, one must engage a text as a "knowing audience," to return to Hutcheon, albeit with some variation to her original point. Hutcheon introduces the concept of "knowing" as a way to distinguish between two audiences: those who know the text being adapted by a later text being encountered and those who do not (120). The latter will encounter the text before them as they "would any other work" (120). The audiences that know the text being adapted will experience "an interpretative doubling, a conceptual flipping back and forth between the work [they] know and the work [they] are experiencing" (139). The "foreknowledge" the knowing audience has presets their encounter with the adapted text, both setting up certain expectations and creating unmistakable surprises when the adapted text becomes something unexpected (121). Hutcheon allows this foreknowledge to include more than just the text being adapted. There are different forms of knowing and "differently knowing audiences" (125). Hutcheon offers the knowledge one can have of a genre, a director, a star, a medium, and a culture as some of the factors influencing different types of knowing.

One can add the knowledge one has of oneself to this list. This is the type of knowledge Wyatt describes in his essay. It is the type of knowledge the characters already described who come to adapt their story rather than simply repeat them have. To know a text involves knowing oneself. Returns of any sort—actual returns to the same text, or the types of indirect returns adaptations provide—can promote this kind of self-awareness or knowing. Each return becomes something like Bazin's family album. An earlier self can be remembered not as an authorial self, a self that writes the story of the person that self becomes, but as an endlessly adaptable self, a self that is set free from what will be. In this way, each return marks what has been and anything else that one could become from that point. In the cinema, the point is an indexical point, a point that signifies nothing as much as a process of signification that begins anew in every *now*, in every encounter.

Spectators must treat movies as something more than puzzles if these more open indexical points are to be encountered. Recent cycles of what David Bordwell (2006) terms "puzzle films" frustrate this break. Puzzle films, after all, exist to be solved. They adopt patterns that Bordwell suggests boast "paradoxical time schemes, hypothetical futures, digressive and dawdling action lines, stories told backward and in loops, and plots stuffed with protagonists" (73). One sees examples of such practices in Quentin Tarantino's *Pulp Fiction* (1994), Bryan Singer's *The Usual Suspects* (1995), David Fincher's *The Game* (1997) and *Fight Club* (1999), M. Night Shyamalan's *The Sixth Sense*

(1999) and *Unbreakable* (2000), and Michel Gondry's *Eternal Sunshine of the Spotless Mind* (2004). Bordwell is careful to ensure that earlier precedents for these films and those like them are not ignored. Bordwell reminds readers of earlier films that possess some puzzle film qualities, films like Orson Welles's *Citizen Kane* (1941), John Ford's *How Green Was My Valley* (1941), Michael Curtiz's *Mildred Pierce* (1945), or John Brahm's *The Locket* (1946). The difference between these early films and the later ones is the way in which the later films exist within a cycle of films that present themselves as puzzles to be solved.

Bordwell claims that entry into the puzzle film cycle is relatively easy: "viewers seem to apply the notion . . . whenever a film asks us to discuss 'what really happened,' to think back over what's been shown, or to rewatch the film in search for clues to the key revelations" (80). Bordwell challenges that the films viewers place in this cycle tend to have certain traits that create the response they do. For instance, the story and the narration will include "gaps" that prevent spectators from being able to see a complete picture; in more extreme examples, like the one in *The Game* or David Mamet's *House of Games* (1987), the plot itself may exist as a hoax (80). Films adopting this quality will often replay key scenes at some pivotal moment where some new significance can be realized. Bordwell offers the final moments of *The Usual Suspects* as an example. The story the main character, Verbal Kint (Kevin Spacey), has been telling turns out to be a lie. The ingredients for that lie—the location of the company that manufactured the bulletin board, the name of the company at the bottom of a coffee cup, the features of a woman in a mug shot—are revealed in dramatic fashion at the end of the Kint's story. The whole of the film changes in that moment.

What is most interesting about puzzle films as they relate to the discussion of the cinematic index this project means to describe is the extent to which they return to a diminished index. Using Singer's film as an example, Kint does demonstrate a kind of inventive storytelling that nearly approximates the reimaginations of some of the characters who reimagine their own traumas, as discussed in earlier parts of the book. The difference between those earlier reimaginations and Kint's act is that the earlier reimaginations lead to a reality that can neither be confirmed nor denied. They are acts that lead to a reality that might be. Kint's act, by contrast, leads to fixed realities. Every element in his story depends on some detail in the detective's office. In this way, the character demonstrates the ongoing play on the point of index this project insists cinematic indices can enact, but he does so at the service of the impoverished or indefinite index. The former depends on the reality depicted in the details presented in the elements found in the office.

Kint's use of those details means to reference them if only to the audience. One could say that these references operate as indefinite indices, bringing the audience to see not the specific element being indexed, but the category to which that element belongs. Either way, Kint's performance eventually limits the indexical range of the elements in specific ways. It does not invite audiences to enter a process of ongoing adaptation. His adaptive work is finished. The indices he uses in that work now exist as puzzle pieces to be set in place. Audiences have nothing left to do at the end of the film but to accept the new reality the surprise ending delivers.

The films this project champions are more than puzzles. They invite spectators into a process of ongoing adaptation that occurs on the point of a cinematic index that not only leads toward intertextual and imaginative indices, but that do so in such a way that the play they perform can be extended by those who participate in it. The reality these films deliver refuses to be fixed. They offer a reality that is always still becoming, and they invite spectators to consider if not participate in that becoming.

Christopher Nolan routinely fashions films that play on this type of self-awareness or knowing, especially as it turns on the point of a cinematic index. As Sorcha Ní Fhlainn (2015) notes, "recent cinema is heavily preoccupied with the manipulation and alteration of subjective memory" (148). Fhlainn offers Singer's *The Usual Suspects*, Fincher's *The Game*, Peter Weir's *The Truman Show* (1998), Lilly and Lana Wachowski's *The Matrix* (1999), and Nolan's *Memento* (2000) as some more prominent examples of this tendency. Fhlainn finds each of these films "grappl[ing] with the themes of reality, simulation, the erosion of certainty and trauma in late postmodernity" (148). Fhlainn claims that Nolan seems especially willing to turn the "perception of events [into] the site of a game, as characters deceive, betray and are driven by trauma of a memory" (149). Fhlainn suggests that *Memento*, *Insomnia* (2002), *The Prestige* (2006), *Inception* (2010), *Interstellar* (2014), and the *Dark Knight* trilogy, which consists of *Batman Begins* (2005), *The Dark Knight* (2008), and *The Dark Knight Rises* (2012), all exhibit these traits. Fhlainn contends that each of these films reject the idea of a "perfect past" (151). The perfect past, which is both a past that can be accessed and a past that finds for the character a favorable self, just does not exist. Fhlainn argues that Nolan prefers to leave his characters "refusing to see," so that spectators can see for themselves the dangers of this refusal (154). The characters' refusal to see comes at a clear cost, which is, above all else, the ongoing belief in a lie.

In Fhlainn's view, the lie at the center of Nolan's films fits the sign of the times. They put on the screen "the deceits and multiplicities that gained heightened cultural emphasis in cinema during the 1990s" (160). Fhlainn suggests that the resulting style that emerges across Nolan's films "provokes us, challenges us and . . . encourages . . . re-entering his puzzle films again and again to solve a mystery or to reveal a hidden truth at its heart" (160). Because Nolan's story so often becomes something of a con—the tension the endings find extends from an admitted and accepted lie, which means that a return can never deliver what it should. For example, spectators do not return to the end of *Interstellar* or *The Dark Knight Rises* to learn if Cooper (Matthew McConaughey) sees a real reality when he sees Brand (Anne Hathaway) or if Batman lives. These questions do not matter as much as the process of signification the whole of the film has favored. Neither film, nor any film from Nolan to date, needs to find a reality in the strictest sense. All of Nolan's films show the way any sense of reality is negotiated and invite audiences to participate in that negotiation.

This claim may come as a bit of surprise to some, as Nolan does not enter discussions of adaptation in the same way other filmmakers might. He is very rarely openly adapting a text that audiences are likely to know. Still, the popular director has engaged in various kinds of adaptation during his filmmaking career. He has directed open adaptations of a short story, as he does in *Memento*; a novel, in *Prestige*; a true story, in *Dunkirk* (2017); and an entire universe of a comic in the *Dark Knight* movies. One also sees a less obvious example of adaptation buried within *The Dark Knight Rises*. As Samrat Laskar (2012–13) and Michał Leliński (2014) note, Nolan allows this last entry in the *Dark Knight* trilogy to be influenced by Charles Dickens, and especially his novel *A Tale of Two Cities* (1859). Leliński proposes that the Bruce Wayne (Christian Bale) character might best be understood as a combination of Sydney Carton and Charles Darnay, two characters in Dickens's novel. Leliński suggests that Wayne most closely matches Carton at the beginning of the film's plot and Darnay at the end. In keeping with the two characters, Wayne "squanders his life away" in the early parts of the film only to sacrifice himself in the end for the couple (320). The sacrifice in *The Dark Knight Rises* is the existence of the Batman. In keeping with Leliński's reading, Wayne "sacrifices his life as Batman . . . to live happily with his newfound lover" (321). Leliński rightly pushes these correspondences through a second source text, namely, the comic books that give rise to Batman. The combination of *A Tale of Two Cities* with Bob Kane's character and world actually realizes a new "original" as it were, a "visionary interpretation of the writers, director and actor . . . [while also being] a direct reference to the source materials" (321). The result follows the tendency established across other adaptations in Nolan's oeuvre, and, more significantly, the process of adaptation Nolan invites his audience to enter as they watch his films.

The clearest example of both Nolan's attitude toward adaptation and the way that attitude draws one into the *Kairos* of ongoing adaptation occurs in *Dunkirk*. *Dunkirk* is a remarkable film for a variety of reasons, but especially for the way Nolan privileges the indexical qualities of a true story. To return to Leitch, one sees how Nolan does this by looking at the qualities Leitch ascribes to movies "based on a true story." Leitch offers that the claim indicates a peculiar form of adaptation since the phrase "indicates a source text that both is and is not a text" (281). A film "based on a true story" is a text since it makes no claim to be "an accurate record of historical events" (282). It is a dramatization that leans into historical events without becoming that event. It stands at some distance, having taken some liberties. Leitch argues, in fact, that the only legitimate historical record a film based on a true story provides is the record it provides about "staging, performance, costuming, set decoration, and even representations of history" (282). It is not, nor does it pretend to be, a return to an actual historical event. A movie based on a true story is a literary representation of an event, even as it attempts to assure audiences that it has some basis in something true.

This basis in something true is as important as the allowance to depart from a true story. From Leitch's view, the phrase "based on a true story" extends artists some literary license, but with the assurance that there is, at the center, some responsible master text. As Leitch explains, movies based on true stories are "authorless, publisherless, agentless" (282). They are often accepted as authentic in the way stories that have such things are contrived or fabricated. On the other hand, the very "category of the true story . . . [creates the impression of] a privileged master text that justifies the film's claims to certain kinds of authority—ideally by placing them beyond question" (286). Viewers assume a movie "based on a true story" will be told as close to how an event actually occurred even as it makes some acceptable adjustments to make things more entertaining. Additionally, any perceived sins of the world set on the screen belong to some actual world, not to any of those who take delight in bringing or seeing a representation of such things on a screen. Some of the more brutal stories, in fact, become acceptable because they tell a story that is "based on a true story." Leitch explains that to alter the horrors of the story would be to misrepresent the atrocities that have been ignored by past generations. Leitch offers Kimberly Peirce's *Boys Don't Cry* (1999) as an example of a film full of barbarisms that would be unacceptable to watch if they did not belong to some past day, to a time when such events were permitted. In this way, a movie "based on a true story" carries with it an essence of truth, a symptomatic truth of a particular time when such stories would be kept private. Those who observe such stories can do so without moral compromise because the events that follow are not a literary text, but a bit of lived experience.

This is not to suggest that those who routinely make movies "based on true stories" mean to let the truth of their stories overwhelm their own auteuristic vision or the discursive aim that extends from that vision. Leitch lists Oliver Stone, Sidney Lumet, Martin Scorsese, and Steven Spielberg as directors who regularly make movies "based on a true story," but who also retain some plain vision and aim. The willingness each of the above shows to base their films on a true story becomes, in fact, part of that vision and aim. Leitch offers Oliver Stone as "the preeminent auteur of films that are based on true stories" (291). Stone earns this title, in part, because even films that are not presented as stories "based on a true story" are circulated with the authority of some actual experience. For instance, Stone's Vietnam films, *Platoon* (1986), *Born on the Fourth of July* (1989), and *Heaven & Earth* (1993), all presume to extend Stone's experiences in Vietnam. They cover some truth even if they are not "based on a true story." Other films announce this quality from the outset, often in an effort to set the record right. Leitch suggests that "from *Salvador* (1986) to *World Trade Center* (2006) Stone's films have aimed to set the historical record straight by quibbling on the relation between fiction and history" (293). Leitch argues that part of Stone's truth is his willingness to intermix truth and fiction in the way he perceives "official American history" to mix these two elements. Stone's films become for Leitch a performance of "true stories" as much as true stories in the strictest sense.

Leitch challenges that something similar happens in the films from Sidney Lumet and Martin Scorsese. In Leitch's view, Lumet presents movies "based on a true story" to show "a fallen and deeply conflicted world . . . [that pits] right against right . . . or, more often, wrong against wrong" (295). The only solution to such a world is the rise of virtuous individual, like Frank Serpico, the hero of *Serpico* (1973), who "can rise at least momentarily above the system that crushes them in Stone's [films]" (296). The stories "based on true stories" Lumet tells play as inspirational tales that show a better system is possible, one that has in fact emerged at times due to the heroics of certain individuals. Leitch finds Scorsese telling a story not unlike the one Lumet tells: "Scorsese is always telling the same story. His heroes and heroines are free spirits struggling for survival in a world determined to crush them into conformity" (297). Such stories gain a certain irony when set on the screen. Following the opinion of critics like Terrence Rafferty (2003), the point of a film is the experience it provides: "when you're sitting in a movie theater, the film is in absolute control of your senses . . . tell[ing] you where to look and for how long" (45). The film becomes the force crushing viewers into conformity. Movies "based on true stories," at least those in the hands of Lumet and Scorsese, create enough of a gap between an actual and imagined reality that the spectator can participate in the process of representation being set on the screen.

Leitch finds Steven Spielberg using movies "based on true stories" in a similar fashion. For Leitch, Spielberg's films are often "allegories of innocents trapped by an oppressive system" (298). The individual feats of the heroes in *The Sugarland Express* (1974), *Catch Me If You Can* (2002), and *The Terminal* (2004) each showcase what an individual can do against imposing systems of control. Each hero serves as another example of what Leitch labels as "Spielberg's little guys [who] are always triumphing over their littleness, their own alleged limitations" (299). Leitch's discussion of Spielberg, as with Scorsese, Lumet, and Stone, is ultimately less interested in the characteristics of any one of these directors than in his insistence that "adaptation studies will rest on a firmer foundation when its practitioners direct their attention away from films that present themselves as based on a single identifiable literary source . . . and toward the process of adaptation" (302). This study agrees with Leitch's conclusion and tries to realize the ways in which film itself can be seen as a medium caught in the ongoing process of adaptation Leitch champions. On the point of the index, spectators are not led to a fixed reality, an event, or a source; instead, they are brought into a series of signifiers where one sign leads to the next, one index leads to another. More than the icon or the symbol, the index avoids a firm notion of reality to keep this process open. As an indexical art, which is to say an art that circulates signs impressed by one reality but leading to other realities, cinema becomes a site of adaptation regardless of whether or not there is a story born in some other medium or some other place behind the one on the screen. Cinema provides spectators a chance to enter this process of adaptation regardless of whether there is a clear source text or not, and it does so by virtue of an index that exists whether the images on screen emerge from a lens-based camera or a computer. In either case, an indexical quality lingers in the frame. The image left on screen is indexical, pointing to some reality beyond itself, regardless of whether that reality actually exists or not. The spectator can perceive that quality and pursue any number of realities on the basis of it.

Christopher Nolan might explore this aspect of cinema more explicitly than anyone else. Interestingly, the director also features stories of characters in the midst of some trauma to highlight the indexical aspect of his stories. One can uncover these qualities in any number of Nolan films, if not every one of them, but three films deserve particular attention: *Dunkirk*, *Inception*, and *Memento*. Taken together, these three films most succinctly illustrate the way that natural and individual trauma can give way to the *Kairos* of ongoing adaptation and do so on the point of a cinematic index that exists between a conjoint desire to document and to animate some world. One only needs to follow the point of the index to see this tension and the opportunity to adapt the reality set on screen.

Dunkirk makes for a good starting point in this discussion, in part because the story is an instance of various kinds of literal rewatching. The story of Dunkirk is a national tale, and it is the tale of individual heroic efforts. As it relates to the national story it helps fashion, Dunkirk helps explain and define the British people in the twentieth century, a people who can rise above impossible circumstances, which also ensures that the story can be told in such a way that it can fit a number of socially constructed ideologies. One might refer to the story at Dunkirk as the truest of true stories, then, a story that it is so complete that one knows what to tell, how to tell it, and when it is appropriate to tell. In this way, nearly every part of the story holds iconic and symbolic value. Anyone retelling these details would be expected to preserve not only a likeness of the events of the evacuation, but the cultural significance of this story in British folklore. Nolan nods to both qualities in the opening moments of his film. The plot opens with nothing but the supertitle, DUNKIRK, in all-capital, white letters set against a black screen. The soundtrack is empty. The lone word speaks for itself. It gathers in one instant all of the iconic, symbolic, and indexical qualities it can. An intercut carries the plot to a single street filled with six Tommy soldiers in uniform. Pamphlets fall from the sky in the way snow-like material floats through a snow globe. The image indicates that Nolan's scenario exists both realistically and non-realistically; it is a presentation and a representation.

A second cut returns the plot to the black screen on which the title had been presented. Nolan replaces the title with a line of exposition: "The enemy had driven the British and French Armies to the sea." The plot cuts to the six Tommy soldiers with a focus on one of the band's members as he reaches into the air to grab one of the flyers falling from the sky. He opens the paper to see a graphic of a map that places YOU in the center of the page, an image of the sea above that pronoun, and a wash of red with the words WE SURROUND YOU below it. Nolan returns to the intertitle to confirm the enemy's message with a second line: "Trapped at Dunkirk, they await their fate." Nolan continues to intercut his images of the group of soldiers with the official history found in his intertitle. After a series of three such intercuts, the scenario and the history are set: "Trapped at Dunkirk, they await their fate./Hoping for deliverance./For a miracle." With the sound of a rifle firing, the plot leaves the intertitle aside and focuses on the men as they literally run for their lives.

Nolan adds machine-gun fire into the scenario and all but one of the six men are struck and presumably killed. The one remaining soldier, the one character that will thread the various parts of the story Nolan writes, a man who will be identified as Tommy (Fionn Whitehead) in the credits, escapes the Germans, moves through a French blockade, and finds himself on the beach where tens of thousands of men stand waiting. In just over three minutes, Nolan establishes the dire circumstances these men face, while acknowledging with only a name what one will learn through extra-diegetic means, the culturally significant value these men and their story amass.

While the opening moments of *Dunkirk* suggest that Nolan is ready to tell a story that deserves reverence with all the veneration one would expect, the writer/director indicates that he will also disrupt this expectation by telling three aspects of this story in three different time signatures. The opening sequence constitutes what will be designated "The Mole" sequence. Its story will stretch across one week. Nolan cuts from this sequence to move the story to a second space and time frame. Just after an air raid that leaves the men on the beach wondering "where is the bloody air force?" the plot shifts to a small English port city where a second line of action begins. Mr. Dawson (Mark Rylance), his son, Peter (Tom Glynn-Carney), and his friend, George (Barry Keoghan), empty their small vessel, the *Moonstone*, to load life preservers for the soldiers they hope to rescue at Dunkirk in response to Churchill's "Operation Dynamo." Nolan designates this space as "The Sea," and announces that its action will unfold in one day.

As the "crew" of Moonstone prepare the vessel for sea, Nolan cuts to the third story, space, and time introduced in his plot. A group of three British planes moves through the skies under the graphic "The Air: one hour." The early parts of Nolan's plot, then, after the above-described prologue of sorts that brings Tommy to the beach, intercuts three story spaces, and sets these stories within three distinct time frames. These introductions intimate that what follows may lack the kind of linearity most mainstream films possess, but one could hardly predict the full extent to which Nolan refuses a linear plot, and, by extension, the kinds of coherence one might expect a film about Dunkirk to realize. The three timelines routinely frustrate rather than favor any sense of coherence. The result is twofold: on the one hand, the film rejects any clear organizing principle; on the other, the plot leaves spectators in the *now* of each segment and sequence. Comprehension and interpretation must take place in each now that follows, as every sense of past and future collapses into the moment of each representation. The significance of any one representation lasts but for the moment it is on screen. Nolan proposes some alternative significance, either by virtue of what amounts to misleading crosscutting or a willingness to restage events, each time some sustainable significance begins to materialize.

Nolan practices what one can designate as misleading crosscutting throughout *Dunkirk*. He tempts audiences to try and establish correlations between competing story spaces happening in different time frames through his crosscutting, only to highlight the incongruence of these stories. One sees this particular point of emphasis in the shifts Nolan makes between stories. For instance, after introducing his audience to all three story-spaces, Nolan returns to "The Mole" to show Tommy and Gibson (Aneurin Barnard) carrying a wounded solider as they pretend to be medics trying to deliver their man to the ship that has been reserved for the injured. Tommy and Gibson make their way down the dock and through the men that crowd out all but a very thin line for the two to pass. The camera begins in a head-on position before cutting first very nearly behind Gibson, the man at the foot of the soldier on the stretcher, then to an image of George's back in "The Sea" segment as the adolescent character carries a suitcase from the *Moonstone*.

The position of the camera suggests some connection between Gibson and George, who are performing the opposite actions. Gibson is trying to load a boat. George is unloading one. The abruptness of the cut further suggests some shared temporality between these two events, but audiences that remember the different time frames of these events must concede that this suggestion misrepresents the story at least as much as it presents it. Nolan provides some clue that he intends his connections between stories to disrupt a sense of coherence a few moments later when he again abruptly cuts from "The Sea" to "The Air." The last image in "The Sea" sequence shows Mr. Dawson looking down the dock at the British soldiers who will soon commandeer the *Moonstone*. From this image, Nolan jumps to the pilots in "The Air" as they complain about how far Dunkirk is from them. This segment ends with an image of the three planes flying over what appears to be the *Moonstone* long enough after she has left the dock that she is now at sea. In this way, Nolan brings the stories of "The Sea" and "The Air" together, but he does so out of time. The connections between the stories turn out to disorient the action rather than align it.

Later instances of crosscutting suggest that this disorientation is very much intentional. Nolan includes in what might constitute the most celebratory moment of *Dunkirk*—that moment when the small vessels reach the shoreline of Dunkirk, an instance of crosscutting that begs for the wrong understanding of the dramatic action. The leader of the British Navy, Commander Bolton (Kenneth Branagh), sees a series of dots along the horizon. The leader of the British Army, Colonel Winnant (James D'Arcy), hands

Bolton a pair of binoculars, and asks him, "What do you see?" After a few seconds, long enough for a look of concern to turn into an expression of delight, Bolton responds, "Home." The plot carries the camera into the midst of small vessels that traverse the sea in rows. A second cut captures a head-on closeup of Mr. Dawson who stands at the wheel of the *Moonstone*. The implication is that the *Moonstone* is among the small vessels nearing the soldiers at Dunkirk, but such is not the case. The *Moonstone* is still at sea, rescuing the men from the ship that has been bombed by a German bomber. The third cut of "home" returns to other small vessels, which again suggests that the *Moonstone* is in this procession. After a series of what amounts to the most celebratory images of the entire film—a ship full of soldiers sounds its horn as the small vessels pass it on their way to the beach, the men see the small vessels nearing them and stand and cheer. A cut to Commander Bolton shows the leader's eyes filling with tears. Nolan inserts a second closeup of Mr. Dawson at the wheel of the *Moonstone*. This second insert ensures that the most scrutinizing spectator understands that the first insert was not an editing mistake. The "inaccuracies" these two inserts suggest become just as important to any message the film tells as anything else. Nolan conveys their importance by ending the segment that shows the small vessels' arrival at Dunkirk with an image of the *Moonstone* and the sounds of the bombs the German bomber drops. Spectators who try to arrange the elements of the plot into the story Nolan tells realize that this segment, which appears later in the plot, occurs earlier in the story, and that the immediately preceding events in the film must take place later in the story and without the *Moonstone*. One is left with what must be understood as competing storylines that are also out of time.

One could argue that Nolan refuses narrative coherence to comment on the nature of war. Wars produce the kinds of disorienting effect audiences likely experience watching and even rewatching *Dunkirk*. The kinds of discontinuities described above do not dissipate the more familiar one becomes with them. Moreover, Nolan's narrative choices seem to fit a desire—developing over the preceding two decades of movies that reflect on what it means to watch and rewatch moving images—to construct and reconstruct differing realities from those images each time one returns to them again. These interests become most apparent in two films, *Inception* and *Memento*. *Inception* considers the ways in which individual images inform a reality one chooses to accept; *Memento* muses over the power the spectator has over those images and, subsequently, that reality. A closer look at the particular focus of each film provides a way to locate the invitation Nolan extends those who watch *Dunkirk* to participate in the ongoing adaptation of the story his film tells.

Inception presents the story of a man, Cobb (Leonardo DiCaprio), who has the ability to enter a person's dreams and to extract information from that person's subconscious. The plot of the film begins with a wealthy Japanese businessman, Saito (Ken Watanabe), hiring Cobb and the most reliable member of Cobb's team, Arthur (Joseph-Gordon Levitt), to perform the reverse trick, to plant the idea in a rival's mind to break up the company he inherits from his father. To perform this act, Cobb claims that he will need to create a dream-within-a-dream-within-a-dream, which, everyone recognizes as a highly complicated maneuver. The team will need a sedative strong enough to keep the dreamers in the real world asleep and a series of mazes, dream worlds genuine enough to pass as authentic worlds to the dreamer. The most interesting complications that arise from these needs are those that relate to what it means to watch a plot that offers viewers a series of worlds-within-worlds. Nolan's plot ultimately invents five layers of reality: the world represented as the real world; dream worlds of the first, second, and third order; and a fifth realm designated as "limbo," which is a space that the characters find themselves should they lose track of what is real or die in one of the dream worlds. Limbo becomes the greatest threat to the characters because it is a space unlike the layers of dreams because the subjects in limbo forget they need to escape it. As such, they are only lost in that space until something reminds them of some other reality.

The plot explicitly makes clear that the greatest threat to those on the inception team that Cobb assembles is their being stuck in limbo. Nolan's script has Arthur and Cobb explicitly define this space. Arthur describes it as an "unconstructed dream space ... [of] raw, infinite subconscious." The only features in this space, Arthur further explains, are the details "left behind by anyone on the team who's been trapped there before," which, in the case of the team, is Cobb. Cobb later clarifies to Ariadne (Ellen Page) how he had found in himself in limbo. He and his wife, Mal (Marion Cotillard), spent decades "exploring dreams within dreams" without understanding how the experience causes one to "lose track of what's real." Once one loses track of reality, there is only "limbo." Cobb admits that Mal was happy to remain in this space with Cobb, but that he knew none of it was "real." He had to leave, so to do that, he planted an idea in his wife's mind that convinced her they had to kill themselves to return to their reality. Cobb's plan reportedly works in that it brings Mal back to their reality, but it goes wrong when the idea that Cobb planted, that "[their] world was not real," remained even when they awoke in reality. Mal was convinced that she needed to die again to find what is truly real.

Cobb's experience in limbo and his means to escape it suggests to him that "an idea" is an even greater threat than limbo. Nolan's plot actually builds itself around repeated recommendations that the most dangerous threat in the world, real or imagined, is an idea. The film begins with Cobb sharing this proposal with Saito. Cobb asks Saito, "What's the most dangerous parasite?" Cobb answers his own question: "An idea . . . resilient, highly contagious, once an idea's taken hold in the brain it's almost impossible to eradicate." Cobb expresses the same belief in the power of an idea in more indirect ways, too. When Saito expresses his desire to have Cobb plant an idea in his rival's mind, Cobb balks. He cautions his potential employer with a description of the seriousness of what Saito is proposing: "this isn't the usual corporate espionage, Mr. Saito," Cobb explains, "this is inception. The seed of the idea we plant will grow in this man's mind. It will change him. It might even come to define him." Cobb insinuates that the act of inception might be too unethical to perform. The implication is that an idea is just too overwhelming a weapon to be played against another.

Cobb's less direct explanation about the power of an idea, and his at least staged hesitation to perform inception, set the dramatic tension in *Inception*, and do so with a bit of irony. The idea of how all-informing an idea can be is, obviously, itself an idea. Any protest against performing inception is undermined by the fact that the protest is a form of inception against (or for) those watching the protest. Understood in this way, the concerns over the comprehensive nature of ideas begin to comment on the nature of stories that often get circulated under a particular idea, an organizing principle that sets all of the action in one particular direction. Noël Carroll (2003) refers to this aspect of cinema as criterial prefocusing, the idea that a film can be "so structured that the descriptions and depictions of the object of our attention in the text will activate our subsumption of the relevant characters and events under the categories that are criterially apposite" (69). In other words, the significance of an object in an image can be set by the idea of that object conveyed in the story or in the society that sees it.

Nolan overtly demonstrates what criterial prefocusing looks like in at least two places in *Inception*. The first demonstration occurs during Mal's suicide scene. Mal wants Cobb to jump from the building with her so that he can join her in their true reality. She constructs a scenario that makes it nearly impossible for Cobb to choose not to jump with her. His life as he knows it is over regardless of whether he jumps or not. Mal has left the room in disarray to suggest the couple has been in a fight. She "filed a letter with [the couple's] attorney explaining how [she is] fearful for her safety, how [he has] threatened to kill [her]." She also had "herself declared sane by three different psychiatrists." Each move ensures that authorities see Mal's death as a murder and not the suicide that in the strictest sense it would appear to be. The scene shows audiences the ways in which an event that is one thing can be staged as another. The significance found in the staging will often overwhelm the actual event. Reality becomes what it appears to be rather than what it is. A director's criterial prefocusing becomes the threat Nolan's films suggest any idea can be when that idea is taken as authoritative rather than arbitrary.

Nolan makes explicit the logic of this danger as it operates in *Inception* through the idea that Cobb is responsible for Mal's death because he was the one that planted the idea in Mal's mind that her world was false. The idea becomes the cause that pushes Mal from the building. This is the position Cobb takes. Ariadne tries to dispel Cobb of this belief when she recognizes Cobb's willingness to blame himself for Mal's death: "It might have been your idea to push the limits, Cobb, but you're not responsible for the idea that destroyed her . . . that her world wasn't real, that was her own idea from her own mind." The statement exists as much as an example of criterial prefocusing as an instance of friendly comfort. Ariadne's words are likely to intensify the sympathy audiences already feel toward Cobb by virtue of *Inception* being Cobb's movie, the fact that Cobb is the one telling the story, and the fact that the character is played by an actor who routinely plays characters with whom audiences sympathize.

Interestingly, Nolan uses Mal's totem to distance audiences from this sympathy in at least two ways. Cobb presumably appropriates Mal's totem as his own after her death. The act violates one of the rules Arthur establishes about totems: they must not be familiar to anyone else, because that way one knows "beyond a doubt that [one] is not in someone else's dream." Given Cobb's use of Mal's totem, neither Cobb nor the audience can say for certain that Cobb is not in someone else's dream. Nolan even brings this doubt to the surface of the film in a late exchange between Mal and Cobb and especially in the final moments of the film. In terms of the late exchange, Mal insists that Cobb is dreaming, that he has lost the ability to "know what's real." She uses the action of the film to support her claim, the "mutable laws of physics . . . the . . . reappearance of the dead . . . persecution of the dreamer." The audience has seen Cobb experience each of these. They could very well decide, as Mal does, that these are not what the plot suggested they were, real or dreamlike attacks occurring outside Cobb. For Mal, they are examples of projections from Cobb's subconscious persecuting the dreamer.

As the plot moves from this contest of realities, this contest of ideas that can alternatively organize the action and significance of the film, the plot seems to reject Mal's contention. The team successfully fulfills its missions. They align the series of kicks required to pull them through the various levels of reality Nolan's script creates. Cobb remains in limbo to retrieve Saito, so that the two characters can return to the plane and Saito can honor his agreement, to make the phone call that will exonerate Cobb from the legal charges that supposedly prevent him from returning home to his children. Cobb returns to the scene of Mal and Cobb's house that has become so familiar to them, the site where Cobb's children wait for their father to return. The ending would seem to resolve all lines of action—only Nolan elects to refuse this resolution in the plot's final image. In the final moments, Cobb sets the top in motion to see if he is, indeed, in reality or in a dream. The sound of his children pulls him from his reality-check before he learns the result of his test. The audience watches the top a few moments longer as the top continues to spin. The object continues to spin through the ending of the film with no indication that it will ever topple. The film stops, in other words, before the audience knows if Cobb is in reality or some fantasy. Nolan leaves that determination in the hands of his spectators. The spectator decides if Cobb is home or not, or if his return is merely dream.

One can argue that Nolan makes the same refusal in *Dunkirk*. The narrative incongruities are so pronounced that audiences are forced to negotiate each narrative segment on their own. Nolan refuses to offer a narrative structure that prefocuses the significance of any one aspect of the film. In fact, his narrative structure frustrates any definitive significance. Every detail exists as a kind of irritant to an otherwise coherent story. These irritants appear in those moments on screen where two realities would appear to be in irrefutable contact. One example of such contact occurs when Collins (Jack Lowden), one of the original three Royal Air Force pilots, gets shot down from the sky. The event is shown two different times. The first instance occurs independently of any other story space, which is to say that it happens in "The Air" segment and in that segment alone. Farrier (Tom Hardy) damages a German plane in one moment, and Collins's plane is hit in the next. The plot jumps to events from "The Mole" segment before Collins actually hits the water. The plot leaves that segment to return to "The Sea" segment, which, interestingly, replays what would seem to be the first overlay of what has otherwise been two different segments of a story, which occurs when the three planes fly over the *Moonstone*. In this moment, the planes appear from behind the *Moonstone* before flying over the vessel. The plot, then, shifts back to "The Air" segment, which has Collins ditching his plane in the sea with no mention of "The Sea" or the *Moonstone*. Farrier simply watches as Collins successfully guides his plane into the water. Only at the tail end of that segment does the *Moonstone* come into sight. The small vessel is, in fact, very nearly on top of Collins's plane by the time it is seen.

Nolan could very easily shift from "The Air" segment to "The Sea" segment to show how the two storylines relate, but the writer/director prefers a return to a moment in the "The Mole" segment, which also brings "The Mole" and "The Sea" segment into contact with one another. The character identified in the credits as "The Shivering Soldier" (Cillian Murphy), a character the *Moonstone* has already rescued earlier in the plot from a boat found sunk at sea, refuses to let Tommy and Gibson board his rowboat for fear that any additional passengers will capsize the boat. Nolan shows that the three competing storylines can relate but refuses to provide any specific relationship between these stories. His refusal leaves spectators to construct rather than recognize whatever meaningful relationships will exist. *Dunkirk* does not provide any meaningful relationship to recognize. Nolan rejects the presence of a stable organizing principle that can hold the whole together. There is only the individual image and sequence of events as they exist on screen in the moment they appear on screen.

Dunkirk can be shown to relate to *Memento* in interesting ways. Even in the relatively early film, Nolan suggests that the significance of any image is always already negotiated, and only ever temporarily. Every image is arbitrary and subjective. Nolan forms this idea about images from the opening sequence in *Memento*, which begins, quite literally, with a photograph. The camera initially frames an instant photo of a blood sprayed scene centered on a man sprawled face down, presumably dead on the floor. The camera holds on the still image for thirty seconds as a series of credits run across the screen, after which the hand holding the instant photo begins to shake the item the way people would help early versions develop faster. When the shaking stops and the photo again sits still at the center of the frame, the audience can see that time is moving in reverse. The image has begun to fade back into the development process rather than clarify. The camera continues to hold as two more alternations occur between holding the photo still and shaking it out of existence. Each time the once fully developed image darkens and becomes less developed. After more than a minute, a cut carries the camera to the underside of the photo. The pace quickens. The events that led to the initial image run in reverse: the print goes back into the Polaroid 690 that produced it; the man returns the camera to his side; the blood on the floor flows toward its source rather than from it; the pistol jumps from the floor into the man's hand; the bullet returns to the chamber; the eventual/previous victim screams, "Wait"; the screen goes black. In roughly two minutes the once clear opening returns to the state of an undeveloped, not yet taken instant photo.

Nolan continues to unfold the main storyline in *Memento* out of sequence. Individual scenes occur in a linear fashion, where the earliest event happens first followed by what one can take as the next event in the scene, but the scenes themselves occur in reverse order. The resulting plot progression requires audiences to make sense of the film in reverse order. Spectators must constantly reconsider the significance of whatever scene they have just observed. Nolan introduces to every scene new context that asks spectators to watch and rewatch the scenes they might otherwise only witness. The structure would seem to fit what scholars typically refer to as "puzzle films," to return to Bordwell, inviting audiences to rewatch what they have seen to find what they have missed, "teasing the spectator to discover the hows and whys of their construction" (82). Elliot Panek (2006) assigns a more particular reason to return to puzzle films, and especially those like *Memento* that center on a traumatized main character. Panek finds such films "possess narratives" that refuse to match "the plot to diegetic reality" in an "immediately clear" manner (65). This lack of clarity "promotes . . . an . . . ambiguity" that prompts spectators to ask a different set of questions than more classical forms of cinematic narration invite: "rather than prompting the viewer to ask questions about characters *within* the diegesis, the narration . . . prompts the viewer to question the relationships among characters, narration, and . . . even the audiences' own . . . social reality" (65). Panek proposes that such films, and *Memento* especially, highlight the importance of "diegetic experience . . . to establishing a unified, coherent character" (83). By telling the story in reverse, and by highlighting the way the narrative presents a "newly motivated causal agent in each scene," Panek proposes that *Memento* reveals just how "meaningless" it is to try and put "every scene back in the right order" (83–84). In this way, then, *Memento* prompts a different kind of spectatorial response, one that asks spectators to consider the inherent contingency in every image.

Every picture possesses the reality it realizes in one story line while never forsaking some other, just as plausible reality. *Memento* prompts this discussion in a number of ways. For one thing, the narrative highlights the individual and instantaneous photo more than just about any other narrative film in contemporary cinema. In addition to the opening, which privileges the instant photo in the ways already described, Nolan places the photograph in over thirty more shots (as many as thirty-eight more shots, depending on what counts as a new instance of the opening). Just as importantly, these photographs provide the only real orientation for the main character, Leonard (Guy Pearce), or the audience. In this way the photograph becomes an essential plot piece rather than just a prop. The photograph becomes the detail on which the plot turns. Most interesting is the way that Nolan refuses to determine the exact meaning or significance of these plot pieces. The image itself rarely stands on its own. Those instant photographs that are never notated are eventually dismissed, destroyed, or otherwise ignored. Those that have notation turn out to support not the reality contained in the picture, but the story that image means to serve. In this way, the reality that matters most in *Memento* is the reality set over the image rather than some sense of significance found in it.

Nolan's suggestion that the ultimate significance of an image is applied to an image rather than found in an image emerges most clearly around two photographs in Leonard's network of images, those marked "Natalie" and "Teddy." Both photographs are referenced repeatedly throughout *Memento*, and even at critical moments in the plot. The most interesting aspect of these images, though, is the way both images are, from the moment they are taken, instances of deception. In the case of Natalie's photo, Nolan arranges the narrative so that the audience knows that Leonard is in the midst of a setup before Natalie's (Carrie-Anne Moss) picture is taken. Natalie is not who she seems to be to Leonard. She mistakenly blames "Teddy" (Joe Pantoliano) for her boyfriend Jimmy's (Larry Holden) death, and she plans to use Leonard to avenge this wrong. Little does she or the audience know that Leonard is a) the actual murderer or b) entangled in the same act of deception against himself.

Neither revelation matters when Natalie's picture is taken. What matters is that Natalie is not who she pretends to be, and that Nolan's script makes her deception explicit to the audience. The same deception surrounds the moment of registration for Teddy's photograph, too. Teddy is presumably working as a nark in a drug bust. He uses the name "Teddy" in that crowd, and in front of Leonard to maintain his cover. His real name, however, is John Edward Gammell. Nolan's script emphasizes the fact that Teddy is a cover when Leonard takes John's photograph. In this way, there is nothing to recover from these moments of registration, nothing authentic or authoritative. There is only deception. There can be, therefore, no real loss in the revisions Leonard makes to the notations over these images. The photographs are, from the moment they are taken, objects to be revised.

Nolan's plot emphasizes the extent to which the images exist to be revised. One sees this point of emphasis when evaluating Natalie's photograph. The first time the audience sees the back of Natalie's photo, her photo displays two notes, one that has been scratched through, and the other that reads "She has lost someone/She will help you out of pity." This second note proves the most persuasive during the film because it is the one that helps Leonard act in Natalie's favor in several key scenes. It also sets up the first real surprise in the plot, the aforementioned revelation that Natalie does not pity Leonard, that she is, in truth, using Leonard. The real take away from the doubly notated photo is twofold. In one sense, the double notation makes plain that the image in the photo does not speak for itself. It requires a notation before it can be prefocused in any significant way. In a second sense, the presence of the two notations also shows that the significance of the photo is always open for reinterpretation. The image can, in other words, bear one significance under one notation, and still another when set beneath some other. These two conditions frustrate lines of argument that tie the index in a photograph to some fixed past. Images only tolerate the interpretative moment of the now wherein some earlier interpretation can either be ratified again or revised in some unexpected way.

The back of Natalie's photograph, with the two notes, shows as much. The first note, which reads, "Do not trust her," has been removed so that some other stance toward this character can be adopted. The same sort of revision takes place on Teddy's photograph. The first time the photograph is seen, it has only the note written on front of the image, "Teddy 555 0134." Later, Leonard flips the photograph to see the notation on the back of the photograph: "Don't listen to him/He is the one/Kill Him." The notes would seem authoritative enough, and they prove to be just that at several key moments in the film. Such is the case in the first segment when Leonard strikes Teddy in the head just before Leonard shoots him. By the end of the film, though, most every notation has lost any sense of authority. The notations are reduced to declarations that are set to expire the moment some other declaration proves more desirable. The image is never bound to any one declaration. The reality every image holds can, after all, be reoriented toward some new reality the moment some new statement is set over it. This is as true for lens-based images pulling from some real world that existed before the camera as it is any other type of image. All images remain open for ongoing adaptation so long as the spectator sees them as such.

Nolan emphasizes this last idea by having Leonard use the photographs to identify and recognize one person from another. The trouble is that the photographs only work when they are definitively notated, and no notation proves definitive. The notations can be false, which is to say that the images can be redirected. This is the conclusion *Memento* encourages one to reach, and, perhaps more interestingly, it is also the conclusion *Dunkirk* encourages. The images brought to the screen in *Dunkirk* are never as dubious as those in *Memento*, but neither are they truly definitive. This quality is most apparent at the end of the film when Nolan elects to have Tommy read Churchill's "We Will Never Surrender" speech from the newspaper, but the words and the images do not match. Tommy reads, for instance, "we shall fight on the beaches," but, rather than have an image of men fighting on a beach, the screen has an image of waves washing over a dead body. The words and the images are set against each other. The spectator is asked to reconcile the difference.

The same thing happens a little more ambiguously when Tommy reads the words "We shall never surrender." Under those words, Nolan places an image of dozens of helmets on the sand separated from the men who had worn them. The combination of image and words could be taken as an explanation of why "We shall never surrender," namely, that the memory of those who have died compels us to continue the fight, but the images could also be seen as one instance of a kind of surrender, death. The exact meaning of the image is not entirely set. In fact, it is unsettled by the notation the voice-over provides it. As such, the image becomes an index begging to be negotiated through a process of ongoing adaptation that only the spectator can perform. That process will entertain images that are in some sense truthful. In other cases, it will entertain images that are more akin to the sorts of truths one wishes were true. The story Peter gives the local paper about George that leads to the headline, "Local Boy, George Mills, Just 17, Hero at Dunkirk," serves as one example. This headline is true, and it is not true. One can examine the truth and untruth of every word. As it existed on the screen, one can direct the evidence the images provide in more than one direction. The pursuit itself moves within and beyond the confines of some truth. It reminds spectators that any truth in the cinema is a truth negotiated rather than received, and that the process of reception will remain open when it is set on the point of a cinematic index that favors rewatching and ongoing adaptation above anything else.

WORKS CITED

Altman, Rick. *Film/Genre*. British Film Institute, 1998.
Amago, Samuel. "Ethics, Aesthetics, and the Future in Alfonso Cuarón's *Children of Men*." *Discourse* 32, no. 2 (2010): 212–35.
The Amorous Guardsman. British Mutoscope and Biograph Company, 1898.
Andrew, Dudley. "Adaptation." In *Film and Literature: An Introduction and Reader*, 2nd ed., edited by Timothy Corrigan. Routledge, 2012.
Apocalypse Now. Directed by France Ford Coppola. Performances by Martin Sheen, Marlon Brando, and Robert Duvall. American Zoetrope, 1979.
Aragay, Mireia, ed. *Books in Motion: Adaptation, Intertextuality, and Authorship*. Rodopi, 2006.
Atkin, Albert. "Peirce on the Index and Indexical Reference." *Transactions of the Charles S. Peirce Society* 41, no. 1 (2005): 161–88.
Avatar. Directed by James Cameron. Performances by Sam Worthington, Zoe Saldana, and Sigourney Weaver. Twentieth Century Fox, 2009.
Avengers: Endgame. Directed by Anthony Russo and Joe Russo. Performances by Robert Downey Jr., Chris Evans, and Mark Ruffalo. Marvel Studios, 2019.
Avengers: Infinity War. Directed by Anthony Russo and Joe Russo. Performances by Robert Downey Jr., Chris Hemsworth, and Mark Ruffalo. Marvel Studios, 2018.
The Avengers. Directed by Joss Whedon. Performances by Robert Downey Jr., Chris Evans, and Scarlett Johansson. Marvel Studios, 2012.
Bacon, Terryl, and Govinda Dickman. "'Who's the Daddy?' The Aesthetics and Politics of Representation in Alfonso Cuarón's Adaptation of P. D. James' *Children of Men*." In *Adaptation in Contemporary Culture: Textual Infidelities*, edited by Rachel Carroll, 147–62. Continuum, 2009.
Baetens, Jan. *Novelization: From Film to Novel*. Ohio State University Press, 2018.
Bambi. Directed by James Algar. Performances by Hardie Albright, Stan Alexander, and Bobette Audrey. Walt Disney Productions, 1942.
Barthes, Roland. *Camera Lucida*, translated by Richard Howard. Hill & Wang, 2010.
Batman Begins. Directed by Christopher Nolan. Performances by Christian Bale, Michael Caine, and Ken Watanabe. Warner Bros., 2005.
Bazin, André, and Hugh Gray. "Ontology of the Photographic Image." *Film Quarterly* 13, no. 4 (Summer 1960): 4–9.
Before Midnight. Directed by Richard Linklater. Performances by Ethan Hawke, Julie Delpy, and Samus Davey-Fitzpatrick. Faliro House Productions, 2013.

Before Sunrise. Directed by Richard Linklater. Performances by Ethan Hawke, Julie Delpy, and Andrea Eckert. Castle Rock Entertainment, 1995.

Before Sunset. Directed by Richard Linklater. Performances by Ethan Hawke, Julie Delpy, and Vernon Dobtcheff. Warner Independent Pictures, 2004.

Beja, Morris. *Film and Literature*. Longman, 1979.

Benjamin, Walter. "The Task of the Translator." In *Illuminations: Essays and Reflections*, edited by Hannah Arendt, translated by Harry Zohn, 69–82. Shocken Books, 1969.

Bernie. Directed by Richard Linklater. Performances by Jack Black, Shirley MacLaine, and Matthew McConaughey. Mandalay Vision, 2012.

Bicycle Thieves. Directed by Vittorio de Sica. Performances by Lamberto Maggiorani, Enzo Staiola, and Lianella Carell. Produzioni De Sica, 1948.

Black Panther. Directed by Ryan Coogler. Performances by Chadwick Boseman, Michael B. Jordan, and Lupita Nyong'o. Marvel Studios, 2018.

Blade Runner. Directed by Ridley Scott. Performances by Harrison Ford, Rutger Hauer, and Sean Young. Ladd Company, 1982.

The Blair Witch Project. Directed by Daniel Myrick. Performances by Heather Donahue, Michael C. Williams, and Joshua Leonard. Haxan Films, 1999.

Bloody Sunday. Directed by Paul Greengrass. Performances by James Nesbitt, Tim Pigott-Smith, and Nicholas Farrell. Bórd Scannán na hÉireann, 2002.

Bluestone, George. *Novels into Film*. Johns Hopkins University Press, 2003.

Body Heat. Directed by Lawrence Kasdan. Performances by William Hurt, Kathleen Turner, and Richard Crenna. Ladd Company, 1981.

Bordwell, David. *Making Meaning: Inference and Rhetoric in the Interpretation of Cinema*. Harvard University Press, 1989.

Bordwell, David. *The Way Hollywood Tells It: Story and Style in Modern Movies*. University of California Press, 2006.

Born on the Fourth of July. Directed by Oliver Stone. Performances by Tom Cruise, Bryan Larkin, and Raymond J. Barry. Ixtlan, 1989.

Boyhood. Directed by Richard Linklater. Performances by Ellar Coltrane, Patricia Arquette, and Ethan Hawke. IFC Productions, 2014.

Boys Don't Cry. Directed by Kimberly Peirce. Performances by Hilary Swank, Chloë Sevigny, and Peter Sarsgaard. Fox Searchlight Pictures, 1999.

Boyum, Joy Gould. *Double Exposure: Fiction into Film*. Olympic Marketing, 1985.

Bride and Prejudice. Directed by Gurinder Chada. Performances by Martin Henderson, Aishwarya Rai Bachchan, and Nadira Babbar. Pathé Pictures International, 2005.

The Brood. Directed by David Cronenberg. Performances by Oliver Reed, Samantha Egger, and Art Hindle. Canadian Film Development Corporation, 1979.

Buchanan, Judith. "Literary Adaptation in the Silent Era." In *A Companion to Literature, Film, and Adaptation*, edited by Deborah Cartmell. Blackwell, 2012.

Burning. Directed by Chang-dong Lee. Performances by Yoo Ah-In, Steven Yuen, and Jong-seo Jun. Pine House Films, 2018.

Butch Cassidy and the Sundance Kid. Directed by George Roy Hill. Performances by Paul Newman, Robert Redford, and Katharine Ross. Campanile Productions, 1969.

Cahir, Linda Costanzo. *Literature into Film: Theory and Practical Approaches.* McFarland, 2006.
Canet, Fernando. "Schizophrenic Twins: A Comparative Study of Hitchcock's *Psycho* (1960) and van Sant's 1998 Remake." *Journal of Film and Video* 70, no. 1 (Spring 2018): 17–31.
Cardwell, Sarah. *Adaptation Revisited: Television and the Classic Novel.* Manchester University Press, 2002.
Carroll, Noël. *The Philosophy of Motion Pictures.* Blackwell, 2008.
Cartmell, Deborah, ed. *A Companion to Literature, Film, and Adaptation.* Wiley-Blackwell, 2012.
Cartmell, Deborah, Heidi Kaye, I. Q. Hunter, and Imelda Whelehan, eds. *Classics in Film and Fiction.* Pluto Press, 2000.
Cartmell, Deborah, I. Q. Hunter, and Imelda Whelehan. *Retrovisions: Reinventing the Past in Film and Fiction.* Pluto Press, 2001.
Cartmell, Deborah, and Imelda Whelehan. *Screen Adaptation: Impure Cinema.* Macmillan International Higher Education, 2010.
Cartmell, Deborah, and Imelda Whelehan, eds. *Adaptations: From Text to Screen, Screen to Text.* Routledge, 1999.
Cartmell, Deborah, and Imelda Whelehan, eds. *The Cambridge Companion to Literature on Screen.* Cambridge University Press, 2007.
Caruth, Cathy. *Unclaimed Experience: Trauma, Narrative, and History.* Johns Hopkins University Press, 1996.
Castoriadis, Cornelius. "The Imaginary: Creation in the Socio-Historical Domain." In *World in Fragments: Writings on Politics, Society, Psychoanalysis and the Imagination,* edited by D. A. Curtis, 3–18. Stanford University Press, 1997.
Catch Me If You Can. Directed by Steven Spielberg. Performances by Leonardo DiCaprio, Tom Hanks, and Christopher Walken. Dreamworks Pictures, 2002.
Chandler, Daniel. *Semiotics: The Basics,* 3rd ed. Routledge, 2016.
Children of Men. Directed by Alfonso Cuarón. Performances by Julianne Moore, Clive Owen, and Chiwetel Ejiofor. Universal Pictures, 2006.
Chumo, Peter. "'You've Got to Put the Past Behind You Before You Can Move On': Forrest Gump and National Reconciliation." *Journal of Popular Film & Television* 23, no. 1 (Spring 1995): 2–7.
Citizen Kane. Directed by Orson Welles. Performances by Orson Welles, Joseph Cotten, and Dorothy Comingore. RKO Radio Pictures, 1941.
Close Encounters of the Third Kind. Directed by Steven Spielberg. Performances by Richard Dreyfuss, Francois Truffaut, and Teri Garr. Julia Phillips and Michael Phillips Productions, 1977.
Clueless. Directed by Amy Heckerling. Performances by Alicia Silverstone, Stacey Dash, and Brittany Murphy. Paramount Pictures, 1995.
Cohen, Keith. *Film and Fiction: The Dynamics of Exchange.* Yale University Press, 1979.
Con Air. Directed by Simon West. Performances by Nicolas Cage, John Cusack, and John Malkovich. Touchstone Pictures, 1997.
Corrigan, Timothy, ed. *Film and Literature: An Introduction and Reader.* Routledge, 2011.

Corrigan, Timothy, ed. "Literature on Screen, A History: In the Gap." In *The Cambridge Companion to Literature on Screen*, edited by Deborah Cartmell and Imelda Whelehan, 29–44. Cambridge University Press, 2007.

Ćosić, Vuk. *ASCII History of the Moving Image*. University of California, Berkeley Art Museum & Pacific Film Archive, 1998.

Cowie, Elizabeth. *Recording Reality, Desiring the Real*. University of Minnesota Press, 2011.

Curtis, Scott. *Animation*. Rutgers University Press, 2019.

Cutler, Aaron. "Love in Time." *Cineaste* 38, no. 4 (Fall 2013): 24–28.

The Dark Knight. Directed by Christopher Nolan. Performances by Christian Bale, Heath Ledger, and Aaron Eckhart. Warner Bros., 2008.

The Dark Knight Rises. Directed by Christopher Nolan. Performances by Christian Bale, Tom Hardy, and Anne Hathaway. Warner Bros., 2012.

The Day After Tomorrow. Directed by Roland Emmerich. Performances by Dennis Quaid, Jake Gyllenhaal, and Emmy Rossum. Twentieth Century Fox, 2004.

deCordova, Richard. "The Emergence of the Star System in America." In *Stardom: Industry of Desire*, edited by Christine Gledhill, 17–29. Routledge, 1991.

de Man, Paul. *Allegories of Reading: Figural Language in Rousseau, Nietzsche, Rilke, and Proust*. Yale University Press, 1982.

Diary of a Country Priest. Directed by Robert Bresson. Performances by Claude Laydu, Nicole Ladmiral, and Jean Riveyre. Union Générale Cinématographique, 1954.

Doane, Mary Ann. *The Emergence of Cinematic Time: Modernity, Contingency, the Archive*. Harvard University Press, 2002.

Doane, Mary Ann. "Indexicality: Trace and Sign: Introduction." *Differences: A Journal of Feminist Cultural Studies* 18, no. 1 (2007): 1–6.

Duchamp, Marcel. *Fountain*. Paris, 1917.

Dunkirk. Directed by Christopher Nolan. Performances by Fionn Whitehead, Barry Keoghan, and Mark Rylance. Syncopy, 2017.

Elliott, Kamilla. *Rethinking the Novel/Film Debate*. Cambridge University Press, 2002.

Elsaesser, Thomas. "Postmodernism as Mourning Work." *Screen* 42, no. 2 (Summer 2001): 193–201.

E.T.: The Extra-Terrestrial. Directed by Steven Spielberg. Performances by Henry Thomas, Drew Barrymore, and Peter Coyote. Universal Pictures, 1982.

Eternal Sunshine of the Spotless Mind. Directed by Michel Gondry. Performances by Jim Carrey, Kate Winslet, and Tom Wilkinson. Focus Features, 2004.

Ex Machina. Directed by Alex Garland. Performances by Alicia Vikander, Domhnall Gleeson, and Oscar Isaac. A24, 2015.

Extremely Loud and Incredibly Close. Directed by Stephen Daldry. Performances by Thomas Horn, Tom Hanks, and Sandra Bullock. Warner Bros., 2011.

Fargo. Directed Joel and Ethan Coen. Performances by William H. Macy, Frances McDormand, and Steve Buscemi. PolyGram Filmed Entertainment, 1996.

Fantasia. Directed by James Algar. Performances by Leopold Stokowski, Deems Taylor, and the Philadelphia Orchestra. Walt Disney Productions, 1940.

Fhlainn, Sorcha Ní. "'You keep telling yourself what you know, but what do you believe?': Cultural Spin, Puzzle Films and Mind Games in the Cinema of Christopher Nolan." In

The Cinema of Christopher Nolan: Imagining the Impossible, edited by Jacqueline Furby and Stuart Joy, 147–62. Columbia University Press, 2015.
Fight Club. Directed by David Fincher. Performances by Brad Pitt, Edward Norton, and Meat Loaf. Fox 2000 Pictures, 1999.
The Fly. Directed by David Cronenberg. Performances by Jeff Goldblum, Geena Davis, and John Getz. SLM Production Group, 1986.
Forrest Gump. Directed by Robert Zemeckis. Performances by Tom Hanks, Robin Wright, and Gary Sinise. Paramount Pictures, 1994.
Furniss, Maureen. *Animation: Art and Industry*. John Libbey, 2007.
The Game. Directed by David Fincher. Performances by Michael Douglas, Deborah Kara Unger, and Sean Penn. Polygram Filmed Entertainment, 1997.
Gaut, Berys. *A Philosophy of Cinematic Art*. Cambridge University Press, 2010.
Geraghty, Christine. *Now a Major Motion Picture: Film Adaptations of Literature and Drama*. Rowman & Littlefield, 2007.
Germany Year Zero. Directed by Roberto Rossellini. Performances by Edmund Moeschke, Ernst Pittschau, and Ingetraud Hinze. Tevere Film, 1948.
Gledhill, Christine. "History of Genre Criticism." 1985. *The Cinema Book*, 3rd ed., edited by Pam Cook, 252–59. British Film Institute, 2007.
Gone in Sixty Seconds. Directed by Dominic Sena. Performances by Nicolas Cage, Angelina Jolie, and Giovanni Ribisi. Touchstone Pictures, 2000.
Gone with the Wind. Directed by Victor Fleming. Performances by Clark Gable, Vivien Leigh, and Thomas Mitchell. Selznick International Pictures, 1939.
The Graduate. Directed by Mike Nichols. Performances by Dustin Hoffman, Anne Bancroft, and Katharine Ross. Lawrence Truman Productions, 1967.
Grease. Directed by Randal Kleiser. Performances by John Travolta, Olivia Newton-John, and Stockard Channing. Paramount Pictures, 1978.
The Great Train Robbery. Directed by Edwin S. Porter. Performances by Gilbert M. "Broncho Billy" Anderson, A. C. Adabie, and George Barnes. Edison Manufacturing Company, 1903.
Greenlaw, Duncan. "'Until Justice is Done': Authenticity and Memory in Paul Greengrass's *Bloody Sunday* and *United 93*." *Canadian Journal of Film Studies/Revue Canadienne D'Etudes Cinematograhiques* 19, no. 2 (October 2010): 2–25.
Grossman, Julie. *Literature, Film, and Their Hideous Progeny: Adaptations and ElasTEXTity*. Palgrave Macmillan, 2015.
Gunning, Tom. "The Cinema of Attraction: Early Film, Its Spectator, and the Avant-Garde." *Wide Angle* 8, no. 3 (Fall 1986): 63–70. Reprinted in *The Cinema of Attractions Reloaded*, edited by Wanda Stauven, 381–88. Amsterdam University Press, 2006.
Gunning, Tom. "Moving Away from the Index: Cinema and the Impression of Reality." *Differences: A Journal of Feminist Cultural Studies* 18, no. 1 (2007): 29–52.
Gunning, Tom. "What's the Point of an Index? Or, Faking Photographs." In *Still Moving: Between Cinema and Photography*, edited by Karen Beckman and Jean Ma, 23–40. Duke University Press, 2008.
Hamlet. Directed by Michael Almereyda. Performances by Ethan Hawke, Kyle MacLachlan, and Diane Venora. Double A Films, 2000.

Hanging Out the Clothes. Directed by George Albert Smith. Performances by Laura Bayley, Mrs. Tom Green, and Tom Green. George Albert Smith Films, 1897.

Harry Potter and the Sorcerer's Stone. Directed by Chris Columbus. Performances by Daniel Radcliffe, Rupert Grint, and Richard Harris. Warner Bros., 2001.

Hearts in Dixie. Directed by Paul Sloane. Performances by Stepin Fetchit, Clarence Muse, and Eugene Jackson. Fox Film Corporation, 1929.

Heaven & Earth. Directed by Oliver Stone. Performances by Hiep Thi Le, Tommy Lee Jones, and Haing S. Ngor. Alcor Films, 1993.

Hello Dolly! Directed by Gene Kelly. Performances by Barbara Streisand, Walter Matthau, and Michael Crawford. Chenault Productions, 1969.

Herman, Judith Lewis. *Trauma and Recovery: The Aftermath of Violence—from Domestic Abuse to Political Terror*. Basic Books, 1992.

Herzog, Amy. "Images of Thought and Acts of Creation: Delueze, Bergson, and the Question of Cinema." *Invisible Culture: An Electronic Journal for Visual Culture* 3 (2000).

Hiroshima, mon amour. Directed by Alain Resnais. Performances by Emmanuelle Riva, Eliji Okada, and Stella Dassas. Argos Films, 1959.

House of Games. Directed by David Mamet. Performances by Lindsay Crouse, Joe Mantegna, and Mike Nussbaum. Filmhaus, 1987.

How Green Was My Valley. Directed by John Ford. Performances by Walter Pidgeon, Maureen O'Hara, and Anna Lee. Twentieth Century Fox, 1941.

Hutcheon, Linda. *A Theory of Adaptation*, 2nd ed. Routledge, 2013.

Imitation of Life. Directed by Douglas Sirk. Performances by Lana Turner, John Gavin, and Sandra Dee. Universal International Pictures, 1959.

Inception. Directed by Christopher Nolan. Performances by Leonardo DiCaprio, Joseph Gordon-Levitt, and Elliot Page. Warner Bros., 2010.

Incredibles 2. Directed by Brad Bird. Performances by Craig T. Nelson, Holly Hunter, and Sarah Vowell. Walt Disney Pictures, 2018.

Inning by Inning: A Portrait of a Coach. Directed by Richard Linklater. Performances by Cathy Clark, Roger Clemens, and Augie Garrido. Detour Filmproduction, 2008.

Insomnia. Directed by Christopher Nolan. Performances by Al Pacino, Robin Williams, and Hilary Swank. Alcon Entertainment, 2002

Interstellar. Directed by Christopher Nolan. Performances by Matthew McConaughey, Anne Hathaway, and Jessica Chastain. Paramount Pictures, 2014.

James, P. D. *Children of Men*. Faber and Faber, 1992.

Jaws. Directed by Steven Spielberg. Performances by Roy Scheider, Robert Shaw, and Richard Dreyfuss. Zanuck/Brown Productions, 1975.

Johnson, David T. *Richard Linklater: An Incisive Analysis of a Popular American Filmmaker*. University of Illinois Press, 2012.

Johnston, Ollie, and Frank Thomas. *Disney Animation: The Illusion of Life*. Abbeville Press, 1981.

Journey to Italy. Directed by Roberto Rossellini. Performances by Ingrid Bergman, George Sanders, and Maria Mauban. Italia Film, 1954.

Jurassic Park. Directed by Steven Spielberg. Performances by Sam Neill, Laura Dern, and Jeff Goldblum. Universal Pictures, 1993.

Jurassic World. Directed by Colin Trevorrow. Performances by Chris Pratt, Bryce Dallas Howard, and Ty Simpkins. Universal Pictures, 2015.

Kaplan, E. Ann. "Pretrauma Political Thrillers." In *Climate Trauma: Foreseeing the Future in Dystopian Film and Fiction*, 59–78. Rutgers University Press, 2016.

Kaplan, E. Ann, and Ben Wang. *Trauma Cinema: Cross-Cultural Explorations*. Hong Kong University Press, 2004.

Kawin, Bruce. "Three Endings." *Film Quarterly* 65, no. 1 (2011): 14–16.

Kilday, Gregg. "Making of *Boyhood*: What You Don't Know About Richard Linklater's 12-Year Shoot." *Hollywood Reporter*, November 20, 2014, 84–89.

The Kiss. Directed by William Heise. Performances by Mary Irwin and John C. Rice. Edison Manufacturing Company, 1896.

The Kiss in the Tunnel. Directed by George Albert Smith. Performances by Laura Bayley and George Albert Smith. George Albert Smith Films, 1899.

The Kiss in the Tunnel. Directed by James Bamforth. Bamforth Films, 1899.

Klein, Amanda Ann. *American Film Cycles: Reframing Genres, Screening Social Problems, and Defining Subcultures*. University of Texas Press, 2011.

Klein, Michael, and Gillian Parker, eds. *The English Novel and the Movies*. Ungar, 1981.

Krauss, Rosalind. *The Originality of the Avant-Garde and Other Modernists Myths*. MIT Press, 1985.

Lady and the Tramp. Directed by Clyde Geronimi. Performances by Barbara Luddy, Larry Roberts, and Peggy Lee. Walt Disney Animation Studios, 1955.

LaRose, Nicole. "The Already Dead and the Posthuman Baby: *Children of Men*, Dystopian Worlds, and Utopian Kinship." *Interdisciplinary Humanities* 27, no. 2 (Fall 2010): 7–23.

La Roue. Directed by Abel Gance. Performances by Gabriel de Gravone, Pierre Magnier, and Georges Térof. Films Abel Gance, 1923.

Laskar, Samrat. "A Tale of Two (Gotham) Cities: Nolanizing Dickens." *Journal of the Department of English: Vidyassagar University* 10 (2012–2013): 105–12.

Last Flag Flying. Directed by Richard Linklater. Performances by Bryan Cranston, Laurence Fishburne, and Steve Carell. Amazon Studios, 2017.

Leitch, Thomas. *Film Adaptation and Its Discontents: From* Gone with the Wind *to* The Passion of the Christ. Johns Hopkins University Press, 2007.

Leliński, Michał. "Dickens's Influence on *The Dark Knight Rises*." In *Reflections on/of Dickens*, edited by Ewa Kujawska-Lis and Anna Laskarzewska. 317–32. Cambridge Scholars Publishing, 2014.

Leys, Ruth. *Trauma: A Genealogy*. University of Chicago Press, 2000.

Live from Shiva's Dance Floor. Directed by Richard Linklater. Performance by Timothy "Speed" Levitch. Detour Filmproduction, 2003.

The Locket. Directed by John Brahm. Performances by Laraine Day, Robert Mitchum, and Brian Aherne. RKO Radio Pictures, 1946.

Longden, Kenneth. "China Whispers: The Symbolic, Economic, and Political Presence of China in Contemporary American Science Fiction Film." *Open Cultural Studies* 2, no. 1 (2018): 151–61.

Lord of the Rings: The Fellowship of the Ring. Directed by Peter Jackson. Performances by Elijah Wood, Ian McKellen, and Orlando Bloom. New Line Cinema, 2001.

Love in a Railroad Train. Directed by Siegmund Lubin. S. Lubin, 1902.

Manchester by the Sea. Directed by Kenneth Lonergan. Performances by Casey Affleck, Michelle Williams, and Kyle Chandler. Amazon Studios, 2016.

Manovich, Lev. *The Language of New Media*, rev. ed. MIT Press, 2002.

Marnie. Directed by Alfred Hitchcock. Performances by Tippi Hedren, Sean Connery, and Martin Gabel. Alfred J. Hitchcock Productions, 1964.

Mary Poppins. Directed by Robert Stevenson. Performances by Julie Andrews, Dick Van Dyke, and David Tomlinson, Walt Disney Production, 1964.

The Matrix. Directed by Lana Wachowski and Lilly Wachowski. Performances by Keanu Reeves, Laurence Fishburne, and Carrie-Anne Moss. Warner Bros., 1999.

McFarlane, Alexander, and Bessel van der Kolk. "Trauma and its Challenge to Society." In *Traumatic Stress: The Effects of Overwhelming Experience on Mind, Body, and Society*, 24–46. Guilford Press, 1996.

McFarlane, Brian. *Novel to Film: An Introduction to the Theory of Adaptation*. Clarendon Press, 1996.

Memento. Directed by Christopher Nolan. Performances by Guy Pearce, Carrie-Anne Moss, and Joe Pantoliano. Newmarket Capital Group, 2000.

Meshes of the Afternoon. Directed by Maya Deren. Performances by Maya Deren and Alexander Hammid. Maya Deren Production, 1943.

Metz, Christian. "On the Impression of Reality in the Cinema." In *Film Language: A Semiotics of the Cinema*, translated by Michael Taylor, 3–15. Oxford University Press, 1974.

Mildred Pierce. Directed by Michael Curtiz. Performances by Joan Crawford, Jack Carson, and Zachary Scott. Warner Bros., 1945.

Miller, Nancy K., and Jason Tougaw. *Extremities: Trauma, Testimony, and Community*. University of Illinois Press, 2002.

Mulvey, Laura. *Death 24x a Second: Stillness and the Moving Image*. Reaktion Books, 2006.

Münsterberg, Hugo. *Hugo Münsterberg on Film: The Photoplay: A Psychological Study and Other Writings*, edited by Allan Langdale. Routledge, 2001.

Münsterberg, Hugo. "Why We Go to the Movies." In *Critical Visions in Film Theory: Classic and Contemporary Readings*, edited by Timothy Corrigan and Patricia White, with Meta Mazaj, 9–17. Bedford, 2010.

Murakami, Haruki. "Barn Burning." Translated Jay Rubin. *New Yorker* 67, no. 39 (1991): 45–54.

Murphet, Julian. "Pitiable or Political Animals?" *SubStance* 37, no. 3 (117, 2008): 97–116.

National Treasure. Directed by Jon Turteltaub. Performances by Nicolas Cage, Diane Kruger, and Justin Bartha. Walt Disney Pictures, 2004.

Nichols, Bill. *Introduction to Documentary*, 3rd ed. Indiana University Press, 2017.

Niessen, Niels. "Lives of Cinema: Against Its 'Death.'" In *Films in the Postmodern Age*, edited by Agnes Petho, 161–84. Cambridge Scholars Publishing, 2012.

Ní Fhlainn, Sorcha. "'You Keep Telling Yourself What You Know, but What Do You Believe?' Cultural Spin, Puzzle Films and Mind Games in the Cinema of Christopher Nolan." In *The Cinema of Christopher Nolan: Imagining the Impossible*, edited by Jacqueline Furby and Stuart Joy, 147–63. Columbia University Press, 2015.

Night and Fog. Directed by Alain Resnais. Performances by Michael Bouquet, Reinhard Heydrich, and Heinrich Himmler. Argos Films, 1956.

Night Cries. Directed by Tracey Moffatt. Performances by Andrew Cymek, Brigitte Kingsley, and Dillon Baldassero. Good Soldier Films, 2015.

O. Directed by Tim Blake Nelson. Performances by Mekhi Phifer, Julia Stiles, and Martin Sheen. Chickie the Cop, 2001.

Olkowski, Dorethea. *Gilles Deleuze and the Ruin of Representation*. University of California Press, 1999.

Panek, Elliot. "The Poet and the Detective: Defining the Psychological Puzzle Film." *Film Criticism* 31, no. 1/2 (2006): 62–88.

Patrick, Robert, and Amy MacDonald. "Symbolism and the City: From Towers of Power to 'Ground Zero.'" *Prairie Perspectives: Geographical Essays* 15 (2012): 14–18.

Paulson, Kris. "The Index and the Interface." *Representations* 122, no. 1 (2013): 83–109.

Peirce, Charles Sanders. "Logic as Semiotic: The Theory of Signs." In *Philosophical Writings of Peirce*, edited by Justus Buchler. Dover Publications, 2016.

Peter Pan. Directed by Clyde Geronimi. Performances by Bobby Driscoll, Kathryn Beaumont, and Hans Conried. Walt Disney Productions, 1943.

Pinocchio. Directed by Norman Ferguson. Performances by Dickie Jones, Christian Rub, and Mel Blanc. Walt Disney Productions, 1940.

Platoon. Directed by Oliver Stone. Performances by Charlie Sheen, Tom Berenger, and Willem Dafoe. Hemdale, 1986.

The Prestige. Directed by Christopher Nolan. Performances by Christian Bale, Hugh Jackman, and Scarlett Johansson. Touchstone Pictures, 2006.

Prince, Stephen. "The emergence of Filmic Artifacts: Cinema and Cinematography in the Digital Era." *Film Quarterly* 57, no. 3 (2004): 24–33.

Psycho. Directed by Alfred Hitchcock. Performances by Anthony Perkins, Janet Leigh, and Vera Miles. Shamley Productions. 1960.

Pulp Fiction. Directed by Quentin Tarantino. Performances by John Travolta, Uma Thurman, and Samuel L. Jackson. Miramax, 1994.

Radstone, Susannah. "Trauma Theory: Contexts, Politics, Ethics." *Paragraph* 30, no. 1 (2007): 9–29.

Rafferty, Terrance. "Everybody Gets a Cut: DVDs Give Viewers Dozens of Choices—and That's the Problem." In *Philosophy of Film and Motion Pictures*, edited by Noël Carroll and Jinhee Choi, 44–48. Blackwell, 2006.

Raw, Laurence, ed. *The Silk Road of Adaptation: Transformations across Disciplines and Cultures*. Cambridge Scholars Publishing, 2013.

The Road to Guantánamo. Directed by Mat Whitecross. Performances by Riz Ahmed, Farhad Harun, and Waqar Siddiqui. Film4, 2006.

Rosen, Philip. *Change Mummified: Cinema, Historicity, Theory*. University of Minnesota Press, 2001.

Rushton, Richard. *The Reality of Film: Theories of Filmic Reality*. Manchester University Press, 2013.

Saving Mr. Banks. Directed by John Lee Hancock. Performances by Emma Thompson, Tom Hanks, and Annie Rose Buckley. Walt Disney Pictures, 2013.

Saving Private Ryan. Directed by Steven Spielberg. Performances by Tom Hanks, Matt Damon, and Tom Sizemore. Dreamworks Pictures, 1998.

A Scanner Darkly. Directed by Richard Linklater. Performances by Keanu Reeves, Winona Ryder, and Robert Downey Jr. Warner Independent Pictures, 2006.

Seger, Linda. *The Art of Adaptation: Turning Fact and Fiction into Film*. Holt Paperbacks, 1992.

Selby, Andrew. *Animation*. Laurence King Publishing, 2013.

Serpico. Directed by Sidney Lumet. Performances by Al Pacino, John Randolph, and Jack Kehoe. Artists Entertainment Complex, 1973.

Shrek 2. Directed by Andrew Adamson. Performances by Mike Myers, Eddie Murphy, and Cameron Diaz. Dreamworks Pictures, 2004.

The Sinking of the Lusitania. Directed by Winsor McCay. Universal Film Manufacturing Company, 1918.

Sinyard, Neil. *Filming Literature: The Art of Screen Adaptation*. Routledge, 1986.

The Sixth Sense. Directed by M. Night Shyamalan. Performances by Bruce Willis, Haley Joel Osment, and Toni Collette. Hollywood Pictures, 1999.

Slacker. Directed by Richard Linklater. Performances by Richard Linklater, Rudy Basquez, and Jean Caffeine. Detour Filmproduction, 1990.

Slethaug, Gordon E. *Adaptation Theory and Criticism: Postmodern Literature and Cinema in the USA*. Bloomsbury Academic, 2014.

Snow White and the Seven Dwarfs. Directed by William Cottrell. Performances by Adriana Caselotti, Harry Stockwell, and Lucille La Verne. Walt Disney Productions, 1937.

The Soldier's Courtship. Directed by Alfred Moul. Performances by Fred Storey, Julie Seale, and Ellen Daws. Robert W. Paul, 1898.

The Sound of Music. Directed by Robert Wise. Performances by Julie Andrews, Christopher Plummer, and Eleanor Parker. Robert Wise Productions, 1965.

Spellbound. Directed by Alfred Hitchcock. Performances by Ingrid Bergman, Gregory Peck, and Michael Chekhov. Selznick International Pictures, 1945.

Split. Directed by M. Night Shyamalan. Performances by James McAvoy, Anya Taylor-Joy, and Haley Lu Richardson. Universal Pictures, 2017.

Stam, Robert. "Introduction: The Theory and Practice of Adaptation." In *Literature and Film: A Guide to the Theory and Practice of Film Adaptation*, edited by Robert Stam and Alessandro Raengo, 1–70. Wiley-Blackwell, 2005.

Stam, Robert. *Literature through Film: Realism, Magic, and the Art of Adaptation*. Wiley-Blackwell, 2004.

Stam, Robert. "Revisionist Adaptation: Transtextuality, Cross-Cultural Dialogism, and Performative Infidelities." In *The Oxford Handbook of Adaptation Studies*, edited by Thomas Leitch, 239–50. Oxford University Press, 2017.

Stam, Robert, and Alessandro Raengo, eds. *A Companion to Literature and Film*. Wiley-Blackwell, 2004.

Star Wars: Episode I—The Phantom Menace. Directed by George Lucas. Performances by Ewan McGregor, Liam Neeson, and Natalie Portman. Lucasfilm, 1999.

Star Wars: Episode IV—A New Hope. Directed by George Lucas. Performances by Mark Hamill, Harrison Ford, and Carrie Fisher. Lucasfilm, 1977.

Star Wars: Episode V—The Empire Strikes Back. Directed by Irvin Kershner. Performances by Mark Hamill, Harrison Ford, and Carrie Fisher. Lucasfilm, 1980.

Star Wars: Episode VI—Return of the Jedi. Directed by Richard Marquand. Performances by Mark Hamill, Harrison Ford, and Carrie Fisher. Lucasfilm, 1983.
Star Wars: Episode VII—The Force Awakens. Directed by J.J. Abrams. Performances by Daisy Ridley, John Boyega, and Oscar Issac. Lucasfilm, 2015.
Star Wars: Episode VIII—The Last Jedi. Directed by Rian Johnson. Performances by Daisy Ridley, John Boyega, and Mark Hamill. Lucasfim, 2017.
Stein, Gertrude. *The Autobiography of Alice B. Toklas*. Vintage, 1990.
Stern, Kevin. "The Filming Locations of Disney's *Saving Mr. Banks*: An East Wing Trip to the West." *Beyond the Marquee*, December 24, 2013.
Stern, Lesley. "*Emma* in Los Angeles: Remaking the Book and the City." *Film Adaptation*, edited by James Naremore, 221–38. Rutgers University Press, 2000.
The Sugarland Express. Directed by Steven Spielberg. Performances by Goldie Hawn, Ben Johnson, and Michael Sacks. Universal Pictures, 1974.
Sutton, David, and Peter Wogan. *Hollywood Blockbusters: The Anthropology of Popular Movies*. Berg Publishers, 2009.
Tape. Directed by Richard Linklater. Performances by Ethan Hawke, Robert Sean Leonard, and Uma Thurman. Detour Filmproduction, 2001.
The Ten Commandments. Directed by Cecil B. DeMille. Performances by Charlton Heston, Yul Brynner, and Anne Baxter. Motion Picture Associates, 1956.
The Terminal. Directed by Steven Spielberg. Performances by Tom Hanks, Catherine Zeta-Jones, and Chi McBride. Dreamworks Pictures, 2004.
Thompson, Kristin. "The Continuity System." In *The Classical Hollywood Cinema: Film Style & Mode of Production to 1960*, David Bordwell, Janet Staiger, and Kristin Thompson, editors, 194–213. Columbia University Press, 1985.
Thompson, Richard F., and Stephen A. Madigan. *Memory: The Key to Consciousness*. Princeton University Press, 2007.
The Three Caballeros. Directed by Norman Ferguson. Performances by Aurora Miranda, Carmen Molina, and Dora Luz. Walt Disney Productions, 1944.
Tibbets, John, and James M. Walsh, eds. *The Encyclopedia of Novels into Film*. Checkmark Books, 2005.
Titanic. Directed by James Cameron. Performances by Leonardo DiCaprio, Kate Winslet, and Billy Zane. Twentieth Century Fox, 1997.
Tommy Atkins in the Park. Directed by Robert W. Paul. Robert W. Paul, 1898.
The Truman Show. Directed by Peter Weir. Performances by Jim Carrey, Ed Harris, and Laura Linney. Paramount Pictures, 1998.
Turim, Maureen. "The Trauma of History: Flashbacks upon Flashbacks." *Screen* 42, no. 2 (Summer 2001): 205–10.
Turnock, Julie A. *Plastic Reality: Special Effects, Technology, and the Emergence of 1970s Blockbuster Aesthetics*. Columbia University Press, 2015.
Unbreakable. Directed by M. Night Shyamalan. Performances by Bruce Willis, Samuel L. Jackson, and Robin Wright. Touchstone Pictures, 2000.
United 93. Directed by Paul Greengrass. Performances by David Alan Basche, Olivia Thirlby, and Liza Colón-Zayas. Universal Pictures, 2006.

The Usual Suspects. Directed by Bryan Singer. Performances by Kevin Spacey, Gabriel Byrne, and Chazz Palminteri. PolyGram Filmed Entertainment, 1995.

van der Kolk, Bessel A., and Alexander C. McFarlane. "The Black Hole of Trauma." In *Traumatic Stress: The Effects of Overwhelming Experience on Mind, Body, and Society*, edited by Bessel van der Kolk, Alexander C. McFarlane, and Lars Weisaeth, 3–23. Guilford Press, 1996.

Vincendeau, Ginette. *Film/Literature/Heritage: A Sight and Sound Reader*. British Film Institute, 2001.

Waking Life. Directed by Richard Linklater. Performances by Ethan Hawke, Trevor Jack Brooks, and Lorelei Linklater. Fox Searchlight Pictures, 2001.

Walker, Elsie, and David T. Johnson. "Letter from the Editors." *Literature/Film Quarterly* 33, no. 1 (2005): 2–3.

Walker, Janet. *Trauma Cinema: Documenting Incest and the Holocaust*. University of California Press, 2005.

Walker, Janet. "Trauma Cinema: False Memories and True Experiences." *Screen* 42, no. 2 (Summer 2001): 211–16.

WALL-E. Directed by Andrew Stanton. Performances by Ben Burtt, Elissa Knight, and Jeff Garlin. FortyFour Studios, 2008.

Ward, Paul. *Documentary: The Margins of Reality*. Wallflower Press, 2006.

Weary River. Directed by Frank Lloyd. Performances by Richard Barthelmess, Betty Compson, and William Holden. First National Pictures, 1929.

Wells, Paul. *Understanding Animation*. Routledge, 1998.

Welsh, James, and Peter Lev, eds. *The Literature/Film Reader: Issues of Adaptation*. Scarecrow Press, 2007.

West Side Story. Directed by Jerome Robbins. Performances by Natalie Wood, George Chakiris, and Richard Beymer. Mirsch Corporation, 1961.

What Happened in the Tunnel. Directed by Edwin S. Porter. Performances by Gilbert M. "Bronco Billy" Anderson and Berth Regustus. Edison Manufacturing Company, 1903.

Willemen, Paul. "Indexicality, Fantasy and the Digital." *Inter-Asia Cultural Studies* 14, no. 1 (2013): 110–35.

Williams, Linda. "Mirrors without Memories: Truth, History, and *The Thin Blue Line*." In *Documenting the Documentary: Close Readings of Documentary Film and Video*, edited by Barry Keith Grant and Jeannette Sloniowski, 379–96. Wayne State University Press, 1998.

The Wizard of Oz. Directed by Victor Fleming. Performances by Judy Garland, Frank Morgan, and Ray Bolger. Metro-Goldwyn-Mayer, 1939.

Wollen, Peter. *Signs and Meanings in the Cinema*. Indiana University Press, 1969.

World Trade Center. Directed by Oliver Stone. Performances by Nicolas Cage, Michael Peña, and Maria Bello. Paramount Pictures, 2006.

Wurth, Kiene Brillenburg, ed. *Between Page and Screen: Remaking Literature through Cinema and Cyberspace*. Fordham University Press, 2012.

Wyatt, David. "The Fate of Rereading." *Kenyon Review* 8 (Spring 1986): 106–12.

The 100-to-One-Shot, or A Run of Luck. Vitagraph, 1906.

INDEX

Abdalla, Khalid, 130
actors, 5, 6, 11, 65, 89–90, 94–95, 96–97, 122
actuality, 3, 7, 9, 12, 13, 16, 18–22, 41, 57, 63–64, 77–78, 85, 97, 101, 118, 124, 133–34, 140, 143–44, 146–48, 162, 169–71
adaptation, 7, 8, 10, 11; and imitation, 82, 149; kairos of, 44, 55, 79, 100, 106, 108, 125, 140, 142, 145, 161, 169, 172; of literary source, 6–7, 9, 13, 27–28, 151–65, 168–71; ongoing, 8–12, 21, 44, 55–56, 65, 100, 103, 106–8, 123, 125, 139–45, 152, 161–62, 164, 167, 175, 183–84; the original, 151–56; studies, 9, 11, 140, 151, 159–62, 171; of true stories, 168–72. *See also under* index; trauma
Affleck, Casey, 113
afterimage, 42–44
Agee, James, 163
Almereyda, Michael, 156
Altman, Rick, 5
Amago, Samuel, 14
Amorous Guardsman, The, 3
Andrew, Dudley, 151–52
Andrews, Julie, 48, 54
animation, 13, 18, 19, 49, 63, 62, 77–78, 81–91, 93–97, 108
Apocalypse Now, 109
Applegate, Curt, 129
archive, 24, 41–42, 44, 55, 104, 108, 142
Arquette, Patricia, 89
ASCII History of the Moving Image, 29–30
Ashitey, Clare-Hope, 15
Atkin, Albert, 30–31, 34–36, 46–47
audience. *See* spectators

Austen, Jane, 156, 157
authenticity, 79–81, 93, 126–28, 132, 141, 143, 169, 176, 182
Avatar, 19, 62, 63
Avengers, The, 62
Avengers: Endgame, 62, 63
Avengers: Infinity War, 62

Bacon, Terryl, 14
Baker, Mitch, 92
Bale, Christian, 168
Bambi, 62
Barnard, Aneurin, 14
Barthes, Roland, 39, 164
Batman Begins, 167
Bazin, André, 23, 25–26, 32, 39–40, 64, 67, 70–75, 106, 151, 165
Before Midnight, 90
Before Sunrise, 86, 90–91
Before Sunset, 88–90
Bello, Maria, 134
Bellour, Raymond, 45
Benjamin, Walter, 11, 126, 154–58, 161
Bergson, Henri, 66
Bernie, 95–97
Bicycle Thieves, 25–26
Black, Jack, 96
Black Panther, 62, 63
Blade Runner, 17
Blair Witch Project, The, 79
Bloody Sunday, 126
Body Heat, 104
Bordwell, David, 10, 68, 159, 165–66, 181

Born on the Fourth of July, 170
Boyhood, 89–90
Boys Don't Cry, 169
Brahm, John, 166
Branagh, Kenneth, 174
Bresson, Robert, 151
Bride and Prejudice, 157
Brood, The, 150
Buchanan, Judith, 6
Buckley, Annie Rose, 50
Buckley, Betty, 110
Bullock, Sandra, 139
Burning, 27
Butch Cassidy and the Sundance Kid, 62, 63

Cage, Nicolas, 133
Caine, Michael, 16
Cameron, James, 19, 37
Canet, Fernando, 149
Carell, Steve, 97, 107
Carrey, Jim, 10, 118, 122
Carroll, Noël, 158–59, 177
Cartmell, Deborah, 157–58
Caruth, Cathy, 124, 145, 147–48
Castoriadis, Cornelius, 61–62
Chadha, Gurinder, 157
Chandler, Daniel, 31–33, 70–71
Chandler, Kyle, 113
Children of Men, 13–19, 29–30, 61
Chumo, Peter, 14
Citizen Kane, 166
Clarke, Dameon, 95
Close Encounters of the Third Kind, 84
Clueless, 156
Coen, Joe and Ethan, 123
Coffey, Izzie, 111
Coltrane, Ellar, 89–90
Columbus, Chris, 158
Con Air, 133
contingency, 36, 40, 42, 44, 48, 60, 74, 78–79, 103, 106, 123, 181
Corrigan, Timothy, 7
Ćosić, Vuk, 29–30
Cotillard, Marion, 176

Cowie, Elizabeth, 78–79
Cranston, Bryan, 97, 107
Cronenberg, David, 150
Cross, David, 121
Cuarón, Alfonso, 13–18, 29, 30, 61
Curtis, Scott, 82–84
Curtiz, Michael, 166
cut, the, 4–5, 27, 41, 50, 52–55, 68, 93, 97, 112, 114–16, 118, 122, 127–36, 172–75, 180
Cutler, Aaron, 90
cycle films, 3–4, 7, 46, 109, 165–66
Cymek, Andrew, 150

Daldry, Stephen, 10, 125–26, 138–41, 143
Damici, Nick, 133
D'Arcy, James, 174
Dark Knight, The, 63, 167
Dark Knight Rises, The, 167–68
Davis, Sonny, 96
Day After Tomorrow, The, 134
deCordova, Richard, 6
Deleuze, Gilles, 66
Delpy, Julie, 90
de Man, Paul, 31, 147
DeMille, Cecil B., 22, 30
Deren, Maya, 150
Derrida, Jacques, 126
de Sica, Vittorio, 25–26
Dial, Rick, 97
Diary of a Country Priest, 151
DiCaprio, Leonardo, 176
Dickens, Charles, 7, 151, 178
Dickman, Govinda, 14
digital cinema, 7, 8, 9, 13–19, 21–22, 28–30, 36, 38, 40, 60, 72, 83–84, 161. *See also* index: digital
Disney, Walt, 48
Doane, Mary Ann, 3, 8, 9, 21–23, 28, 40–44, 51, 55, 78–79, 104, 108, 142
documentary, 5, 6, 24, 66, 77–82, 85–89, 94–97, 108, 134
Don Quixote, 154
Dotrice, Karen, 55
Duchamp, Marcel, 40–41
Dunkirk, 11, 168, 169, 171–75, 179–80, 183–84

Ejiofor, Chiwetel, 16
Elliott, Kamilla, 160–61
Elsaesser, Thomas, 117–18, 124–25
Emma, 156
Eternal Sunshine of the Spotless Mind, 10, 113, 118–23, 125, 166
E.T.: The Extra-Terrestrial, 63
Ex Machina, 17
Extremely Loud and Incredibly Close, 10, 125, 138–41, 143
eye, the, 20, 28, 42–43, 81

Fantasia, 62
Fargo, 123–24
Farrell, Colin, 52
Ferguson, Chamblee, 94
Ferguson, Normal, 85
Fhlainn, Sorcha Ní, 167–68
Fight Club, 165
Fincher, David, 165, 167
Fishburne, Laurence, 97, 107
flashback, 50, 53, 68, 110–11, 113, 115, 135–36, 140, 141, 145, 147
flashforward, 68
Fly, The, 150
Foer, Jonathan Safran, 138
Ford, John, 166
Forrest Gump, 14, 79
Freud, Sigmund, 38, 148
Furniss, Maureen, 82, 85

Game, The, 165–67
Gance, Abel, 19, 37, 161–62
Garber, Matthew, 55
Garland, Alex, 17–18
Gaut, Berys, 10, 60–61
Genette, Gérard, 156–57
genre, 5–6, 11, 46, 65, 86, 156, 165
Germany Year Zero, 71–72
Gledhill, Christine, 5
Glynn-Carney, Tom, 173
Godard, Jean-Luc, 24
Gombrich, E. H., 152
Gondry, Michel, 10, 113, 118, 123, 125, 166
Gone in Sixty Seconds, 133

Gone With the Wind, 62, 63
Graduate, The, 62, 63
Grease, 63
Great Train Robbery, The, 4
Greengrass, Paul, 10, 125–33, 134, 141, 142
Greenlaw, Duncan, 126, 128
Griffith, D. W., 22, 30
Griffiths, Rachel, 64
Grossman, Julie, 161
Gunning, Tom, 3–5, 8, 9, 19, 20, 22–23, 26–28, 46, 59, 77, 101, 104
Gyllenhaal, Maggie, 135

Hamlet, 156
Hancock, John Lee, 9, 47–48, 50, 54, 55, 57–58, 64, 65, 107
Hanging Out the Clothes, 3
Hanks, Tom, 14, 49, 64, 138
Hardy, Tom, 179
Harry Potter and the Sorcerer's Stone, 158
Hathaway, Anne, 168
Hawke, Ethan, 88–90
Hearts in Dixie, 5
Heaven & Earth, 170
Heckerling, Amy, 156
Hedges, Lucas, 113
Heise, William, 3
Hello Dolly!, 18
Hen Hop, 85
Henke, Brad William, 111
Henry, Gregg, 128
Herman, Judith Lewis, 144
Hernandez, Jay, 134
Herzog, Amy, 66, 108
Hiroshima, mon amour, 150
Hitchcock, Alfred, 91, 149, 150
Holden, Larry, 182
Holocaust, the, 112, 124, 150
Hong, Kyung-pyo, 28
Horn, Thomas, 10, 126, 143
House of Games, 166
How Green Was My Valley, 166
Hugo, Victor, 7
Hutcheon, Linda, 163–65

icons, 11, 14, 19–20, 23–25, 31–34, 43, 48, 68, 89, 93, 103, 125, 141, 146–47, 152, 172
Imitation of Life, 38–39
Inception, 11, 167, 171, 175–79
Incredibles, The, 62
index: and adaptation, 8, 9, 10, 11–12, 141, 145, 152, 161, 162, 171, 184; and art, 7–8, 9, 22, 89; and death, 45–46; deictic, 21, 40–41, 57, 63, 73, 85; digital, 7–8, 9, 15, 19–20, 23, 27, 36–38, 41, 77; diminished, 9, 11, 20–25, 27, 47, 48, 50, 104, 113, 142, 145, 166; imaginative, 8, 21, 47–48, 50, 55–59, 61, 64, 73, 76, 80, 90, 102–3, 105–6, 162, 167; impoverished, 8, 11, 21, 47–48, 51, 53, 55, 57–59, 61, 64, 76, 80–81, 88, 90, 102–4, 151, 161; indefinite, 8, 11, 21, 47–48, 51, 53–55, 57–59, 61, 64, 73, 76, 80–81, 90, 102–5, 162, 167; and interpretation, 19, 20, 31–32, 34, 36–37; intertextual, 8, 12, 21, 47–48, 50, 54–55, 57–59, 61, 64, 73, 76, 80, 90–91, 102–3, 105–6, 162, 167; Peircean, 22–26, 30–31, 35–38, 43–45, 87, 103; and play, 11, 20, 21, 47–51, 65–67, 76, 126, 162, 166; and reality, 8–11, 13, 16–17, 19–22, 25–27, 29, 33–34, 43–46, 57–59, 63–65, 69, 72–73, 76, 80, 85, 88, 100–103, 108, 141, 146, 171; and sign, 11, 19, 21, 23–25, 29–34, 36–37, 47, 59, 73–74, 87, 101–4; and spectators, 8–11, 26, 29, 43, 46, 65, 90, 151, 157; and time, 11, 20, 32, 37–44, 46, 53, 88–90, 104–6, 108, 123; as trace, 22–24, 32, 38, 43–46; and trauma, 8–10, 45, 47, 97–100, 104–9, 117, 142, 150–51; yet-to-be determined, 20, 25, 33, 35–36, 74. *See also* adaptation; digital cinema; Peirce, Charles Sanders; spectators; time; trauma
Inning by Inning: A Portrait of a Coach, 86
Insomnia, 167
Interstellar, 167–68

Jackson, Peter, 158
James, P. D., 13, 29
Jameson, Fredric, 104
Jaws, 14, 63
Jeon, Jong-seo, 27

Johnson, David T., 86–87, 89, 91–92, 99–100, 162
Johnston, Ollie, 82–83
Journey to Italy, 71–72
Jurassic Park, 63
Jurassic World, 62

Kaplan, E. Ann, 18, 123, 149–51
Kasdan, Lawrence, 104
Kaufman, Charlie, 121–23, 126
Kawin, Bruce, 19, 23, 37
Kelly, Gene, 18
Keoghan, Barry, 173
Kilday, Gregg, 89–90
King, Stephen, 151
Kirkpatrick, Karen, 128
Kiss, The, 3
Kiss in the Tunnel, The, 3
Klein, Amanda Ann, 3
Krauss, Rosalind, 40

Lady and the Tramp, 62
LaRose, Nicole, 17
Laskar, Samrat, 168
Last Flag Flying, 97–99, 107–8, 118, 126
Lee, Chang-dong, 27
Leitch, Thomas, 164, 169–71
Leliński, Michał, 168
lens-based camera, 7, 22, 36, 39–41, 69, 73–75, 81, 84–85, 104, 146, 171, 183
Levitch, Timothy "Speed," 86–88
Levitt, Joseph-Gordon, 176
Leys, Ruth, 144–49, 152
Linklater, Lorelei, 89
Linklater, Richard, 8, 10, 66, 72, 76, 85–99, 107
Live from Shiva's Dance Floor, 86–87
Locket, The, 166
Lonergan, Kenneth, 113–18, 125
Longden, Kenneth, 162
Lord of the Rings: The Fellowship of the Ring, 158
Lowden, Jack, 179
Lubin, Siegmund, *Love in a Railroad Train*, 3
Lucas, George, 29
Lumet, Sidney, 112, 113, 115, 170–71

MacDonald, Amy, 31
MacLaine, Shirley, 97
Madigan, Stephen A., 59
Mamet, David, 166
Manchester by the Sea, 113–17, 122, 125
Manovich, Lev, 7, 13, 18–19, 23, 28–30, 40–41
Marcel, Kelly, 48, 52
Mary Poppins, 47–48, 50, 53, 54, 58
Matrix, The, 77, 167
McAvoy, James, 110
McConaughey, Matthew, 97, 168
McFarlane, Alexander C., 142–43, 149
Méliès, George, 82
Memento, 11, 167, 168, 171, 175, 180–83
memorial, 124, 131, 137, 141, 144, 149
memory, 52–55, 58–59, 65–69, 79, 100, 120–22, 124–30, 147, 167
Meshes of the Afternoon, 150
Metz, Christian, 10, 23, 27, 59, 70, 75–77
Mildred Pierce, 166
Miller, Nancy K., 108–9
Moeschke, Edmund, 71
Moss, Carrie-Anne, 182
motion, cinematic, 23, 28, 38, 58, 60, 67–68, 77–78, 81, 84–85, 101, 105, 106. *See also under* spectators
Moul, Alfred, 3
Mulvey, Laura, 9, 38–40, 44–46, 51, 101, 104–7, 146
Münsterberg, Hugo, 10, 66–70, 72, 84–85
Murakami, Haruki, 27–28
Murphet, Julian, 17–18
Murphy, Cillian, 180
music. *See* soundtrack
musicals, 5, 63, 156

National Treasure, 133
Nelson, Tim Blake, 156
Nichols, Bill, 79–81
Niessen, Niels, 19–20, 21–22
Night and Fog, 150
Night Cries, 150
Nolan, Christopher, 8, 11, 167–69, 171–83
Novak, B. J., 52

now, the, 55–56, 88, 100, 106, 122, 125, 173, 183. *See also* present; time

O, 156
O'Brien, Ben, 113
Odyssey, the, 154
Oh, Jung-mi, 27
Olkowski, Dorothea, 66
100-to-One Shot, The, 4–5
Othello, 156
Owen, Clive, 15

Page, Ellen, 176
painting, 7, 13, 18, 32, 75
Panek, Elliot, 181
Pantoliano, Joe, 182
Pastrone, Giovanni, 22, 30
pathos, 42, 44, 55, 104, 108, 142, 147
Patrick, Robert, 31
Paul, Robert W., 3
Paulsen, Kris, 9, 36–40, 60
Pawnbroker, The, 112–13, 115, 116
Pearce, Guy, 181
Peirce, Charles Sanders, 7–9, 20, 22–26, 30–31, 33–35, 37–39, 43–44, 47, 74, 146. *See also* index: Peircean
Peirce, Kimberly, 169
Pellicane, Peter, 129
Peña, Michael, 133
Peter Pan, 62
Phantom Menace, The, 29
photography, 6, 19, 25, 32, 36–37, 39–41, 43–45, 48, 61, 64, 72–75, 80, 100, 105, 180–82
photorealism, 13, 19, 60–61, 84
Picasso, Pablo, 32
Piccininni, Anthony, 134
Pinocchio, 62
Plato, 153–54
Platoon, 109, 170
Porter, Edwin S., 3, 4
present, the, 28, 36–37, 39, 42–44, 46, 52–53, 59, 68–69, 73–74, 87–88, 100, 104–5, 112, 115–16, 121, 140, 145
Prestige, The, 167, 168

Pride and Prejudice, 157
Prince, Stephen, 72
Psycho (1960), 91, 149
Psycho (1998), 149
Pulp Fiction, 165

Radstone, Susannah, 117–18, 123–24
Rafferty, Terrence, 170
Raw, Laurence, 162–63
Rawna, Angela, 94
realism, 10, 14, 19, 23, 41, 60–100
Reeves, Ann, 97
Reeves, Keanu, 92–93, 95
Resnais, Alain, 150
retina. *See* eye, the
rewatching, 4–7, 46, 51, 78, 108, 142–43, 161, 166, 181, 184; and anxiety, 13–14; context, 3, 11; and reality, 11, 59, 106; and return, 152–53, 161, 163–65; and trauma, 8, 57, 107. *See also* index: and trauma
Riesco, Armando, 136
Road to Guantánamo, The, 79
Robbins, Jerome, 156
Robichaux, Richard, 97
Robinson Crusoe, 154
Romeo and Juliet, 156
Rosen, Philip, 70–74
Rossellini, Roberto, 26, 71
Roue, La, 19, 161–62
Rowling, J. K., 151
Ruffalo, Mark, 121
Rushton, Richard, 10, 61–63, 65, 67, 70–77, 144
Ryder, Winona, 95
Rylance, Mark, 173

Saving Mr. Banks, 9, 47–55, 57–59, 61, 63–64, 66, 72, 99, 107, 118, 126
Saving Private Ryan, 109
Scanner Darkly, A, 91–95
Scorsese, Martin, 170–71
Scott, Ridley, 17–18
Selby, Andrew, 82
Serpico, 170
Shakespeare, William, 7, 151, 156
Shannon, Michael, 137

Shrek 2, 63
Shyamalan, M. Night, 109–11, 165
Singer, Bryan, 165, 166–67
Sinking of the Lusitania, The, 82
Sixth Sense, The, 165
Slacker, 86
Sleep, 85
Sliney, Ben, 128
Smith, George Albert, 3
Smith, Sue, 48, 52
Snow White and the Seven Dwarfs, 62, 85
Soldier's Courtship, The, 3
Sound of Music, The, 62
soundtrack, 17, 32, 69, 86, 115, 121, 126–27, 129, 131–33
Spacey, Kevin, 166
spectators, 4–6, 8–10, 27, 38; active, 26, 30, 45–46, 50, 56, 117, 145, 153, 159, 162, 164–65, 180–81; and emotion, 69–70, 81, 108, 126, 128–30, 132, 134–36; imagination, 16, 20, 21, 58, 64, 66–67, 74, 76, 103, 145; knowing, 128–30, 134, 136, 139, 164–65; and motion, 23, 28, 59; participation of, 28, 29, 50, 67–69, 71, 75–76, 91–92, 107, 125, 139, 161, 167–68, 171; perception, 77–78, 105–6; and reality, 11, 75–76, 103, 134, 181. *See also* index: spectators; motion, cinematic
Spellbound, 150
Spielberg, Steven, 14, 170–71
Split, 109–12
Stam, Robert, 153–54, 156–57, 161
Star Wars: Episode I—The Phantom Menace, 63
Star Wars: Episode IV—A New Hope, 63, 84
Star Wars: Episode V—The Empire Strikes Back, 63
Star Wars: Episode VI—Return of the Jedi, 63
Star Wars Episode VII—The Force Awakens, 62, 63
Star Wars: Episode VIII—The Last Jedi, 62
Steiger, Rod, 112
Stein, Gertrude, 32
Stern, Kevin, 48
Stern, Lesley, 156

Stone, Oliver, 10, 125–26, 133–38, 141, 142, 170–71
Sutton, David, 14
symbols, 11, 14, 19–20, 23–25, 31–34, 36, 43, 68, 89, 103, 125, 141, 146–47, 152, 172

Tale of Two Cities, A, 168
Tape, 99–100
Tarantino, Quentin, 165
Taylor-Joy, Anya, 110
Ten Commandments, The, 62
Thomas, Frank, 82–83
Thompson, Emma, 47, 57, 107
Thompson, Kristin, 4
Thompson, Richard F., 59
Three Caballeros, The, 85
time, 44, 52–53, 69, 87–90, 102, 104–7. *See also* index: time; present
Titanic, 62, 63
Tomlinson, David, 55, 58
Tommy Atkins in the Park, 3
Tougaw, Jason, 108–9
trauma, 8–10, 76; adaptation, 107, 139, 143–44, 149–50, 152–53, 164; celebration of, 109–11; moving through, 10, 57, 100, 107, 109, 113, 117–18, 124–26, 132–33, 135–36, 139–41, 145, 151; ongoing, 104, 142–43; and reality, 109, 117–20, 132, 150; and repetition, 47, 109, 113, 117, 124, 139, 147–48; representation, 109, 143–48; stuck in, 53, 113, 116–17, 142; and the event, 123–24, 142, 147–48, 153, 162; and truth, 99–100, 123–24. *See also* adaptation; index: trauma
Travers, Pamela, 48
Truman Show, The, 79, 167
Turim, Maureen, 112–13
Turnock, Julie A., 84
Tyson, Cicely, 98

Unbreakable, 166
United 93, 10, 125–33, 141, 142, 144
Usual Suspects, The, 165, 166–67

van der Kolk, Bessel A., 142–43, 145–49

Van Dyke, Dick, 55
Van Sant, Gus, 149
viewer. *See* spectator
von Sternberg, Josef, 23
Voyage to Italy, 71–72

Wachowski, Lana and Lilly, 167
Waking Life, 87–89, 91
Walker, Elsie, 162
Walker, Janet, 10, 109, 123, 135
Wall-E, 18
Wang, Ban, 123, 149–51
Ward, John Quincy Adams, 86–87
Ward, Paul, 81–82
Warren, Robert Penn, 163
Watanabe, Ken, 176
Weary River, 5
Weir, Peter, 167
Welles, Orson, 166
Wells, Paul, 82
West Side Story, 156
What Happened in the Tunnel, 3
Whelehan, Imelda, 157–58
Whitehead, Fionn, 173
Whitford, Bradley, 51–52
Whitney, Ryan, 122
Wiggins, Wiley, 87
Wilkinson, Tom, 121
Willemen, Paul, 8, 22–23, 28, 30, 76–77
Williams, Linda, 99–100
Williams, Michelle, 115
Winslet, Kate, 118, 122
Wise, Robert, 156
Wizard of Oz, The, 62
Wogan, Peter, 14
Wollen, Peter, 23–26, 40, 73, 125
World Trade Center, 10, 125, 133–38, 141, 142, 144, 170
Wright, Jeffrey, 140
Wyatt, David, 162–63, 165

Yoo, Ah-in, 27
You and Your . . . , 82

Zemeckis, Robert, 14

ABOUT THE AUTHOR

Allen H. Redmon is professor of English and film studies at Texas A&M University–Central Texas. He is editor of *Next Generation Adaptation: Spectatorship and Process* (2021) and coeditor of Clint Eastwood's *Cinema of Trauma: Essays on PTSD in the Director's Films* (2017). Redmon serves as president of the Literature/Film Association, an organization that supports and promotes cinema study by encouraging a wide variety of approaches that explore, among other things, the relationship of literature and film.

www.ingramcontent.com/pod-product-compliance
Lightning Source LLC
Chambersburg PA
CBHW030623230426
43661CB00053B/2116